TO AN

UNKNOWN

GOD

ALSO BY GARRETT EPPS

The Shad Treatment

The Floating Island: A Tale of Washington

GARRETT EPPS

ST. MARTIN'S PRESS ❧ NEW YORK

TO AN

RELIGIOUS

UNKNOWN

FREEDOM

GOD

ON TRIAL

www.stmartins.com

Design by Kathryn Parise

ISBN 0-312-26239-6

First Edition: March 2001

10 9 8 7 6 5 4 3 2 1

FOR MY CHILDREN, DANIEL AND MAGGIE,

*and for the next generation of
Blacks, Farrell-Smiths, Frohnmayers,
and Smiths,*

the living and the dead

CONTENTS

Men of Athens, I perceive that in every way
you are very religious. For as I passed along,
and observed the objects of your worship, I
found also an altar with this inscription, "To
an unknown god."

—*The Apostle Paul*
preaching to the Athenians,
ACTS 17:22–23

TO AN

UNKNOWN

GOD

PROLOGUE

WEIGHED IN THE
BALANCE

On November 6, 1989, Dave Frohnmayer, the attorney general of Oregon, awoke early at the Phoenix Park Hotel in Washington, D.C. November 6 was a Tuesday, one of those splendid fall mornings that partially redeem Washington's swampy summer— fluffy white clouds dancing across a woozy deep blue sky, the air moving in cool gusts across the sidewalks and among the cherry trees along the Mall. It was the most important day of Dave Frohnmayer's legal career. He didn't know that; in fact, he didn't know that the case he would argue that morning before the U.S. Supreme Court would radically change the law of religious freedom. As he prepared his notes, he repeated two phrases to himself: *Drugs are bad; slippery slope*. These phrases, to Frohnmayer, summed up the case at hand, which was blandly titled *Employment Division, Department of Human Resources* v. *Smith*. It was

1

an unemployment-compensation case, not quite routine, because the constitutional issues were somewhat novel. But Frohnmayer expected them to be disposed of easily under existing precedent; he had no hint—no one did—that Smith would become the landmark case on religious freedom, the mother document of a radically new interpretation of the First Amendment's guarantee of the "free exercise" of religion.

In November 1989 Dave Frohnmayer was forty-nine years old. He was well over six feet tall, with springy brownish hair beginning to gray. With his ready smile and slightly chubby cheeks, Frohnmayer bore a striking resemblance to professional basketball player Larry Bird. No one would have mistaken him for an athlete, though: he was fit enough—he could spend all day on skis at Mount Bachelor when he got the chance—but he still walked loosely, with a faint touch of the gangly adolescent he had been, the class brain who played the trumpet in the Medford High School band while his brother John performed on the football field.

Frohnmayer had been attorney general of Oregon since 1981. He had no reason to consider *Smith* the most important case he would ever handle. He had already argued six other cases in front of the Supreme Court, some of which seemed to pose issues more sweeping than whether two workers in Roseburg got their unemployment benefits. Those cases had concerned the fishing rights of Indian tribes, the legal immunities of prison guards who shoot or kill prisoners during riots, the protection of prisoners who confess to police officers while under arrest. Frohnmayer often told young lawyers that arguing a case before the Supreme Court was by far the greatest professional thrill a lawyer could hope to experience. He was delighted, then, to be back in Washington, but the *Smith* case was not even the most important matter he was dealing with in the fall of 1989. He had just announced his candidacy for governor of Oregon in 1990. He expected a tough fight against a wily incumbent, Democrat Neil Goldschmidt. He also had three daughters at home all suffering from the same potentially fatal genetic disease. The *Smith* case was almost a distraction.

Frohnmayer had been willing to settle the case at the last minute. He had negotiated a settlement that broke down only when Al Smith, the Native American unemployment claimant who was one of the two men on the other side, refused to accept it. So, over breakfast at the Phoenix Park, Frohnmayer found himself repeating like a legal mantra, *Drugs are bad, drugs are bad. Slippery slope, slippery slope.*

Al Smith was in Washington that morning as well. The morning of oral argument was his seventieth birthday; despite a life full of hard knocks, he looked younger. His appearance was as different from Frohnmayer's as one can imagine. Where Frohnmayer was tall, Al Smith was short; Frohnmayer was fair, Al Smith, dark; Frohnmayer wore his brown hair short, Al Smith's, iron-gray shot with black, spilled to his waist. In contrast to Frohnmayer's shambling gait, Al Smith walked carefully, planting his feet deliberately and shifting his weight with care. Perhaps because he had suffered damage to his inner ear, which controls the sense of balance, Al Smith reminded an observer of something said by a blind man whose sight Jesus restored. Seeing people for the first time, the man had said they looked like trees walking. That was Al Smith. He was not a tall tree, but he had weathered the wind and the lightning.

Unlike Frohnmayer, Al Smith had no doubt that this would be the most important day of his life, at least as it would be known to history. In the world where Dave Frohnmayer was prominent, Al Smith was obscure: a penniless Native American whose very tribe had once been contemptuously wiped out of existence by congressional vote. He was well known in his own community, among Indian people in the Pacific Northwest and around the country—a man who had beaten alcohol and then spent his life helping others do the same. But in this world—the world of documents and courts—he knew that if he was remembered at all in years to come, it would be because of what happened in the case the Court would hear that day.

The Phoenix Park sits across the square from Washington's magnificent Union Station, only a few blocks from the Supreme Court's even grander palace at First Street N.E. and East Capitol Street. As the Oregon legal team walked past on its way to the Court, the brisk November wind rattled the lanyards of the fifty state flags that fly in front of the station. Frohnmayer was accompanied by three bright lawyers from his staff. Each was familiar with the case; each stood ready to proffer a quick reminder if Frohnmayer's memory failed. No one expected that, though; most of them would have agreed that Dave Frohnmayer was one of the most impressive appellate lawyers in the country. His memory was razor-sharp, and his ability to construct impromptu legal arguments when challenged by a court was so powerful that it could seem overwhelming to his co-counsel as well as to the other side. Further, Frohnmayer's demeanor in court had none of the truculence or sarcasm that curdles far too many lawyers' arguments. In court, as in his daily life, he projected only genial good nature and acute interest in the matter at hand. Judges enjoyed his arguments, and pleasing the judges is half the secret of winning.

Al Smith traveled to the Court with his wife, Jane Farrell-Smith, thirty-seven years younger than he was, and their two children. Also with Smith was Stanley Smart, a Northern Paiute Indian medicine man. Smart was also a "Road man," a ceremonial leader in the Native American Church. Under the traditions of the Church, Stanley Smart held the keys to the kingdom; he was entitled to administer the sacred sacrament, the peyote buttons that embodied God. He was empowered to conduct the ceremonies by which worshipers ate Grandfather Peyote and used the wisdom it provided to maintain themselves in a sober and holy way of life—the "Peyote Road." Stanley Smart was the only leader of the Church who had come forward to support Al Smith's decision to come before the Court.

Other leaders of the Church, and other prominent Native American activists, were gathering at the Court, too. Many of them gave Al Smith a wide berth. They had asked him not to stick with the case; they had pressured him to withdraw his claims. When he had hesitated, some had let it be known, behind his back, that they didn't think much of Al Smith.

Al Smith sat in a special section reserved for parties to the case and for friends of the justices and the attorneys. Smith had never been inside the temple of justice before, and when the justices took their seats, his reaction was sharp. This case was no longer about him, or about his religion. Indeed, these nine people would not recognize Al Smith if they saw him on the street. "It was showtime for them," he said. He imagined the justices idly wondering, *Who is Al Smith? He is just a little nobody who got sent to the Court.* As he looked up at the nine oracles of the law, he resented them. "How did they get so high and mighty?" he found himself asking.

In the Supreme Court chamber, Dave Frohnmayer gathered with his aides at the petitioner's table and prepared his argument. He looked across the courtroom and saw the Native people gathered there. The night before, they had held a worship ceremony across the street, drumming and singing peyote songs, calling on God to guide the Court in its decision. Now they were sitting on the other side of the chamber as Frohnmayer prepared to argue for the state of Oregon. Some of those present were Native lawyers and activists Frohnmayer had come to know; a few had become good friends. In his years as attorney general of Oregon, he had tried a number of ways to mend fences with the Indian tribes of the Northwest, who had often been treated with contempt by state government in the past. Now he saw that work unraveling. Frohnmayer looked at his legal team and said somewhat sadly, "How did we get to be the Indian bashers?"

Just for that second, Frohnmayer sensed that the case he was about to argue had gotten away from him. It was a foretaste of the understanding that would come to him slowly, over the months and years after the Court's decision, that the justices had done something no one had asked or expected them to do and that their decision would become the meaning of the case; and further that that meaning, because of the notice, the anger and dismay the decision would provoke, would become in a way the meaning of Frohnmayer's public career. It would be what lawyers and laypeople remembered when they heard his name. Nothing he had done, nothing he would do, would loom larger in the memory of history than this day's work. But it was just a foretaste of that knowledge, and it was fleeting; he focused again on the key points of his argument.

Employment Division v. *Smith* was the second case of the day. The first was a highly technical dispute about conflict-of-interest rules for federal defense contractors. As the lawyers in that case slipped away, the clerk of the Court called out the *Smith* case's number. Frohnmayer moved to the petitioner's table and arranged his notes, thinking of drugs and of slippery slopes, reviewing in his mind the facts he wanted to emphasize in the record. Before him, on the lectern at which lawyers stood to address the Court, was a laminated sheet bearing, for the benefit of lawyers struck mute by the Court's majesty, the required opening, "Mr. Chief Justice, and may it please the Court."

Frohnmayer was not awed by the Court. He knew just what he wanted to say. But as philosopher Søren Kierkegaard once wrote, life must be lived forward, but it can only be understood backward. Dave Frohnmayer knew what he would say, but neither he nor anyone else present knew what the words would come to mean. This case would not be about drugs, or even about slopes. It would come to define the limits of America's religious freedom.

Chief Justice William Rehnquist nodded formally and invited him to begin. "General Frohnmayer?" the chief justice said.

Dave Frohnmayer rose to meet his destiny.

1

A GOD I DIDN'T UNDERSTAND

No one who sees Al Smith doubts that he is a full-blooded Native American. He is compact, wiry, and athletic; his face is a study of light and angles; and his skin is the color of rust. His hair (black when he was young, iron-gray now) hangs nearly to his waist, thick and straight even though, a decade after the Supreme Court case that bears his name, he is eighty years old. His eyes have a distant look, as if he is seeing something others cannot. The overall effect is formidable, almost iconic.

But the bland name—Al Smith—clashes with his appearance. Al knows it, and he senses that strangers are disappointed when they hear it. In order to live up to his appearance, Al Smith long ago chose what he calls his "restaurant name"—Red Coyote. In public, among strangers, he will give that name, so that when the hostess calls "Red Coyote, table for four," onlookers will not be disappointed.

Alfred Leo Smith Jr. is a member of the Klamath tribe of southern Oregon—a people who have lived by the great Klamath Lake since Kamukamts, the Ancient Old Man who made the earth and the sky, brought them forth to win a bet with Pocket Gopher. Anthropologists say the Klamath people have lived there at least ten thousand years, making them one of the oldest settled tribes in the New World. But in the nineteenth century, federal Indian agents took away the Klamath people's descriptive names and gave them "American" names to make them easier to keep track of. One historian recorded the renaming process, in which a government clerk, who did not speak Klamath, made up new names for Klamaths and wrote them down on documents the Klamaths could not even read. " 'This is your name,' he would say [through an interpreter], writing it on a card, 'and if you forget what it is, ask anyone who can read, and he will tell you.' "

Al Smith's "true" name, like so much about his culture and his language, is lost. In fact, he sometimes imagines arriving in the spirit world after he dies. The spirit people ask his name, and when he gives it, the answer comes back: *We never heard of any Al Smith.* "They don't even know my Indian name in the spirit world," he once said.

Al Smith's Indian roots run deeper than his appearance, however. He is a kind of twentieth-century Indian Everyman; his lined face bears the scars of every betrayal and false turning of post-"frontier" Indian history. He was born into a largely intact culture but—like thousands of other young Indian boys and girls—was torn away from his home and sent to boarding school to learn to be "American." Religious schools and government teachers made sure he did not learn his own language, the history of his people, or the rituals that Klamaths had used to mark the seasons for more than ten thousand years. Stripped of these things, he graduated from boarding school to alcoholism, petty crime, prison, and disease. Finally, the federal government "terminated" his people and sold off the rich timberlands of the Klamath reservation.

White Americans have long regarded Indians as the "Vanishing Americans"—and when America's aboriginal people show a distressing reluctance to disappear, whites have often been eager to hasten the "inevitable" process. But Al Smith, like Native America generally, has refused to vanish. Drinking didn't kill him; neither did tuberculosis nor the army nor the federal penitentiary. And the wonder is that, like many other Indian people, he not only refused to disappear but began to recover, and then even to thrive, until, as he grew older, he began to live a "normal" middle-class family life. Most of his early years were marked by struggle—often violent and blind—against the forces that were trying to write him and those like him out of American history. And in the end Al Smith won; he wrote himself in. When Americans in the 1990s talk about religious freedom, they are, whether they know it or not, talking about Al Smith.

He was born on November 6, 1919, in Modoc Point, Oregon—a tree-shaded landing where the Williamson River flows down out of the mountains and into Upper Klamath Lake. For someone with a metaphorical cast of mind, Modoc Point might mark the dividing point between the heavens and the marshy earth of the Klamath cosmos. Twenty miles northwest, up the Cascade Range, is Crater Lake—the eeriest landmark in Oregon's stark geography. The lake is what remains of a volcano called Mount Mazama. More than six thousand years ago, the top blew off the mountain. Klamath legend—which geologists regard as a startlingly accurate record of the eruption—tells how the tribe sought shelter in caves from the lethal rain of fire and ash. Today, what remains is a dazzling clear lake, the deepest in North America, six thousand feet above sea level, with ice-blue water that reflects the colors of the sky. As late as a hundred years ago, Klamaths did not like to go near Crater Lake; it held bad memories.

But just below Modoc Point is the vast expanse of Upper Klamath Lake, which has been the center of Klamath life for thousands of years. Twenty miles long, as wide as eight miles at some points, it is the largest body of water in Oregon. At its deepest, though, it is barely four feet deep, and for much of its expanse it is more like a marsh than a lake—broken by the green of glistening reeds and the mud brown of sandbars. Upper Klamath Lake makes the area the largest refuge for migratory birds in the continental United States; each spring, thousands of eagles, ducks, geese, and other birds gather on or near it, along with ghostly white pelicans, often six feet from wingtip to wingtip, that nest there, a hundred miles from the sea. Like the birds, the Klamath people lived off the lake. It was the source of the *wocus*, which is what they call the butter-yellow seeds of the floating pond lily. Millions of seeds appeared each spring, and the Klamaths harvested them in dugout canoes. Dried and boiled, the *wocus* was their staple food—so important in their culture that the Klamath language has five different words for *wocus*, depending on how ripe the seeds are when the harvesters come by.

The lake and the rivers that feed it were home to the suckerfish, who came upstream like salmon each spring to spawn and to feed the Klamath people, who caught them in dip nets and dried them in the sun. The Klamath people had a rich traditional diet: *wocus*, camas root, and suckerfish; antelope and mule deer; pine nuts, sweet resin, blackberries, cherries, wild plums, gooseberries, and huckleberries that grew wild in the summer in their lush home country. They ate them fresh in summer and dried them in the sun or made them into jam to eat during the long, wet winter nights.

Twelve miles south of Modoc Point is the city of Klamath Falls, which is the center of the other culture Al Smith grew up with—the white Americans who had come down the Applegate Trail beginning in the 1840s to fish, mine, and log the rich hills and streams of the Klamath Basin. Twenty miles from the California line, Klamath Falls was and is a tough frontier town, with more than its share of saloons and dance halls, built by people with a taste for home-brewed law enforcement. Even today, Main Street in Klamath Falls looks a bit like the set for *High Noon*, and much of the city's social life revolves around institutions like the Leatherneck Club and the Bum Steer Saloon.

The white people of Klamath Falls did not have much interest in the Klamath, Modoc, and Yahooskin Indians who lived in the hills around them—or much love, either. Oregon in general is not a state that has opened its heart to nonwhite people. Its first territorial constitution barred black people, "Chinamen," and Hawaiian natives from its borders—an official proscription the state repealed only in 1922. But even other Oregonians regard the white people of Klamath Falls as a bit harsh in their racial attitudes. As late as 1957 an investigator for the American Friends Service Committee reported to his headquarters in Portland that he was stunned by the readiness of respectable white people in the town to express their contempt for Indians—and to express it in earthy terms that weren't polite even forty years ago. "One gets the feeling of very intense feelings just below the surface here," he wrote.

As late as 1974 Indian-white relations boiled over into what many people called an "Indian war." Native people marched through town to protest mistreatment of Indian customers by local bartenders. A few months later Klamaths were charged with two separate murders, both of customers at downtown bars. *The Oregonian* reported that gun sales were on the increase and that some diners were afraid to go downtown at night. The mayor of Klamath Falls was nonchalant about the situation: "Indians as a whole—with a few exceptions—are a pretty irresponsible group," he told a reporter.

The whites of the Klamath Basin resented the easy life they saw the Indians living. Because of a treaty signed at the time of the Civil War, the Klamath people held title to hundreds of thousands of acres of prime old-growth forest; they logged a part of it each year and allotted the proceeds to tribal members. As more and more of the valley was fenced off for ranches and farms, the Klamaths found it hard to pursue their traditional no-madic occupations; each generation came to depend more heav-ily on the timber allotments as their means of support.

But to white people, this way of living was wrong; indeed, it was pretty close to immoral. Even when Al Smith was young, there were mutterings about what people today would call "wel-fare" or the "culture of dependency." It was time for the Indians to stop sitting around and living on timber checks, people said; it was time for the Indians to make something of themselves, to become Americans. If that meant selling off the reservation for commercial logging, so much the better.

Al Smith knew little of this as a child. Even today when he speaks of his childhood, a wistful note creeps into his voice; he sounds like an Indian Adam remembering Eden. He lived with his mother, Delia, and his grandparents in a small wood-frame house beside the Williamson River. He played by the riverbank and hunted birds and squirrels with his slingshot. He had a dog named Pal and a fishing rod, and he spent the long, bright sum-mer days on the river in his grandmother's dugout, "fishing," though today he can't remember catching much of anything. The family would pile into his grandfather's old Ford and travel down to the lake to gather the *wocus*; Al's job was to spread the seeds in the sun and keep birds from eating them while they dried. They would go over the mountains to catch suckerfish or pick huckleberries and apples or wild plums for jam. Every now and then they would hire out—the whole family, little Al, too—to help a white farmer in the Willamette Valley to the north pick his hops.

But otherwise, Al Smith spent his first seven years in a Klamath world. He had little awareness of the white culture, or of the forces that were closing in on the Klamath way of life. There were some troubling signs; his grandparents would talk to each other in Klamath, but they wouldn't teach him the language. It would hold him back, they said. When the men got together to play the traditional gambling games or to hold a traditional sweat in a wooden lodge at the riverbank, they were secretive about it; white people didn't approve of these "primitive" ways.

None of this prepared Al Smith for what happened to him at the age of seven. He was sent away from home to live at St. Mary's Academy, the Catholic parochial school in the middle of Klamath Falls. The Indian agents at the Klamath Agency had told Klamath parents to send the children to boarding school to prepare them for futures as real Americans—futures that didn't involve sweat lodges, *wocus*-gathering, or traditional religion. Writing a few years after Al Smith entered St. Mary's, a Catholic historian explained the mission of Oregon's Catholic boarding schools: to "take the child away from the barbaric surroundings of the teepee and . . . mold him in the ways of civilization."

Eden was over. Years later Al Smith remembered Catholic school as a kind of prison. There were high walls and locked doors, and white women in strange black robes gliding silently around. But it was at St. Mary's that Al Smith's true character began to emerge. To put it simply, he was a stubborn boy. He did not back down, and he did not give up. He began to resist the new life the nuns had planned for him.

His first act of resistance was passive but profound: when the nuns asked him whether he had been baptized, he lied. By telling his teachers that he was already baptized, he avoided the formal entry into white religion. But there was still compulsory chapel and catechism class and the switch for Indian boys who did not learn their lessons to the nuns' satisfaction. Very soon Al Smith began to run away, trying to get home to the happiness he remembered beside the Williamson River.

Most of the time he didn't get far; the sheriff's men would spot the small Indian boy on the street and lead him back to St. Mary's. As he grew older, he was transferred to a school in Beaverton, nearly two hundred miles to the north, but that didn't stop him. He lit out for the highway over and over, and the state police would bring him back. After one attempt when he was twelve, an angry priest beat Al and a friend with a leather strap. The other boy went back to his room, so bruised and humiliated that he would not even look Al in the eye. But Al Smith took his whipping and just lit out again, and this time he caught a freight train south through the Willamette Valley, then over the Cascades and down to Klamath Falls. Yard bulls would catch him and throw him off the train, and he'd hide and wait for another southbound freight, until he finally made it home. After that, he enrolled at the Stewart Indian School, a boarding school in Nevada run by the Bureau of Indian Affairs (BIA).

The Indian boarding schools of the 1930s were better than Catholic school—but not much. Their purpose was still to assimilate their students, to teach them "American" ways; but at least Al Smith was now among Native students, even though they were mostly Paiutes from Nevada, who tended to look down on the Klamaths. Al determined to show them that he was someone to be taken seriously. He and a few other students from Oregon sneaked off one night to a neighboring farm. The farmer kept gallons of homemade wine in his barn, and Al and his friends hoisted a few jugs over their shoulders, carried them back to Stewart, and hosted a campfire and drinking party for the student body. He got in trouble, of course; but he also got respect from the southwestern Indian students. And there was something about the taste of that homemade wine that stuck with him. It was as haunting, in a different way, as the memories of fishing the Williamson River.

Al Smith did well at Indian school—first at Stewart and then at Chemawa, another BIA school in Oregon. He played basketball and ran track, and in his senior year he was captain of the football team, an undersized but scrappy tight end. He got good grades in math. But he was also sneaking beer and cheap wine whenever he could, getting drunk, getting into fights. The dark side of white life was growing more and more important to him.

When he left Chemawa in 1938, he was drawn irresistibly to the big-city skid row of Portland, near the docks where the river barges tied up. He and his friends lived by panhandling, cadging drinks, and rolling drunks. He would first hear the word *alcoholic* five years later, after he was drafted, when an army doctor diagnosed him as one. By then he was on his way to federal prison for drinking on duty; when he got out in 1946, he hit the street again.

It got harder, though, as the years went on. In 1950 Al's mother, Delia, fell to her death over a banister and through a skylight in a Portland hotel. His sister had died eight years before. He married, for the first of three times; still, like most alcoholics, he was always alone. He got sick, too; in the early 1950s he ended up in a tuberculosis sanitarium near Salem, Oregon, where doctors collapsed one lung and removed two ribs. Nothing stopped the progression of the disease until they tried a new "miracle drug" called streptomycin. Slowly Al began to regain his health and strength—enough to walk one step, then two, then enough to visit the bathroom alone, and finally enough to go outside and sit in the sunshine. But though he got well, he wasn't a model patient:

> I was sitting out in the sun. I just got there it seems like, I was there maybe five minutes, ten minutes. But they says, "You got to get back inside," and I says, "Screw you people, I'm sitting outside." The doctor came along later on and told me that if I couldn't abide by the rules there that I could leave. I said, "Oh, okay, thanks," so I just got up, asked for my clothes, phoned my wife to come down and get me. And that was it.

He stayed sober for a year or two, but after that it was back to the street. Things were getting worse, though: the strepto-mycin had affected his inner ear, so when he drank he staggered and sometimes fell. Meanwhile, the federal government sent him a notice that he wasn't an Indian anymore.

The 1950s were the "termination era" in federal Indian policy. Congress, like the good people of Klamath Falls, had decided that it was time to get Indian people off the reservations and into the "mainstream." Their approach was simple. Tribes who were considered "ready" for assimilation were "terminated": the federal government closed their tribal rolls, sold off their tribal lands, and sent each tribal member a check for his or her share of the proceeds. The Klamaths were one of the first tribes se-lected for termination. Advocates of termination argued that the Klamaths were ready—educated, acculturated, Christianized. Opponents claimed that the zeal for termination was less a cul-tural judgment than an appraisal of the acres of virgin timber that would be opened for private exploitation when the tribe's land was sold. Some tribal members wanted their lump-sum checks, and some white timber barons wanted the chance to clear-cut the Klamath old growth.

After a bitter battle that split the tribe and the town, the advocates of "Americanism" prevailed; 70 percent of the tribe agreed to accept a $40,000 per capita payment for their timberland. Al Smith was one of them. Termination might have been the end of him; white society had taken his history, his language, his tribe, and his religion. Any further down, and Al Smith, like his mother and sister, would be dead.

But Al Smith had begun to turn himself around. One day in early 1957, he woke up in an alley in Sacramento, bruised and broke and hung over, and decided that he wasn't ready to die yet. If America wanted him out of its history, he wouldn't go along. He would live. He had been around enough to know that AA offered the only hope of survival for a man who had been drinking on the street for nearly twenty years. He had heard the Twelve Steps read out at meetings, and now he decided to try them. On January 15, 1957, he went back to AA. Four decades later he still celebrates the date as a solemn anniversary.

"I had to learn to live all over again," he recalled. "How to behave different. How to treat people. How to treat myself. Learn about different values I knew about but was not really practicing until I was sober. It was a whole new ballgame called life. I finally decided to play by the rules, and the rules were that you had to work the Twelve Steps of Alcoholics Anonymous."

But that was a problem, because the Twelve Steps weren't just about not drinking, they were about filling the emptiness inside him; Al Smith didn't know how to do that, or even whether he wanted to—particularly since Step Two required him to turn to some kind of god, some "higher power." Inside himself he couldn't find one; just an angry, stubborn void, a memory of fighting off the nuns and the Christian God. He knew nothing of his people's religion. His only memory was of his grandmother;

every night before going to bed, she would walk through the house by the Williamson chanting a prayer in Klamath. Al didn't know what she had been saying; he didn't know who she was saying it to. But he had no time to find out; he needed help now. And so he decided to turn to that power, that Indian Creator, or perhaps merely to the sound of the words and the memory of a time when the sun had sparkled on the river and his life and his people had seemed whole. For the first time in his life, Al Smith began to pray. "That will be my God," he said to himself. "A God that I didn't even understand."

2

VALLEY OF THE

SHADOW

Every Fourth of July the city of Eugene, Oregon, holds a municipal fireworks display. Eugene, a city of about 130,000 people, is surrounded by hills. Residents who live in the higher parts of town can sit on their porches or in their front yards and watch as delicate traceries of light streak across the jewel-like Oregon summer sky, casting the shadows of Douglas firs, maples, and oaks across their houses and yards.

The Fourth of July is a special holiday in the western part of Oregon. After the constant rains of winter and spring, the Fourth marks the definitive beginning of the dry season. This time of year is close to being the earthly paradise of which the prophets dreamed: sunny, dry days—warm but seldom hot—ended by long, purple twilights and silken, starry nights. Oregonians as a

VALLEY OF THE SHADOW

group move out of doors: hiking, camping, running, canoeing, kayaking, or playing golf on one of the state's scores of courses.

On July 4, 1983, Dave Frohnmayer; his wife, Lynn; and their three children seemed to be standing at the gates of paradise in more ways than one. As they watched the colors rise and fall above them, the future of the Frohnmayer family must have seemed as bright and broad as the sky around them. The Frohnmayers were a handsome and accomplished couple, each with a successful career. He was attorney general of Oregon, with the prospect of higher office; she was a social worker who had risen to head the Eugene office of the state Children's Services Division (CSD). Their three children—Kirsten, Mark, and Katie—were standouts in the local public schools; the elder two were straight-A students and leaders of student government. Truly, their family must have seemed blessed.

In hindsight, however, it is clear that July 4, 1983, was what classical dramatists would call the climax of Dave and Lynn Frohnmayer's life—the point at which their fortunes had reached flood tide and then began inexorably to recede. Each day that passed after July 4 would take them further away from the brightness of their lives before then, and deeper into the valley of the shadow of death.

David Braden Frohnmayer was born on July 9, 1940, in Medford, Oregon, just north of the California state line. He was the second child of Otto Frohnmayer and MarAbel Braden Frohnmayer, a couple known locally as "the first family of Medford." Otto Frohnmayer had come to Oregon as a boy with his parents, immigrants from Germany. Otto Frohnmayer's life had been a true American pageant of immigrant success: working as a bellboy at the Eugene Hotel, he put himself through the University of Oregon and then through U of O law school. He settled in Medford in 1933 and built a successful small-town law practice.

When he first arrived in town, he later recalled, it wasn't uncommon for lawyers to carry pistols in their jacket pockets—a habit carried over from the turbulent days of the teens and twenties, when Jackson County, torn by party violence and an active Ku Klux Klan, had come close to actual civil war. But Otto Frohnmayer remembers the early days of his practice as a golden time. In those days before legal specialization and megafirms, it was not uncommon for a successful law office to handle real-estate transactions, business and corporate work, personal-injury litigation, and even criminal-defense work. Otto Frohnmayer did all of that, and flourished.

Otto Frohnmayer had won some distinction as a criminal defender, in fact. Once, during the 1950s, he took on the case of a local woman who had shot her husband with the family rifle. No one back then had heard of battered wife syndrome; violent women usually fared poorly in court. But Otto Frohnmayer— tall, dignified, and imposing—made a formidable advocate. He produced experts to testify that his client had undergone a seizure brought on by the flicker of a woodstove. He put on evidence of the husband's systematic abuse—how he had blackened both her eyes repeatedly and even finally broken her dentures. In the end, the jury deliberated only briefly. Otto was pleased by the verdict of not guilty, but he had expected no less. What truly tickled him was that the jury had taken up a collection to buy the defendant new false teeth.

But most of Otto Frohnmayer's practice was business-oriented, and he had a golden touch. His clients included Harry & David during the early years of the fruit empire; he was personal attorney for Glenn Jackson, the utility magnate who merged California-Oregon Power Company with Pacific Power & Light, now PacifiCorp. Frohnmayer was also active from the first in public affairs, a loyal member of the Republican Party, and a friend and adviser to the genial Republican establishment that ran Oregon. He became particularly close to Mark Hatfield, the cerebral political-science professor who became governor of Oregon and then served for thirty years as its maverick senator.

Otto installed his growing family in a tree-shaded home on the northern edge of town, surrounded by acres of forest. (Though the Frohnmayers later donated part of their land to the city for a park, even today their little empire includes thirty-eight acres of prime undeveloped real estate not far from what has become downtown Medford.) His wife, MarAbel Braden, taught music to a generation of Medford children, and she made sure that her own children grew up surrounded by music. So successful was she that two of her four children—Philip, her third son, and Mira, her only daughter—grew up to be professional musicians.

Dave and his brother John also loved and appreciated music. Dave played the trumpet in the Medford High band; John played the trombone and contributed a tuneful baritone to the Frohnmayer Family Singers, who gave a cappella serenades on family occasions. But the two eldest boys followed Otto into the family trade of law. (John, who entered private practice, later became chairman of the National Endowment for the Arts and the author of several books on free expression, including *Leaving Town Alive: Confessions of an Arts Warrior*.)

John Frohnmayer was the star athlete, named to a high-school all-America team in his senior year for his performance as an offensive guard for the Medford High School Black Tornado. Dave was no athlete, but he was a high scorer in the classroom and student body president. He entered Harvard College in 1958, and played in the Harvard Band, which was noted, then as now, for its silly hijinks at halftime during Ivy League football games. But Frohnmayer was still serious in the classroom. As an undergraduate, he published a paper called "The Concept of the

Elite in Liberal Democratic Thought." He was fascinated by figures who understood and used power—Nietzsche and Lenin
were the subjects of his senior thesis. In 1962 he was awarded
a Rhodes scholarship to Oxford, where he won a second B.A.,
in philosophy, in 1964.

After Oxford, Frohnmayer entered the Boalt Hall School of
Law at the University of California at Berkeley. Frohnmayer
graduated in 1967, winning admission to the Order of the
Coif, law school's counterpart of Phi Beta Kappa. He at once
snagged a plum job with the elite firm of Pillsbury, Madison &
Sutro in San Francisco. But public law and constitutional
questions interested Frohnmayer more than the corporate and
commercial work of the law firm. From his father he had inherited a firm but moderate Republicanism and a wide network
of ties to the state and national parties. When Richard Nixon
was elected president in 1968, he named California Republican
Bob Finch his first secretary of Health, Education, and Welfare;
Finch tapped Dave Frohnmayer as his special assistant and one
of his speechwriters.

By now, Dave Frohnmayer was twenty-nine years old and still
single. Otto and MarAbel, proud of their talented and accomplished son, thought it was time for him to settle down, prefer-
ably with a nice girl from Oregon. One evening in 1969, they
were eating at Callahan's, a popular restaurant south of the resort
town of Ashland, a few miles from Medford. There they ran into
old friends, Sue and William Johnson, from Grants Pass, thirty
miles northwest of Medford. William Johnson, like Otto, was a
successful small-town lawyer, and a former district attorney of
Josephine County, of which Grants Pass was the county seat.
The Frohnmayers learned that the Johnsons' daughter, Lynn, had
recently gotten her master's in social work and was working at a
mental-heath clinic near Washington, D.C. Otto made a note to
call Dave. Dave had met Lynn years before, but only briefly. Now

he dutifully called her for a first date. Twelve months later, on December 30, 1970, Dave and Lynn were married in the white wooden Methodist church the Johnsons attended in Grants Pass.

Lynn Diane Johnson was twenty-eight when she and Dave were married. The two in many ways seemed a perfect, almost dynastic, match. He was tall, rangy, and genial; she was blond, petite, and vibrant. Besides their shared backgrounds in small southern Oregon towns, they shared the same kind of intelligence—an almost steely focus on the questions that seemed important to them, an ability to pursue long-term interests and projects without becoming distracted by the minutiae of daily life.

Lynn was also strong-willed and independent. Her parents came from Minnesota originally but had picked Oregon as their home because of its mild climate and glorious summers. When Lynn was born, the family lived in a 520-square-foot shack by the Rogue River; she remembers her early years as a symphony of chuckling water and flashing sunlight. But when she was still in grade school, her mother, expecting her fourth child, insisted on a larger house in town. Shortly after they moved, William Johnson had a sudden heart attack. From then on, the family lived under the shadow of his impending death. Men in Bill Johnson's family died early—in their thirties and forties—and the doctors often told him he had little time left. Bill Johnson, in fact, lived to be sixty-two—but every day of that time seemed to him and his family to be borrowed.

Though her father was a prominent Republican, when Lynn turned twenty-one she went to the courthouse and registered as a Democrat. When the party began sending mailings to the Johnson home, Bill Johnson exploded. "There is no Democrat at this address!" he said. Lynn politely defied him. She defied him again a few months later, when she graduated from Stanford with a degree in history and a minor in French. She wasn't sure what to do next, she told her parents; she had even thought about

President Kennedy's new Peace Corps, perhaps working in French-speaking Africa. Out of the question, said Bill Johnson. Too far away, too dangerous, too Democratic—that was one thing she was not even to consider. "I don't ever want to hear the words *Peace Corps* spoken in this house," he said. Lynn later remembered, "I said, 'That's it! I know what I'm going to do! I'm going into the Peace Corps and show him that he was wrong again.'"

Lynn spent two years in the Ivory Coast teaching French to African schoolchildren who needed the language to go on to high school under the educational system created by the French colonizers. Compared with those she taught, she lived in luxury, with pure water and wholesome food and an apartment, and later an entire house, all to herself. In the summer after her first year, she headed out on her own to see the real Africa. She took no one with her; if she had an English-speaking friend along, she reasoned, she wouldn't learn to talk to the people. Often she would be the only non-African person aboard an ancient lorry or a rickety bus winding its way around the Sahel—through Niger, Upper Volta, and Nigeria. Once, she recalled, the lorry tilted in the sand at the side of the road, finally coming to rest at a precarious angle. They couldn't go farther without a tow, so the entire group waited three days by the side of the road for a passing driver who could pull them out. They ran out of food; a passing shepherd sold them a lamb, which they butchered and ate family-style. All in all, she was a long way from Grants Pass.

Back in the United States, she enrolled in graduate school at Columbia to study French literature but quit after only seven weeks. She couldn't forget the children she had seen in Africa or the children she saw around her on New York's Upper West Side. These kids didn't need French lessons—they needed food, clothes, warm homes, loving caretakers. Lynn went to work for an adoption agency. Soon she had enrolled in social-work school, with the aim of becoming an adoption specialist. She was living in Washington's Mount Pleasant neighborhood and commuting to a mental-health center in Springfield, Virginia, when Dave called her for their first date.

Dave and Lynn spent their honeymoon skiing at Mount Bachelor, near Bend, Oregon. It was a short honeymoon; Dave had been hired as an assistant professor at his father's alma mater, the University of Oregon law school. He started teaching early in January of 1971. "After I finished writing thank-you notes for all those beautiful gifts," Lynn said later, "I went to work myself."

Lynn had hoped to find a job at a small mental-health clinic for children. But in Eugene in 1971, there was no such center. She took a job as a child-abuse investigator for Oregon's Children's Services Division.

The Frohnmayers flourished in Eugene. Dave quickly became known as a rising star in academic constitutional law; he won the American Bar Foundation's prestigious Weaver Essay Competition twice in three years. Lynn became pregnant, and they moved into their family home on Baker Boulevard shortly before their first daughter, Kirsten, was born in 1973. Mark followed a year later, and in 1978, a second daughter, Katie.

The children were as remarkable as their parents. "We felt so lucky and so blessed," Lynn Frohnmayer recalls. "We'd talk about it: 'Look at our kids, they are just terrific kids.' They all loved school. They were all great students. It wasn't a matter of urging them to work, or bribing them to do well. They just took off on their own. They had interests, they had friends, they were very happy children. We were just sailing along. Were we smug? Maybe we were."

Certainly the Frohnmayers had their worries—but they were the kind of worries that parents pray for. The three kids were all outstanding—how would their parents pay for first-rate colleges? How could they fit in enough time for family life and the demands of their careers?

One worry would sometimes keep Lynn up at night, and sometimes led her to come down hard on those who worked for her at CSD when they fell short of her high expectations. She could not forget that she and her staff held children's lives in their hands. If they made a mistake—left a child in an abusive home or mistakenly put one in an unsafe foster placement—a child could die. To Lynn, with her lifelong commitment to children, the needless death of a child was unimaginably sad. She could not tolerate even the thought, and so she lay awake at night, heart pounding, or woke up early and went to the office to drive her staff. "I don't think I was an easy person to work for," she said later.

To Lynn, it seemed natural to take on a sense of responsibility for the community they lived in. Dave felt the same about work and public life. The feeling that second- and third-generation Oregonians have for the state is hard to understand for those who were born in more populous parts. Even though it has as many square miles as Italy, the state of Oregon during the forties and fifties was more like a small city than a state. In 1940, the year Dave Frohnmayer was born, the population of Oregon barely topped a million. In 1970, the year Dave and Lynn were married, its population had grown to only 2 million. The state lacked any trappings of aristocracy. Almost all its children, for example, went to public school. But there was a kind of Jeffersonian upper crust—those who by education and hard work had risen to positions of influence. That group included the Frohnmayers and the Johnsons; they tended to feel that their community extended beyond their home and family to encompass public life.

Politics and government in a small state are fundamentally different from the same activities in a megastate like New York or California. A politician, a civil servant, a businessman, or a lawyer could rise to the top rank of influence without sacrificing the values of private life. Even today, when Oregon's population is enough to make up a fair-size borough of New York, Oregon politics has some of that small-town flavor; it's not uncommon to catch sight of the current governor, John Kitzhaber, shopping for groceries by himself in a supermarket.

So politics and community service have always seemed to the Frohnmayers compatible with family life—indeed, in a way, an extension of it. In 1974 Dave Frohnmayer had almost impulsively filed as the Republican candidate for the Oregon House of Representatives. His home lay in District 40, a university neighborhood that was one of the most liberal and Democratic districts in the state. But he had tackled the campaign with his usual thoroughness, ringing doorbells and buttonholing voters, peppering the newspapers with closely reasoned position papers. It was the year of Watergate: he didn't really expect to win; the idea was to spread his name before the public, in preparation for another race at a better time. On election night he took Lynn to Tino's Spaghetti House, a local restaurant with checked tablecloths and candles in Chianti bottles on every table, to celebrate the return to normal life. Emerging from dinner, the Frohnmayers heard on the radio that Dave, improbably, had won.

Frohnmayer quickly became a respected member of the Oregon legislature and a key part of a moderate-liberal bipartisan establishment that made Oregon a watchword for progressive state government in the 1970s. His speeches and votes helped prevent reinstatement of capital punishment, passed court reforms, and supported Oregon's sweeping system of land-use controls, designed by Governor Tom McCall to keep development from "Californicating" the state.

Frohnmayer made his name in the legislature with his intelligence, his readiness with language, and his level head. He had the one skill a politician needs most—he could suffer fools gladly, listening with grave attention to colleagues or constituents who might not be rocket scientists but were flattered that this eminent, brilliant man seemed to be thinking about what they had to say. In the rough-and-tumble of legislative debate, he managed to keep an even temper; even when receiving bad news, his strongest oath was often "Oh, for heaven's sake." (Though not always: on one memorable occasion, Frohnmayer was point man for a bill to limit the number of fields that could be burned as part of the process of beginning a new year's grass-seed crop in the Willamette Valley. The late-summer burning often caused people near Eugene to suffer teary eyes, dry coughing, and even asthma attacks; the thick smoke sometimes caused massive traffic pileups on Interstate Highway 5. Grass-seed farmers protested bitterly when the state began to clamp down on the practice; after one hearing, a scientist from Oregon State University got right in Frohnmayer's face and called him a liar. A quarter century later, Frohnmayer is still embarrassed at how close the incident came to an old-fashioned fistfight, as he leaned right back into the other man's face and eloquently described his intelligence, personal hygiene, and family background.)

Dave Frohnmayer enjoyed politics—its blend of high ideals, late nights, and cheap cigars. Politics even allowed Frohnmayer an outlet for the love of music he had learned from his mother; each year at the GOP's annual Dorchester Conference, Dave and the Frohn Tones would entertain the assembled activists with song parodies satirizing the foibles of both parties.

In 1980 Frohnmayer ran for attorney general of the state. He won handily, and by July 1983 his reelection was a foregone conclusion. Beyond that, it was assumed, lay the governorship, and then perhaps a seat in the U.S. Senate. By July 4, 1983, some people had even begun to wonder whether Oregon—whose closest brush with the White House had come when Richard

Nixon briefly considered Senator Mark Hatfield as a replacement for disgraced Vice President Spiro Agnew—might have a president in its future.

On July 5 Dave Frohnmayer rode with his usual carpool for the hour-long commute up the valley to Salem, the state capital. When he got back home that evening, he found the family babysitter waiting for him, all but hysterical, in the driveway. Kirsten had collapsed, she told him. The doctors didn't know what was wrong, but it was serious. She was at Sacred Heart Medical Center downtown, and Dave was needed there right away.

Dave and Lynn had worried about Kirsten recently, but only in the way that high-achieving parents gifted with a nearly perfect child often somewhat idly imagine what would make her truly perfect. Kirsten was small, to begin with. Not abnormally so; her growth was in the fifteenth percentile for her age. And Lynn was petite. That wasn't really a problem, even though Katie and Mark seemed to have inherited the Frohnmayer gene for height. But sometimes Kirsten seemed to lack energy—not for her studies, at which she excelled, or for school activities, but sometimes when the family took a long bike ride or a hike up Spencer Butte, Kirsten would lag behind. She probably needed vitamins, they thought; or maybe it was some kind of anemia. In fact, just a year before, they had had her blood counts checked, and everything came back normal. So they had filed it away; no parent could really worry about a girl like Kirsten, who was so clearly exceptional in almost every way.

But when he reached the hospital, Dave learned that Kirsten was running a high fever, and her white count—the measure of infection-fighting blood cells—had fallen through the floor. The doctors suspected leukemia, and they were worried enough to order a bone-marrow biopsy, a painful and scary operation in which a bit of marrow is sucked out through a large needle, to confirm their initial diagnosis.

The results came back that night, and Dave and Lynn Frohn-mayer waited anxiously in the hospital room for the news. The doctor entered, looking grim. "It's not leukemia," he said. Lynn reacted visibly, with relief bordering on euphoria. Then the doctor went on. It was something worse, he said—aplastic anemia, a rare, often fatal blood disease in which the bone marrow stops making enough healthy blood cells. Although all of the causes of aplastic anemia are still unknown, it has been linked to everyday toxins and viruses. And the prognosis—well, there was no prognosis, really. Aplastic anemia was usually incurable and fatal, and with counts as low as Kirsten's, the horizon would be measured in weeks or months, not years. Kirsten would be dead by Christmas. Her only chance would be a bone-marrow transplant from a family member, if one could be found whose marrow matched closely enough to give a transplant a fighting chance.

Dave and Lynn and their children were tested to see whether any of them could provide a match. The answer was no; there was no matching donor. Kirsten was transferred to Doernbecher Children's Hospital in Portland, part of the Oregon Health Sciences University, the state's only teaching hospital complex. Immune-suppressing drugs produced no improvement. Meanwhile, the Frohnmayers began frantically reading about her condition, which was called idiopathic aplastic anemia, meaning aplastic anemia for which there is no obvious cause. They took Kirsten to the Fred Hutchinson Cancer Research Center in Seattle—the Hutch, as cancer patients call it—in search of a new therapy. The doctors there could only suggest androgens, male hormones that might slow the progress of the disease. The Frohnmayers were troubled by that prospect. Kirsten was only ten, just about to hit puberty; massive doses of male hormones might distort her growth forever, and without much chance of success.

Sunday mornings in the Frohnmayer household had been

carefree times, when Dave would go for doughnuts and the entire family would saddle up the bikes or head for the river. Now the main business was reading medical journals, making notes on promising therapies, jotting phone numbers of researchers working on new theories. Dave and Lynn drew inspiration from Kirsten, who reacted to her illness with a ferocious determination to go on with her schoolwork and her sports as if nothing at all were wrong. Summer gave way to fall; Kirsten's blood counts got no better, but they didn't get worse, either. December came, and she was still alive and, to the untrained eye, blooming. Her counts were low, but she didn't need transfusions. Something was wrong with the diagnosis.

Early in December Dave and Lynn took Kirsten to Portland for some new tests. Doctors there had a suspicion they hadn't shared with the Frohnmayers; they performed a test on her chromosomes to see whether they broke easily in the presence of test chemicals. The results came back on December 30, the Frohnmayers' fourteenth wedding anniversary. Lynn took the doctor's call in the midst of a dinner party for friends; when she heard what the doctors had to say, she became hysterical: Kirsten had something called Fanconi anemia.

Fanconi anemia, or FA, is a rare disease, discovered in 1927 by Swiss pediatrician Guido Fanconi. An FA patient's bone marrow gradually stops making the three key ingredients of blood—red cells, which carry oxygen to the rest of the body; white cells, which fight off infection; and platelets, which clump together and coagulate to stop internal or external bleeding. The child—FA is almost invariably a childhood-onset disease—has a high chance of developing leukemia. Eventually the bone marrow fails altogether.

Barring a miracle, FA children did not live to become adults. And unlike aplastic anemia, FA was not an idiopathic disease.

Doctors knew the cause—a recessive gene. If both parents carried the genetic trait, there was one chance in four their child would have FA.

It was a stunning diagnosis in many ways. First of all, it meant Kirsten had gotten the disease from her parents. Neither family had any history of FA; no one on either side had even heard the name before. But it was their heritage: two people who had come together to give their child a fatal gift. The guilt, the sense of impurity, was hard enough to bear. But there was another implication: Katie and Mark were at risk, too. Each had one chance in four of developing FA. Neither child showed any sign of the disease, however. Unlike Kirsten, Mark and Katie were tall, big-boned. And Kirsten's features were dysmorphic—slightly different from her siblings, a bit smaller, not as cleanly shaped. The Frohnmayers had Mark and Katie tested, just to be on the safe side.

Kirsten's only hope was a bone-marrow transplant. And now the failure of the family to provide a genetic match became an ominous portent. In 1983 the science of bone-marrow transplantation had not progressed, as it has now, to the point at which a patient can safely receive a transplant from an unrelated donor. The Frohnmayers would have to broaden their search for a donor, to look for cousins who might provide a match for Kirsten's marrow.

And then the tests came back. Mark was fine. But Katie, five years old, had FA, too.

Katie and Kirsten were alike in their intelligence and drive; otherwise, they were as different as siblings could be. Kirsten was serious, an organizer, and something of a philosopher. She had decided early that she would be a lawyer like her father and her grandfathers. Katie was high-spirited, a clotheshorse, a planner of parties. She was the one in the family who began planning the Christmas decorations as soon as Thanksgiving was over. Her mind was almost scary, too. She had more than two dozen My Little Pony dolls, each one a little different, with its own name and its own traits. Lynn had noticed early that if she sent Katie out of the room and took away one of the ponies, Katie could tell at once which one was gone: "It's Firefly, the blue one with the stars on the tail."

As she grew older, she collected young readers' series books, the numbered paperbacks recounting the adventures of the Baby-Sitters Club or Sweet Valley High. She had the books in her room, neatly shelved in order, and sometimes Dave or Lynn would test her. "Katie, what's on the cover of *Nancy Drew Files* number ninety-six?" And she would describe the color, who was pictured, and what they were doing. Or they would describe a picture from a book cover, and she would give the title and volume number and recap the plot. "She was never wrong," Lynn remembers. Katie was a prodigy on skis; she played soccer; and when she played the piano, she could make you cry.

None of this was fair. Dave and Lynn decided to try to protect Katie, who was only five when they got the news. They said nothing to either child about the results. Let Katie have her childhood years before she realized what lay before her. She had no symptoms; besides, they thought with the desperate optimism of parents everywhere, by the time she was ten, there might be a treatment—even a cure.

And so the months wore on. Kirsten was in school, and her counts were stable. Katie showed no symptoms. Dave and Lynn began to teach themselves about the disease that had suddenly come into the center of their lives. Research was ongoing in bone-marrow transplantation, which is the key to treating leukemia and other blood diseases as well as FA. Doctors hoped soon to be able to match unrelated donors, but so far they couldn't. And when they finally were able to, how would the proper donors be found? Dave got involved in starting the National Bone Marrow Donor Program, a registry of information on people all over the country who had had their tissues typed in an attempt to provide a donor for someone. Even if there was no match, there was no sense throwing away the data. Someday potential donors might save the life of someone they did not even know.

Dave decided that the Frohnmayers should start a support group for FA families. FA was so rare and obscure that families faced with a diagnosis—a death sentence, really, for one of their children—usually had no one but their physicians to turn to for information or support. The doctors usually weren't much help; most of them had never seen an FA patient before. The families needed a central clearinghouse for information and support. Lynn reluctantly agreed; she was still trying to go on with life as if it were normal. She was still working at CSD, still driving the kids to soccer and to music lessons, and she was reading the journals, calling researchers at night, trying to learn whatever she could about FA. (Eventually she left her job and devoted herself to taking care of the girls.) Dave was attorney general, busy every day with a series of crises; where would they find the time? But Dave insisted; his way of coping with unimaginable pain and fear was to work, to charge straight at the demons that were tormenting their little girls.

Until the group began, there had been no one to lobby for research funding, no group helping coordinate research. The informal group became the Fanconi Anemia Support Group, the only national organization devoted to FA support and research, with a family newsletter, a scientific bulletin, and a yearly camp for FA patients and their families.

Dave was still attorney general; friends and supporters were urging him to run for governor in 1986, to replace Republican Vic Atiyeh, who was retiring. It would be a tough primary, though, against his fellow Republican Norma Paulus; months on the road, nights on the telephone raising money. So in 1985 Dave decided to put politics on hold. He would run for reelection as attorney general in 1988 (his poll numbers were so high that the election was a formality) and concentrate on his family.

Also in 1985 Lynn gave birth to a son. Pregnancy had stirred many conflicting feelings. Lynn loved children; they were her life, private and professional, and she had sometimes wished that she had married younger so that she could have had a dozen. Life with Mark and the girls was fun, every day bringing some new adventure. But she had also brought two girls into the world who had to suffer, and perhaps die, because of the genes she and Dave had passed along to them. It seemed unfair to let that happen again. On the other hand, a healthy child might grow to be a donor for one of the girls. Lynn had the fetus tested by amniocentesis; it was a baby boy (they would name him Jonathan), perfectly healthy and free from FA—but not a match for either of his sisters.

The next year, 1986, Katie's innocence came to a brutal end. One day her parents noticed a small infection on her leg—something that looked like a spider bite. But it wouldn't go away, and with an FA patient there are no minor injuries. Her doctor noticed, too, that she had petechiae, small outbreaks of bleeding under the skin. Katie entered Sacred Heart, where a surgeon excised the infected spot. Within days it grew back larger than before. Sores also popped out on her face. A second surgery excised it again, and this time it returned as a putrefying sore. Meanwhile, the doctors put Katie through a battery of tests, including X rays; one day, when she was in a wheelchair on her way down to radiology, a harried nurse sought to save a few steps by putting Katie's chart in her hand and asking her to give it to the X-ray staff. Katie did, but being bright and inquisitive, she read it first; written in block letters across the cover sheet was a notation that the patient had FA.

"Why didn't you tell me?" she asked Lynn. Her parents tried

to explain that they had hoped to give her a few good years, to save some of her innocence. Katie didn't stay angry; that was not her way. But the Frohnmayers resolved that if—God forbid—they ever had to do it over again, they would level with a child from the first day of illness.

Katie was referred to a specialist in Seattle, who diagnosed her with signs of impending leukemia. Doctors gave her prednisone, an anti-inflammatory that would control the infection and inflammation, even though it would probably stunt her growth. She got better. A few weeks later she was back on skis, back at school, reading and playing soccer as if she had not had to read her own death sentence in an unknown handwriting, alone in a cold hospital corridor.

In 1986 Lynn Frohnmayer found out she was pregnant again. Once again, she was determined to take every precaution—to make sure the baby would be healthy. This time the doctors suggested a new technique, as reliable as amniocentesis but earlier in the pregnancy. It was called chorionic villi sampling (CVS)—a procedure by which a technician inserts a tiny needle into the uterus. The needle is passed into the developing placenta. During the entire procedure, the position of the needle is observed and guided by ultrasound. Once the needle is properly positioned, small fragments of the developing placenta are drawn up the needle with a syringe. The sample is then immediately examined under a microscope to determine if enough cells have been obtained to run a test.

Lynn went to San Francisco for the procedure, which was so new that it wasn't offered in Eugene. But when the doctors did a preliminary ultrasound, they found that Lynn was carrying not one baby, but two. Because the center would not do a CVS on a twin pregnancy—they weren't sure about the risks—Lynn traveled to Philadelphia, where physicians gathered sample tissues from both babies. Lynn carried the samples herself to New York

City to a leading authority on prenatal testing for FA. The tests produced good news—neither child bore the FA trait. Then the cells were sent on to Texas, where another lab examined them for compatibility with Katie and Kirsten. A few weeks later, the really good news came in. There were two children, a boy and a girl. The female fetus was a match for Katie; the boy would be a match for Kirsten.

For a few short weeks, then, Dave and Lynn began to think that their dreams had come true, the dreams they had begun to have since the day Kirsten got sick. Maybe the whole nightmare could just go away; maybe it was all a mistake. Maybe the twins would be born, and in a few years the girls would have bone-marrow transplants and would be well again. Maybe Dave and Lynn would wake again to a house full of healthy children, of music and sunlight, with nothing more to worry about than politics and when to go for doughnuts.

At sixteen weeks Lynn went to Portland for an amniocentesis to confirm the earlier findings. But the results, when they came, were useless. Something had contaminated the fluid, and the lab could not grow a culture of cells to test. It was a slight worry, but still, they had the CVS results. Then a few weeks later, another ultrasound revealed that the male twin had died. Something—probably the amniocentesis needle—had caused the placenta to separate from the wall of Lynn's uterus. She was carrying only one live fetus, the baby girl. When Lynn told the children the news, Katie burst into tears. Her match had not died; she was crying for her sister, for Kirsten, who now did not have the lifeline the female twin offered Katie.

In February 1987 Lynn gave birth to a tiny blond girl. They named her Amy. A few days after she was born, Lynn got a call from the specialist in New York. They had sent a small sample of blood from Amy's umbilical cord, just to confirm the CVS results. Now the doctor was calling to ask for just one more blood sample. "Why in the world would you need another test?" Lynn Frohnmayer asked.

The cord blood had clotted, the doctor replied. Just a formality. We need a little more.

In fact, the cord blood sample was okay; but the tests showed that Amy had FA. The earlier test had missed this. The specialist was hoping against hope that something in the second test was wrong—perhaps as a result of contamination in the lab. But the second test confirmed the worst.

"Which shock is the worst I can't tell," Lynn Frohnmayer recalled. "But that has to be right at the top of the list. I would have three children with the same illness. There would be no way to help Katie. And to have three daughters with it—not a life-threatening disease but a disease described in all the literature as a fatal disease. It was just overwhelming. I was incredibly depressed."

Lynn Frohnmayer had never believed in hiding the pain her daughters' illness caused her. She would tell the world that this wasn't fair, that this was awful. Dave was more circumspect, more stoic. He didn't believe in dwelling on the negative. But he admits that the winter of 1987 was a low point. Lynn was forty-four; it was unlikely she'd ever have another child. They had three sick girls to care for. There would be no awakening from the nightmare. Whatever light and music came from this ordeal, the Frohnmayer family would have to make on their own.

3

THE LAST OF
THE KLAMATHS

In the fall of 1975, Al Smith drove back into the Klamath Basin. He was a very different man from the young hell-raiser who had lit out for Portland nearly forty years before. He was driving a new pickup truck, he had money in his pocket, he had decent clothes on his back. He hadn't had a drink in nearly twenty years, and he had made a national reputation—and a good living— helping other Indian people deal with alcohol- and drug-abuse problems. He had seen the world—far more of it than he had ever imagined he would as a young man. And he had begun to see himself as an Indian, whatever the Bureau of Indian Affairs said about the Klamath tribe. But Al Smith still didn't really understand the world he had come from, the world that—in what seemed to be its final flickers of existence—beckoned him back to where his people still lived.

For eighteen years Al Smith had "worked the program," as AA members say. AA's Twelve Steps are not simply about ways of not drinking; in fact, many AA publications warn that becoming sober without undergoing a spiritual rebirth is far more agonizing and destructive than continuing to drink. AA members need to enter "recovery"; they must, in essence, rebuild themselves from the ground up as moral beings. Much of their energy must go into taking responsibility for the harm they have done to others and into making amends to anyone they have wronged.

For Al Smith, recovery meant learning to stand on his own and do something he had not done in all his thirty-seven years— hold a job for longer than it took to earn the price of a binge. He had done that—first as a janitor, then as a furniture finisher. People in AA had gotten to know him and his story. Up and down the West Coast, he became a sought-after speaker at AA meetings and conferences. AA counsels its members against seeking status inside the organization, and Al sometimes became angry when he thought others were putting him on a pedestal. Nonetheless, Al Smith was well known for his dynamic presentation and the fierce determination with which he would urge others to work the Steps. Helping other alcoholics is an important part of recovery, AA teaches.

One day in 1970, his AA work had opened a new career door for him. A group in Portland was starting a program to counsel alcoholics, and they asked Al Smith to help them write their grant application. The group had liked his suggestions so much that they ended up offering him a job with their new agency, which they called the Alcoholism Counseling and Recovery Program. Al Smith became the agency's first alcoholism counselor.

In moving from furniture finishing to alcoholism counseling, Al Smith was getting in on the ground floor of an enormous growth industry. America in the seventies was like a binge drinker awakening with a hangover. The chemical excesses of the sixties had left a lot of wreckage in their wake. And alcoholism had just recently been recognized by medical science as a disease rather than a moral failing. Governments and foundations were eager to fund experiments that showed promise of helping drinkers turn their lives around. Al Smith offered his own story, his own example of sobriety, and his knowledge of the Twelve Steps.

By 1973 Al was offered a job with the newly formed American Indian Council on Alcohol and Alcohol Abuse, funded by the federal government and headquartered in Denver. Within four years, Al Smith's name was known all over Indian country. He would travel to reservations, meet with tribal officials, and teach all who would listen how to set up AA meetings, how to work the Steps, how to stay sober and help others. Native people were as eager for sobriety as anyone else in the seventies. Al's work sowed the seeds of a huge upswelling of self-help in Indian communities across the West.

The reservation work also brought Al into the world of what he calls "national Indians." He had never flown in a plane before; now he became a frequent flyer, hopping by commercial airliner in and out of reservation towns across the country. He stayed in motels and drove rental cars. All the apparatus of middle-class life—which his colleagues took for granted—was daunting to Al Smith. And while he was learning to function like a white man, Al Smith was also learning more about how to be an Indian.

The job with the council came at a time when Indian country was stirring in a variety of ways. After the termination era, Richard Nixon inaugurated a federal policy of support for tribal self-determination. To this day, many Indian activists remember the Nixon administration as a golden era, a time when federal funds were available for reservation projects and when Indian people were genuinely included in planning and carrying them out. And at the same time, Indians all over the country were feeling the aftershocks of the civil rights and antiwar movements. Indian militancy and Indian power became catchphrases, particularly on the big reservations of the Great Plains. A new generation of activists emerged—angry, flamboyant, and at least potentially violent; men like Russell Means, a Lakota Sioux, and Clyde Bellecourt and Dennis Banks, both Chippewas. In 1969 a group of these activists seized Alcatraz Island in San Francisco Bay, demanding its return to Indian ownership and offering the federal government twenty-four dollars' worth of beads in exchange. For nineteen months the protesters held the island, in direct view of America's most-visited waterfront, and received delegations of sympathetic clergy, civil-rights activists, and film actors. Although they abandoned the island in June 1971, the group, which called itself Indians of All Nations, had managed to put a face on Indian activism and raise the profile of Indian militancy across the nation.

Indian activists in Minnesota in 1968 had formed a group called the American Indian Movement (AIM) to protest police harassment of Natives in the Twin Cites. AIM's first large-scale operation was a nationwide caravan of protesters called the Trail of Broken Treaties. They crossed the country in the fall of 1972 and, just before the presidential election, occupied the Bureau of Indian Affairs office at 1951 Constitution Avenue N.W. in Washington, D.C. AIM had twenty demands, most of which centered on restoring the old treaties to give Native communities increased independence and self-determination. Nixon administration officials were anxious to avoid television footage of federal marshals attacking Indian protesters, so the administration negotiated, and at length persuaded the occupiers to leave the BIA by guaranteeing federal reimbursement of their travel expenses.

AIM next took its campaign to the huge Pine Ridge Reservation in South Dakota, where Means challenged the leadership of Oglala Sioux tribal chairman Dickie Wilson. Wilson fought back with the support of his Guardians of the Oglala Nation, or

GOON squads, and something very much like civil war raged across the prairies. In February 1973 AIM members seized the tourist complex at Wounded Knee, South Dakota, site of the 1890 massacre of Ghost Dance followers and a symbol of white mistreatment of Native peoples. The occupation led to an armed standoff between AIM and the FBI, which ended on May 8, after two occupiers were killed.

The political stirrings of the early seventies were matched by a religious stirring among Native peoples. Not since the Ghost Dance swept out of Paiute country in the nineteenth century had so many Native people found themselves reexamining their religious beliefs and practices. The days were gone when BIA officials took it upon themselves to suppress traditional ceremonies and songs. Beyond that, the boarding-school era had produced a radical change in Indian religious thinking. The designers of the boarding-school policy had hoped that throwing together young people from different tribes would eradicate their tribal beliefs and lead them within the consensus of American Christianity. But in fact, the diverse tribal members at the boarding schools had learned how much they had in common. Until the twentieth century, much of Native religion was specific to individual villages or tribes; but by the time Al Smith went to work for the council, the sharing at boarding schools, powwows and conferences, and in the major cities (where BIA policy had relocated Indians during the 1950s) had produced a new Native tradition that scholars were beginning to call pan-Indian—a complex of rituals and beliefs that served to identify adherents not as members of a given tribe but as Native Americans, partakers of a common tradition opposed to the white culture that dominated it.

At conferences and meetings, Al Smith began to learn the elements of this new Indian spirituality. One of the most important he was already familiar with: the sweat lodge, which was indigenous to the Northwest, including Klamath country. The sweat lodge is a round, low structure, usually made of willow saplings, and covered with hides or blankets, which keep light out and heat in. Outside the lodge, leaders light a sacred fire and heat stones in its flames until they are red-hot. Participants enter the lodge and seat themselves in a circle—men wearing shorts and women wearing sheets or special "sweat dresses." Hot stones are then passed into the tent and placed in a hole in the center. When the lodge has been closed, the leader, in the darkness, ladles water onto the hot stones to make steam. Inside, the people sing and pray while the steam and heat brings forth impurities from their bodies. Four times during the ceremony the lodge is opened to give participants a chance to cool off; then new stones are brought in and the prayer and sweating begin again. Sweating can be a vigorous experience; usually a ceremony takes three to four hours, and the events around it can occupy an entire day. Indian people all over North America—everywhere except the desert Southwest—had known and used the sweat lodge for hundreds of years. It was a way of purifying the body and the spirit; the sweat seemed to carry off much of the dross of daily life, leaving those in the lodge strengthened in their efforts to change and improve.

Al Smith was exposed to these traditions. Like a lot of people in the field, he noticed that Native people tended to do better when their recovery was anchored in specifically Native spirituality and ritual as well as the Twelve Steps of Alcoholics Anonymous.

AA is very much a product of Protestant Christianity. It emphasizes words—both the words spoken by members in meetings and the words of the "Big Book," the collection of essays about the Twelve Steps written by Bill Wilson and other founders of AA. AA members spend a lot of time getting in touch with their feelings and sharing them with the group. That wasn't exactly the

Indian way. The Big Book is much like a Bible to AA members; some meetings begin with a set reading, like the Scripture in a Christian church. But words were not as important in the Indian religious tradition. Indian prophets did not write sacred books, and Native people often found more meaning in music, dance, and other ritual behavior than in Scripture lessons and hymns.

Alcoholism is endemic in Indian country. On some reservations rates are well above 50 percent. Any Native person—or indeed any non-Indian who knows more than a few Native people—can tell stories of lives blighted or snuffed out by alcohol and drug abuse. The federal American Indian Policy Review Commission in 1977 had called alcoholism "the most severe and widespread health problem among Indians today." A contemporaneous study showed that more than 50 percent of the Indians surveyed had either experienced alcohol abuse themselves or encountered it in their own families. Often they can also point to friends and family who have triumphed over alcoholism and begun to help others do the same. But many stories end in tragedy.

There is almost certainly no one explanation for this phenomenon. For one thing, alcoholism and drug abuse, no matter what the setting, are complex public-health problems with many causes, some biological, some social. For another, America's Native population is, within itself, nearly as diverse as the nation as a whole, consisting of hundreds of tribes with radically different histories, cultures, and genetic heritages. Some theorists posit an evolutionary or genetic basis to the susceptibility of Native people to alcoholism; European cultures, they argue, have used liquor for many centuries longer than have Indian people. Individuals in alcohol-using cultures tend to die earlier if they are unable to control their drinking; thus, because these unfortunates have fewer children, the number of individuals with a genetic susceptibility to alcohol declines over the generations. Beyond this speculative explanation, researchers in recent years have realized that heavy drinking by one or both parents may biologically predispose a child to abuse alcohol as well, thus setting up a familial basis for alcoholism that is devastating among some Native tribes.

Others who study the problem, however, see the epidemic of Indian drinking as the result of complex cultural causes. To begin with, they note, many Indian people have long accepted altered states of consciousness as an important source of enlightenment. When they encountered alcohol, some decided it was a quicker and easier way to a vision quest, requiring no fasting or isolation. In addition, they often learned about alcohol from white conquistadors, explorers, or frontiersmen, who were themselves accustomed to binge drinking and regular intoxication as a normal part of life. Since that first introduction, group drunkenness has become such an important part of life among Indian communities that individuals who refuse to drink may find themselves shunned by friends and even family members.

But there is, of course, another dimension to alcoholism. The poisonous consolation of drinking became available to Indians at the moment when white settlers were systematically destroying Native culture. Through disease, military defeat, displacement, and cultural warfare, whites humbled once-proud Indian nomads and dispossessed once-settled Indian farmers. Native people were taught to look on their languages, their religions, and their families as inferior constructs, destined to disappear without a trace. It is hardly surprising that many people subjected to such a view of the world chose to hide from the pain in drunkenness and drugs.

As early as the beginning of the nineteenth century, white missionaries and officials began seeking to combat drinking among Indians by giving them yet another hefty dose of white culture: temperance societies and anti-alcohol tracts, some written in Native languages. By the 1970s some alcohol specialists had begun to theorize that the cultural aspect of alcoholism might be addressed if Native religious concepts and cultural patterns were adapted for the new field of substance-abuse counseling, rather than simply shipping AA concepts onto reservations.

But as Al Smith was beginning to learn about ways to adapt Native religious beliefs to alcoholism and drug-abuse treatment, money for Indian programs began to dry up once again. In 1977 Al Smith left the council and closed his apartment in Denver. Before he left town, he went to a car lot and traded his Porsche for a pickup truck. He was going home again.

The Klamath nation had legally ceased to exist in 1958. But erasing history is not as easy as passing a law; Klamath people remained, as fractious, confused, and proud as before. The termination fight had split the tribe down the middle, to the point that some Klamaths welcomed the loss of tribal status as a way of ending the conflict. But even in the afterlife, the Klamaths continued to fight among themselves. Those who had accepted termination had taken their share of the tribal assets and "withdrawn" from the tribe. Others were "remaining Indians"—they had left their share in the common pot, which the federal government assigned to U.S. Bank of Oregon to manage as trustee. Every five years the remaining Klamaths would vote again on continuing the trust arrangement. Every five years the issue would split the community anew, until in 1969, by a narrow margin, the majority voted to close the trust. Congress then voted to purchase the 135,000 acres of tribal forestland and incorporate it into the national forest system, and by 1974 each remaining tribal member received a first payment of nearly a hundred thousand dollars.

The name the Forest Service chose for the new parcel was drawn from Klamath history: Winema National Forest. Winema, whom the whites had called Toby Riddle, was a Klamath woman

who had served as translator and peace negotiator during the
most dangerous moments of the Modoc War of 1873. The nam-
ing of the forest was intended as a graceful salute to a disap-
pearing people.

But at the moment when the spark of Klamath identity
seemed to be dying out, another name from Klamath history
arose to keep it burning. Edison Chiloquin is the grandson of
Chiloquin, one of the Klamath people's greatest nineteenth-
century leaders. Chiloquin was revered as a man of wisdom and
a warrior, and the old people still told miraculous stories of his
bravery and prowess in battle. "Old chief Chiloquin was quite a
man, short but very strong," one elder told a historian. "He was
a *chief!*" The story ran that Chiloquin had slept in his tent all
day while battle against another tribe raged around him. At sun-
set he awoke, washed his face, and rode forth to win the battle
single-handedly.

Now another Chiloquin single-handedly took on the U.S. government. Edison Chiloquin didn't want money and wasn't
impressed that the white people wanted to take Klamath land
and name it after Winema. He refused his hundred thousand
dollars. He asked instead that the Forest Service give him his
share in land—enough to build a traditional Klamath village
where young people could get a glimpse of their people's history.
The Forest Service at first agreed, but they wanted Chiloquin's
village to be a kind of "living history" exhibit, where white tourists
could photograph the ceremonies. Ed Chiloquin refused. One
day in 1974, he went into the forest, built a tipi, and lit a sacred
council fire. The fire, he said, would not go out until the land
had been restored to Indian ownership.

In the aftermath of Alcatraz and Wounded Knee, Chiloquin's
camp became a center of Native resistance. There was no armed
standoff, like the one at Wounded Knee, so the national media
showed little interest. But to Native activists and sympathizers,

the spectacle of a Klamath with a historic name peacefully defying both the good and bad intentions of white society was electrifying. Day after day the council fire burned in the clearing near the town of Chiloquin, named after his grandfather; Indians from all over the country came to be part of this reoccupation of Indian land.

Al Smith came to Chiloquin's camp in 1975 and ended up staying ten months. Once again, he was exposed to Indian beliefs and ceremonies from all over the West. At the camp, too, Al Smith got a vivid look at how the sweat lodge could serve to define and protect Native identity. Max Bear, a Lakota Sioux who was the security coordinator for the camp, used the sweat lodge as a kind of counterintelligence tool. Many of those who flocked to the camp were either part Indian or white—members of what Indians have called for years the Wannabe tribe. But the aim of the camp was to make a serious statement about Native people and their ways, and part-timers weren't welcome or useful. Once or twice a week, Bear would collar Al Smith and a couple of other members of the camp and drag a prospective recruit into an ordeal by sweat. "He would put on six hot stones," Smith recalled. "A lot of those guys would just freak out and panic and then crawl over the rocks to find the door. He'd tell them, 'Don't unpack, just get dressed and leave, because we do this every day.'"

Of his time at Chiloquin's camp, Al Smith says simply, "I got grounded again." That short sentence covers a big change—from "national Indian" to Oregonian, from dispossessed urban Native to Klamath—and it mirrors what was happening to the Klamath people during the years when Edison Chiloquin kept the council fire lit inside the national forest. In 1980 President Carter signed the Edison Chiloquin Act, by which Congress bestowed beneficial title to 580 acres of the national forest surrounding his camp. It was only a symbol—a tiny land base for a tribe that officially didn't exist. But Chiloquin's victory heartened the forces within the tribe who believed that the Klamath nation survived, and a long and patient campaign for restoration of tribal status began. With the aid of Oregon's Senator Mark Hatfield, the Klamaths persuaded Congress to restore their tribal status in 1986. Klamath people were officially Indians once again and tribal members were eligible for federal Indian services, but the bill didn't bring back the land base.

After much haggling with the bank, and a lawsuit to enforce a proper valuation of the forestland sold to the federal government, the tribe collected $81 million above the "down payment" made in 1974. Klamaths have formed a new tribal government and begun to lobby for return of some their ancient lands. As surely as Al Smith came back from the brink of death in 1957, his people narrowly missed destruction in the 1980s.

Al Smith left Edison Chiloquin's camp in 1978 and began yet another new life. He went to work for Sweathouse Lodge, a new alcoholism and drug-abuse treatment facility in Corvallis, 280 miles north of Klamath Falls.

Sweathouse Lodge represented a victory Native people had won during the AIM upheavals of the early seventies. During the fall of 1972, a number of Indian and Chicano groups asked the federal government to let them start a "Chicano-Indian Study Center" on the grounds of Camp Adair, an obsolete Air Force base near Corvallis, Oregon, that had been closed in 1969. The government seemed to be dragging its feet; then, on November 8 (the day Richard Nixon was triumphantly reelected president over Senator George McGovern), seventy-five to a hundred Indian militants took over the gymnasium at Camp Adair in support of the study center project.

The occupation of Camp Adair followed right on the heels of AIM's withdrawal from the BIA office in Washington. Within a day, federal officials had agreed in principle that some of the base would be made available. Some Native activists used part of the base to start an alcoholism and drug-abuse treatment facility specifically for Indian people.

When Al Smith went to work as treatment coordinator at Sweathouse Lodge, he found a vibrant experimental facility that probably could not be re-created in today's insured, regulated, professionalized environment. Native people were adapting the Twelve Steps, discarding the dominant-culture overlay in the field of treatment, and experimenting with their own spiritual traditions as treatment for the modern plagues of whiskey and drugs.

Treatment at Sweathouse Lodge lasted ninety days. Al Smith's job was to meet with new clients, orient them to the program, and assign them to a counselor. Janet Dair, a counselor at Sweathouse Lodge during that time, remembered Al as a charismatic figure who laid down the law for new arrivals. "He let them know what they needed to do and he didn't believe in babying people," she said.

The "tough love" approach carried over to the staff. Dair recalled that many clients would come to the program with unresolved feelings of rage toward whites. Al would invariably assign these clients to Dair, the only non-Indian counselor. "He'd tell them, 'If you're going to get well, you need to deal with this racism that you have,'" she recalled. "He told me that either I was going to be able to handle that or not, but that he had a sense that I could. And then he laughed."

Clients could attend two AA meetings a week at Sweathouse Lodge. But more important in many ways were the daily sweat lodges and the other Native ceremonies with which the program tried to heal clients' injured spirits. "Al found value in ceremony," Dair recalled. "I think he recognized that he was still sober because of the red road and ceremony as well as AA. He wanted the people there to have as many opportunities as they could."

Even today, Al Smith will not claim status for himself as a
Native spiritual leader. He says over and over that he knows little
about Indian traditions. But the fact is that he had learned a lot
during his years traveling the country bringing AA concepts to
reservations. And he was and is an indefatigable networker,
reaching out far and wide to those who could teach new facets
of the traditional ways. One of those he brought into the program
was Devere Eastman, a Lakota elder. Everyone called Eastman
"Papa-san," but he later took the name Brave Buffalo. Brave Buffalo had the title "cultural adviser." He and a visiting Lakota
medicine man, Martin Highbear, would run sweat lodges and
talking circles, in which participants shared their concerns and
struggles in recovery. And Brave Buffalo introduced Al and his
clients to the Sun Dance.

This dance, which originated in the Great Plains, is one of
the most sacred expressions of the new Native spirituality. A
four-day event, it is usually not open to spectators or casual seek-
ers. Dancers cut a sacred tree and carry it into a circular arbor,
where they erect it in the center. The next day at daybreak, the
dancers gather and tie colorful "prayer ties" to the tree, and dancing begins. Men who are not dancing gather around a sacred
drum, while women sing to accompany the dancing. The dance
goes on for four days.

Native people today are protective, sometimes even secretive,
about the Sun Dance. Many of them find it a powerful expression
of healing and union with the earth. But they know that it is a
tradition that most whites do not understand, and that some
white missionaries found frightening or ungodly. In part that's
because some male Sun Dancers make shallow incisions, or
piercings, in the flesh of their upper chests and insert hand-
carved hardwood pegs that are tied to the sacred tree. The pain
and the minor blood loss of piercing, some people explain, is a

kind of male equivalent of childbirth—the pain and bleeding that women undergo to renew life on earth.

But Christian missionaries and Indian agents did not see the inner meaning in the Dance. They saw only a cultural nightmare, a pagan, primitive ritual to be stamped out for the good of all concerned. Sun Dances were forbidden on reservations, but the ritual survived in secret. When, in the sixties and seventies, Native spirituality reemerged, the Sun Dance moved out of the Plains to become an important focus of traditionally minded Indian communities across the country.

Al Smith found the Sun Dance a moving experience, and continues to participate today. But it was not the only semi-underground ritual he was learning about. Some of the clients came from another religious background. "Sun Dance is not our way," they said to him. "Sweats are new to us." Well, Smith asked, what is your way? They told him they followed the Native American Church.

Al Smith knew very little about the Native American Church when he began work at Sweathouse Lodge. The Church—which is actually a very loose confederation of denominations with differing ceremonies and beliefs—has kept a low profile by intent, both in American society generally and in Indian country. Many whites and Native people alike object to its ceremonies because they involve peyote.

Peyote religion is one of the most important and distinctive religious traditions to emerge from the New World, but it is also one of the most obscure and least understood. In part, this is because of the nature of Native American religion generally. Unlike Western religions, Native traditions do not revolve around the written—or even the spoken—word; Indian people often experience religion more through music and dance than do most Christians or Jews. A certain reticence, or even secrecy, also attends many Indian religions. Many of them arose as rituals of membership for bands or tribes, with no "great commission" from the Creator to evangelize the world. Indeed, many Native traditions don't place much emphasis on membership in "churches" or "denominations" and don't define themselves in opposition to or distinction from other traditions.

White missionaries were often amazed at the ease with which Indians accepted the Gospel, whether as individuals or in tribal or village units. They sometimes took this as comforting evidence that the Indians had not had any real religion until they were "converted." But Indians did not see conversion as the shattering new beginning that Protestant Christians did. There seems no conflict to many Native people between the worship of Jesus and the "pagan" practices that so appalled His emissaries. It is the Creator who is at the basis of it all, they reason. Christians have been taught that there is but one way to salvation and that any practice not sanctioned by Christ's church or taught in His name is idolatry. And because Indians tend not to talk about the Creator much, it was easy for the missionaries to miss that almost all Native American religions believe in and honor Him.

In fact, white Americans have often been unable to grasp that Native religion is religion at all. Because there are no Bibles, no creeds, no sanctuaries, and no hierarchies, it is much easier to regard Native beliefs as a matter of superstition and custom, devoid of any "real" religious content. It comes as no surprise that the early settlers of the New World, who had no particular regard for freedom of religion in their own societies, should be scornful of Native American practices as "devil worship" or "idolatry," to be extirpated by preaching if possible and by force if necessary. What is more startling to contemporary Americans is that the very founders of the American republic—proud of the new country's value of liberty of conscience—saw no contradiction in denying that liberty to the continent's Native people.

This myopia goes back at least to Thomas Jefferson, drafter of the Virginia Statute for Religious Freedom and, with James Madison, one of the two principal architects of American religious freedom. In his Second Inaugural Address, Jefferson assures the American people that "free exercise" of religion "is placed by the constitution independent of the powers of the general government." In the very next paragraph, however, he laments that the "aboriginal inhabitants of these countries" have been misled by those among them who "inculcate a sanctimonious reverence for the customs of their ancestors" and teach "that their duty is to remain as their Creator made them."

If Jefferson had been pressed, he would probably have said that "free exercise" extended to the Indians; what he would have found incomprehensible is the argument that "the customs of their ancestors" were anything but a kind of prereligious vestige destined to be brushed away by exposure to fully developed (that is to say, Western) religious and philosophical concepts. The key to this contradiction lies in the Enlightenment idea of progress, strengthened by the doctrine of biological and social evolution, which was emerging even in Jefferson's time. Decades later, writing of his trip to the Galapagos, Charles Darwin assured European readers that the Native people he encountered had no religion, no concept of God at all, a finding that subsequent scholars regard as grotesquely wrong.

It's no accident that Darwin, the theorist of natural selection as the mechanism of evolution, should take such a disparaging attitude toward Indian religion. Darwin's evolutionary ideas blended easily with Western ideas of progress. Religion, like every other aspect of human civilization, seemed to the nineteenth-century mind to be moving from a primitive, "lower" state inexorably through intermediate stages to a "higher" state—an evolutionary zenith that looked a good deal like liberal American Protestanism. Indian religion was dismissed as animism, a form of nature worship that hardly qualified as religion when compared with the "advanced" religions of the West.

Even those who encountered Indian worship at close hand were often unable to put aside their cultural presumptions and see it as a genuine alternative to the Judeo-Christian tradition. Kate McBeth, a Presbyterian missionary to the Nez Perce in the late nineteenth century, wrote that "whatever religion those people may have had to start with, had degenerated into a kind of devil worship." In fact, she suggested, the Nez Perce had not even begun to worship the sun and the earth until after the arrival of whites in the Northwest. Until then, the Nez Perce "did not have any idea of the worship of God." Another Presbyterian missionary at the same time penned a careful description of Choctaw beliefs in the afterlife, witchcraft, burial customs, and ceremonial practices but then immediately concluded that "they had no worship" and were "[a]s completely, almost, as possible . . . a people without God."

Of course, white people making contact with Native culture sometimes noticed the reverence the Indians felt for the Creator and the way in which their religious practices sought to honor Him. But they had an explanation for that as well; these savages had simply heard from afar the good news brought to America by Europeans and had begun to worship the God of Abraham in a distorted, even ridiculous fashion. Thus, even evidence of Indian beliefs served to reinforce the certainty whites felt of the superiority of their traditions and of the need to Christianize the Indians in order to bring them out of savagery.

As late as the 1950s—a decade in which many of today's judges and government officials were educated—it was common for prominent historians of religion and educators to dismiss Native religion as a vestige doomed to prompt extinction and thus unworthy of serious study.

That brings us to another characteristic of Native religion that whites have trouble grasping. American culture, when it thinks of Indian religion at all, tends to think of it as a kind of fossil, preserved unchanged over hundreds and thousands of years. Native people themselves are not above playing to this stereotype, emphasizing the antiquity of their traditions as a means of arguing for their legitimacy. It is an effective rhetorical strategy, but it has had the side effect of creating a static image of Native spirituality that is radically wide of the truth.

In fact, Indian religion no less than Christianity has always been, and remains today, a dynamic and indeed volatile field. From the earliest recorded times, Indian tribes have seen the rise and fall of new prophets and new revelations, such as Wovoka, the Northern Paiute medicine man whose vision of a reconstructed world without white people launched the Ghost Dance religion in the nineteenth century. Individual tribes and bands of Indians have borrowed from other tribes, adapting rituals, myths, and beliefs freely to fit their circumstances. And one of the fastest-spreading adaptations of the nineteenth and twentieth centuries is the worship of Grandfather Peyote.

Peyotists like to claim that their religion is ten thousand or more years old—older than any major non-Native faith. In a sense, that's true. Archaeologists have documented the use of peyote by humans in North America stretching back nearly as far as the evidence of human occupation of the New World. But it's also a bit misleading, because peyote religion as it is practiced in the United States today is a relatively new form of peyotism, heavily influenced by Christianity and by the demands of religious survival in a country dominated, until recently, by Protestant Christians who had little patience for traditions truly different from their own.

The plant itself, a small, spineless cactus that grows close to the ground, is found mostly in northern Mexico, although there are some productive stands of peyote in southern Texas, where

American *peyoteros* harvest most of the peyote used in this country. The plants, which may be used green or dried, contain a
potent blend of naturally occurring hallucinogens, whether they
are eaten or made into a hot infusion to be drunk. The taste,
however, is bitter and often nauseating, which has limited the
popularity of peyote as a recreational drug.

Peyote religion originally arose among the Native people of
what is now northern Mexico and southwest Texas. One legend
related that an Indian woman, wandering across the desert without food or water, was on the point of death when she received
a vision that the unappetizing small plants growing nearby would
save her. She ate peyote and received the strength to find her
way back to her village. Her people soon began using the cactus
to obtain strength, to cure disease, and to gain visions of the
future. Accounts by Spanish explorers tell of the peyote ritual
they evolved—a furious dance that involved ritual scarification
with knives and hooks.

In 1620 the Inquisition banned this "pagan" rite. But the worship of peyote was deeply rooted, and sometime in the nineteenth century it crossed the Rio Grande and moved into what
was then Indian Territory (present-day Oklahoma), where for-
merly nomadic tribes like the Kiowa and the Comanche, deprived
of their land and their way of life, were ripe for a new religious
revelation. Sometime in the 1880s, a new peyote ceremony
emerged. It blended aspects of Christian ritual and theology with
the music and ritual of the tribes of the Southwest. John Wilson,
a Caddo-Delaware who was an important leader of the emerging
peyote cult, described a vision in which Christ showed him the
road He had walked from the empty tomb to the moon on his
way to Heaven. Those who partook of the new peyote ceremonial
and who followed this Peyote Road would one day ascend themselves into the presence of Christ.

The ceremony that emerged from the new revelation has remained essentially the same for the past century, although each ceremonial leader, or Road man, incorporates individual elements. A peyote service is often called a tipi ceremony because it is usually held in a Plains-style tipi (though peyote ceremonials may be held in many different kinds of shelters). The participants gather at sundown, freshly bathed and wearing clean clothing, to sit all night in the tipi around a ceremonial fire. The Road man officiates, with the help of a Fire man, who tends the fire; a Cedar man, who spreads the aromatic cedar incense on the fire; and a Drummer, who maintains a steady cadence on the drum during the night. At several points during the night, the participants are offered the opportunity to eat peyote, and participants sing ceremonial songs in turn. The rest sit motionless, watching the fire and meditating on the gifts of peyote. Several times during the night, the participants drink consecrated water. At sunrise a chosen woman (usually the Road man's wife), opens the tipi and brings in water and a ritual meal. Once the sun has risen, the participants leave the tipi, eat breakfast together, and disperse.

Peyote meetings do not occur on a schedule. Often the congregation gathers for a special reason—to seek protection for a family member who is leaving home, for example, or to pray for healing for a loved one who is ill. Sometimes, in remote parts of the country, the ceremonies simply coincide with the passage through town of a Road man. But whether they participate often or seldom, peyotists agree that the tipi ceremony is a powerful experience.

Outsiders often construe that statement in the most simplistic way. Of course it is powerful—the worshipers are gathering to take a potent hallucinogen. The image is of a kind of Native American LSD, with celebrants' minds pinwheeling through sensations and images in uncontrolled gyrations. But those who have been through the ceremony tend to describe it in more subtle terms. The peyote increases concentration; worshipers find themselves fascinated by the ceremonial fire and focused inward, on their own weaknesses and flaws and on spiritual tasks they need to perform. The peyote also allows them to ignore the discomfort of sitting cross-legged with no back support for twelve to fifteen hours. Actual hallucinations, or visions, are relatively rare, and most Road men regard them as a bad sign. A very few peyotists may have a true mystical experience—a collapse of ego boundaries, a timeless sense of unity with the cosmos and its Creator. But very few participants, in the safe and structured environment of the tipi ceremony, with the counsel of the Road man available, have any kind of "bad trip." Accounts of lasting bad effects are all but nonexistent.

Peyotists are united in their ethical code as well. Members are to be faithful to their spouses, to care for their families, to be self-supporting and honest. Peyote itself is to be used only in the ritual context; anything else is the gravest of sacrilege. And alcohol in any form, or any kind of illegal drug, is strictly off-limits. Grandfather Peyote forbids them; through the tipi ceremony, He gives His people the strength to live without them.

No sooner had this new form of peyotism emerged in the 1880s than white missionaries and Indian agents began trying to ban it. To whites, peyote was just another way for Indians to get drunk; it was on a par with the savage dances and pagan rituals American civilization could not tolerate. Peyotists in Oklahoma proved adept at lobbying for its survival, however. Early in the twentieth century, they accepted a suggestion from James Mooney, a Smithsonian anthropologist who had written the definitive chronicle of the rise of the Ghost Dance. Mooney recommended that the Road men and their followers do what white people would do—organize a church. In 1918 a group made up of Oklahoma tribes incorporated the Native American Church, "mother church" of all contemporary peyote sects. The Church created a hierarchy, and its leaders explained to members of

Congress and Christian clergy that theirs was simply a new patch in the American quilt of Christianity. Church members worshiped Jesus, and peyote was their "sacrament," just as wine or grape juice was the sacrament for their white Christian brothers. Much of the Christian theology was a skilled form of camouflage, to shield white society from the knowledge that peyotism was a distinctly Native spiritual tradition. Peyote leaders were careful, too, to keep a low profile, never to challenge authority directly, and to keep Church matters within the group. Publicly, they insisted that peyotism was nothing very different and presented a facade of unity; inside the Church, there were disagreements and divisions.

One of the most searing disputes concerned whether non-Indians could belong to the Church. The mother church had always tolerated whites, if they were sincere; James Mooney had taken part in ceremonials, and another anthropologist, J. S. Slotkin, had been on the Church's governing board. But some groups insisted that the Creator, having given whites so many other things, intended Grandfather Peyote for Native people only. This doctrine was most strongly held in the desert Southwest, where populous Indian communities could maintain their separation. By the 1980s this group had coalesced around a Navajo Road man named Emerson Jackson and organized itself as the Native American Church of North America (NACNA). To the world at large, the NACNA spoke in categorical terms—only Indians could be members of the Church. But Native people, on the whole, do not take well to centralized authority, and many congregations followed the beliefs of their own Road men, allowing whites to take part if they were judged sincere.

By the time Al Smith first heard about peyote, whites had become interested for another reason. Starting in the 1960s, some doctors in the Indian Health Service had noticed that Native patients who turned to the Church had a far better chance

of recovering from alcoholism than those who did not. Robert
Bergman, a psychiatrist and head of mental-health programs for
the Health Service, later reported treating close to a thousand
peyotists during his nine years with the IHS. In 1971 he published a study of peyotism among the Navajo. The practice, he
wrote, was apparently safe and was no threat to the sobriety of
alcoholics who engaged in it. Two years later he went further,
authoring a chapter in a psychology textbook that recommended
peyotism as a system for healing some Native alcoholics. In 1977
three authors in the *Journal of the New York Academy of Sciences*
reported on their observations of Native alcoholics seeking recovery through the Church. They often succeeded, the authors
wrote—not because of pharmacological effects of the sacrament
but because of the "orderly, constructive, and stimulating" structure of the congregation and the ritual. Native peyotists used "the
drug-induced altered state of consciousness for insight and
exchange." For these peyotists, the "attraction to peyote and the
ritual is similar to the patient's reliance on the analyst and does
not constitute an addiction in any sense of the word."

Al Smith began to find out about peyote, but he was not sure
the Peyote Road was for him. "To me peyote was a drug," he
testified a few years later. "I'm not about to jeopardize my sobriety, I've got years and years and years of sobriety and I ain't
going to mess with that." Al Smith's spiritual way had been AA.
AA teaches that all drugs are alike, that recovering alcoholics
cannot risk altering their consciousnesses in any way, lest they
lose their spiritual balance and relapse into drinking. So he
watched at the ceremonies, passing the buttons when they came
around. He did not eat peyote—at first. But he could tell that
the clients benefited. In 1979 he took the sacrament at a ceremony on the Makah Reservation in northwestern Washington.
Not long after, he went to a workshop on treatments for Indian
alcoholism and ate peyote again. He didn't fall off the wagon;

indeed, he saw the benefits. "I have been assisted to a place where I have a better understanding, or led to an understanding, which helps me become a good person," he testified later.

When Brave Buffalo left Sweathouse Lodge, Al brought in Stanley Smart, a Northern Paiute who was a Road man in the Native American Church. Al and Stanley formed a close bond; even today, Al often refers to his friend and mentor as "Mr. Smart," as if in recognition of his wisdom. Stanley Smart began to hold tipi meetings at Sweathouse Lodge. Al took part, and respected the ceremony. But to him, the Native American Church was only one part of the lost religious heritage he was rediscovering. Native American Church membership was fairly loose, but even so, Al Smith said later, "I never did [consider myself a member]. Still don't. Just the white man and the white man's laws saying that I, as a Native person, couldn't go to church. That's what started the whole thing."

4

EAST OF EDEN

Only Eden could be greener than the Willamette Valley, which runs down the west side of Oregon from Portland at the state's northern edge to below Eugene, 160 miles to the south. Seven months of steady rain and five months of sunshine each year make the valley a lush incubator of plant life of all kinds, where berries grow as big as apples and roses bloom like cabbages.

But east of Eden is another Oregon, as bleak and hard as sun-bleached bone. Driving east from Dave Frohnmayer's home in Eugene, a traveler takes vertiginous mountain passes through the Cascade Range and then descends to the high desert, a waste-land of sagebrush, ponderosa pine, and lava beds as brown and mysterious as the Sonoran plain of Arizona or El Malpais of eastern New Mexico.

The farther east and north the traveler drives, the bleaker and stranger the land becomes until, crossing from Jefferson into Wasco County, the highway might almost be crossing the moon. Saints and anchorites have always sought visions in wild places, and the harsh desert light can sometimes mislead the traveler as well. In summer when conditions are just right, road and light may combine to etch evanescent visions on the road ahead—phantoms of reflection the eye translates into blue lakes, oncoming cars, or even the fantastic spires of nonexistent cities.

Like one of these desert visions, a real city rose and fell in eastern Oregon during the 1980s. For many Oregonians, and for Dave Frohnmayer in particular, the rise and fall of Rajneeshpuram framed the issues of religious freedom and government neutrality in a stark and unforgettable way.

Americans have always built holy cities in the "empty" land of the New World: from Plymouth Plantation to Salt Lake City and beyond, the map of North America is dotted with new Jerusalems and shining cities upon hills. But even amid the unparalleled exuberance of American religious history, the story of Rajneeshpuram is one of the strangest ever told. Like Nauvoo, Jonestown, or Waco, Rajneeshpuram might have ended in fire and blood; that it did not is due, in large part, to caution and adroitness on the part of Oregon's authorities, prominent among them Dave Frohnmayer.

Rajneeshpuram was the American dream of Bhagwan Shree Rajneesh, an Indian philosopher and holy man who had acquired the nickname "the progressive guru" for his embrace of the psychological theories of Fritz Perls, Abraham Maslow, Wilhelm Reich, and other icons of the human potential movement of the 1970s. Bhagwan built an ashram in Poona, India, that became a magnet for Europeans and Americans seeking a reassuringly familiar glimpse of the exotic East. Disciples at Poona were initiated into a form of discipleship—Bhagwan called it *sannyas*, and his disciples *sanyassin*—that required them to sacrifice almost nothing except their capacity for independent thought. Bhagwan revealed the religious truth that religion has no truth, the belief that all beliefs are false, the rule that rules stifle our "true" selves and protect the hypocrisies and oppressions of society. *Do what thou wilt shall be the whole of the law*, Bhagwan seemed to preach—as long as it was understood that it was the will of Bhagwan, the Awakened One, that took precedence over every other imperative.

Residence at Poona had little of the tedium and asceticism of life at other Indian retreats. *Sanyassin* did not need to master Sanskrit or immerse themselves in the *gitas*; instead, they practiced Bhagwan's "dynamic meditation" (a form of dance and breathing designed to break down inhibitions and focus the seeker's consciousness on love of Bhagwan); attended Bhagwan's discourses, which blended parable, paradox, and Ericksonian hypnosis; and spent their time (and money) in group-therapy sessions and encounter groups. When Richard Price, director of the Esalen Institute, visited Poona in 1977, he was appalled by the use Rajneesh was making of the "humanistic psychology" Americans had pioneered. "It is as if the worst mistakes of some inexperienced Esalen group leaders of many years ago had been systematized and given the stamp of 'God,' " he wrote in a letter to Bhagwan.

Because Rajneesh's revelation was that there are no rules, his Western devotees found Poona a place of sexual freedom and indeed of freedom to enact many forbidden fantasies. Without rules, social life turns dangerous, as surely for educated adults as for the children of William Golding's *Lord of the Flies*. And where the only authority is an unaccountable, inaccessible, and semidivine dictator, some people retreat into childlike obedience while others flower as full-blown psychopaths. Some Poona therapy groups degenerated into violent assault or forcible rape. Some *sanyassin* snapped under the stress;

Rajneesh and his lieutenants escorted them to local mental hospitals and walked away.

Many of the features of Bhagwan's organization seem to have
been designed to offend his Hindu neighbors; the term *sanyassin*,
for example, was an appropriation of a word that Hindus use for
holy men who have attained godhood. Bhagwan, meanwhile, began expressing his disdain for his "old, ancient and rotten country" and systematically picked fights with Indian officials,
beginning with local planning officials and working his way up
to the country's prime minister, Morarji Desai. By 1980 officials
were blocking his plans to expand the ashram and were refusing
visas to Westerners en route to Poona. An enraged Hindu reared
up from the audience at one of Bhagwan's speeches and tried to
stab him. In May 1981, without mentioning his plans to the
remaining members of his ashram, Rajneesh slipped out of Poona
and found refuge in Montclair, New Jersey, where his followers
had bought a mansion for his use.

But Montclair was only a way station. Bhagwan dreamed of
a new city of *sannyassin*, so far from society's rules that no one
would interfere. He dispatched his top lieutenant, a young Gu-
jarati woman named Sheela Patel but renamed Ma Anand
Sheela, on a scouting trip to find such a place. In June 1981
Sheela agreed to pay $5.75 million for the Big Muddy Ranch, a
64,000-acre spread near Antelope, Oregon, on the west side of
the John Day River as it passes through Wasco and Jefferson
Counties in the Oregon high desert. Like many pioneers before
her, Sheela seems to have conceived of this huge desert empire
as a place where any dream could be made real. But geography
and climate made the Big Muddy a problematic site for paradise.
Overgrazing by cattlemen and the John Day's frequent floods had
eroded the valleys and ravines around it, and in the bare, dry soil
it might require a hundred acres of pasture to support one head
of cattle.

There was another constraint that Sheela did not suspect. When she got back to Montclair and announced that she had bought the Big Muddy, one of her fellow *sannyassin* asked her whether the land was zoned for the uses Bhagwan planned. Sheela's reply was puzzled: zoning? "It was suddenly very clear to me," the other disciple recalled, "that Sheela had just paid almost six million dollars for a piece of land without bothering to enquire about any restrictions that may be in force concerning its use."

In fact, Oregon's land-use laws were a more formidable obstacle than even floods and drought. The state maintains the strictest zoning regulations in the nation, designed to protect open space and farmland from urban sprawl. Under the system, cities are assigned "urban growth boundaries" within which new development can take place after local approval; outside these boundaries, any change in land use must be approved by the powerful statewide Land Conservation and Development Commission (LCDC), whose decisions can be appealed to the Land Use Board of Appeals (LUBA) or, beyond that, to the Oregon Court of Appeals. Any citizen may challenge an LCDC decision to allow development, and the framers of the land-use system founded a watchdog group, 1000 Friends of Oregon, whose mission was to do just that whenever a landowner anywhere in the state appeared to be contemplating changes that would threaten the character of the land.

Thus, when Sheela and other *sanyassin* arrived in Antelope in July 1981, they promised publicly that no more than forty people would be employed on the Big Muddy, renamed Rancho Rajneesh. But the *sanyassin* seemed to be preparing roads and structures for many times that number. 1000 Friends of Oregon immediately warned the commune's leaders that the ranch, as agricultural land, could not be used for commercial or industrial activity. Such enterprises would have to be located in Antelope, fourteen miles away. Though the town was only four blocks square, with less than fifty full-time residents, Antelope had an urban growth boundary and thus could give approval for new building without LCDC action.

Thus began the battle of Antelope, which set the pattern for the commune's contentious dealings with county and state. The locals had been somewhat nonplussed by the arrival of the *sannyassin*, who wore "sunrise colors"—pink, orange, red, and purple—and beaded necklaces with photographs of Bhagwan. Some locals were offended; many Oregonians are fundamentalist Christians, and to them, as to the Hindus of Poona, the guru's airs of divinity smacked of sacrilege. But others were more tolerant; Oregon is a place where people come in part because they are eccentric, and some neighbors were prepared to welcome Hindu misfits as cheerfully as they welcomed American nonconformists.

It took only a few months for tolerance to turn to alarm. Rajneesh followers began to move into Antelope, and by the fall of 1981, the organization had applied for permits to open a printing plant and an office complex. When the city authorities refused permission, the Rajneeshees went to court and won an order permitting them to build.

The Rajneesh movement was mainly drawn from the upper middle class of the United States, Germany, England, Italy, and other Western countries. Bhagwan could call upon expert and devoted legal help. His general counsel, Swami Prem Niren, had previously been a partner in the Los Angeles law firm of Manatt, Phelps, Rothenburg & Tunney. The firm had produced, among other things, a chairman of the Democratic National Committee, and Niren was a skilled advocate with a large and devoted litigation staff and only one real client. These clever lawyers found in the Oregon land-use statutes a new strategy to bypass the restrictions on development outside Antelope; Rancho Rajneesh would apply to the county commission for permission to incorporate the ranch itself as a new city, with its own growth boundary. Unlike development outside a boundary, this incorporation did not require LCDC approval.

Antelope, meanwhile, began to fight back against the Rajneeshee "invasion." Most of the town's residents were retired, the sort of people who had come there to be left alone. The Rajneesh followers, mostly young, well-educated people, dressed oddly, made noise, and, worst of all, seemed to plan to make this quiet little town a site of pilgrimage and bustle. To prevent that, the part-time members of the Antelope City Council quickly scheduled a vote of the people to "disincorporate" the town. If the city of Antelope ceased to exist, its urban growth boundary would disappear, and the orange-clad strangers would have no choice but to leave them in peace.

Rajneesh's followers countered by making use of Oregon's voter-registration laws, then among the most liberal in the nation. Any voter who had spent one night in an Oregon precinct and showed an intent to remain could register to vote, even on election day. Accordingly, the commune sent *sanyassin* into Antelope to live. In April 1982 the disincorporation measure failed by a vote of 55 to 42. Not long before, the county commission had approved an "election" on the ranch to incorporate the commune as a city. LUBA had rejected a petition by 1000 Friends to delay incorporation until the group could litigate the land-use issues. The Rajneeshees, it seemed, were on a roll.

But their victories in these early skirmishes set up a pattern they would exhibit until the very end. The Rajneeshees played for keeps, whether the issue involved was large or small; and whether they won or lost, they made enemies along the way. During the disincorporation fight in Antelope, the *sanyassin* began photographing residents at polling places, ostentatiously noting license-plate numbers at pro-disincorporation rallies, and videotaping public meetings where the issue was discussed. Ra-jneeshees took up covert posts with views of polling places and videotaped each voter who entered, laying the groundwork for a possible future challenge to the election. Many residents felt threatened in their own hometown. Then, when the issue of city status for Rajneeshpuram came before the county commission, the commune quickly made a very favorable bid for seventeen thousand dollars' worth of cattle owned by the swing member of the three-member commission; residents who opposed the plan to build a city on the Big Muddy felt that they had been defeated by corrupt means. Some were so outraged that they complained to the state ethics commission. When that body decided that state statutes did not forbid the commissioner from voting, the anti-Bhagwan forces took their quarrel to a higher authority. The commissioner was an active Mormon; after the opposition com-plained to Church authorities, they decided to send the hapless sixty-one-year-old official on an immediate mission to Nigeria, removing him from local politics for good.

So far, nothing in the dispute had involved Dave Frohnmayer's office. But he had picked up early rumbles of concern about the commune's leadership and tactics. In 1982 people west of the Cascades were not quite sure what to make of the unfolding drama in the desert. Some regarded the sanyassin as a dangerous and aggressive crowd, but others knew from experience that some eastern Oregonians could be a bit close-minded. Rajneesh and Sheela were not shy about claiming that the opposition to their plans stemmed from bigotry and religious prejudice, and many people were inclined to believe them.

Frohnmayer had his own source, however. The Bowerman family, whose roots lay in the desert soil beside the John Day, were as much a part of Oregon's elite as were the Frohnmayers. Bill Bowerman was the legendary track coach at the University of Oregon whose program had produced Steve Prefontaine and other world-class runners. Bowerman had also borrowed his wife's waffle iron and used it to produce the first waffle running-shoe sole, bringing into existence the multibillion-dollar Nike shoe empire and cementing Eugene's reputation as Track Town, the long-distance running capital of the world.

Bill Bowerman's son Jon, a childhood friend of Frohnmayer, lived on the family ranch, which bordered on Big Muddy Ranch. When the Rajneeshees first arrived, Jon Bowerman had been one of the voices urging patience and hospitality for these strange new pioneers. But his goodwill soon evaporated. *Sannyassin* appeared on his land, making obscure threats; the commune took to shining a brilliant searchlight into his bedroom window at night, in what he took to be an effort to drive his family off their land. Bowerman had shared his misgivings with Frohnmayer. Jon Bowerman was no bigot, Frohnmayer knew, so he was inclined to be skeptical about Sheela's claims of persecution.

Rancho Rajneesh was now the city of Rajneeshpuram, complete with a city government and a pink-clad Peace Force headed by a graduate of the Oregon State Police Academy and enjoying full access to the state's law-enforcement information network. By now there was no more pretense that the guru planned an agricultural co-op; construction was well along on a huge meditation hall, dwelling units for two thousand full-time residents, a hotel and discotheque, a medical center, and temporary shelters for five thousand or more people who were expected to attend Rajneeshee festivals.

But the Rajneesh Neo-Sannyassin International Foundation, as the religious body that owned the ranch was now called, was taking no chances; the incorporation of the city was still being challenged in court by 1000 Friends, who viewed the creation of Rajneeshpuram as an end run that threatened to gut the land-use regulation system. Throughout 1982 the orange-clad devotees continued their odd migration into Antelope. By November

the Rajneeshees had enough votes to take over the city government, which they did with an enthusiasm that shocked people
around the state. Though the *sannyassin* at first fielded only three
candidates for the seven-member city council, on election day
they wrote in names for all the other city offices and ended up
controlling nine out of ten, including mayor, treasurer, and town
marshal. "We are going to paint Oregon red!" a commune spokesman told a TV interviewer after the vote.

Once they took office in February 1983, the new majority
immediately changed the name of the city to Rajneesh, renamed
all the city streets after Hindu holy men, raised taxes in an apparent attempt to drive out the old-line residents, and filed a
lawsuit to gain control of an Episcopal church that had been
restored by volunteers as a community center. Most ominous to
the commune's neighbors, the new council majority also contracted out the town's police service to the Rajneesh Peace Force
from the ranch. Soon the streets were patrolled by pink-clad *sannyassin* toting assault rifles. The Peace Force was not passive—
nightly patrols shone brilliant searchlights into the windows of
non-*sannyassin* residents. On several occasions they forced their
way inside the homes of outspoken critics of Rajneesh to make
threats and even arrests.

Bhagwan himself was becoming more active at the same time.
He had entered the United States on a temporary medical visa;
his followers told the Immigration and Naturalization Service
(INS) that their guru was at death's door and in need of immediate medical treatment. Away from his political and financial
problems, however, Rajneesh made a rapid recovery and never
consulted any doctors except the *sannyassin* who traveled with
him. Then, as work began on the ranch, Bhagwan filed a new
application for permanent residence as a "religious worker." In
December 1982 the INS refused the application. Bhagwan had
defrauded the government, the INS suggested, by claiming ill-

ness when he had always intended to remain permanently. Besides, the service added with the literal-minded logic of low-level bureaucrats around the world, Bhagwan preached a religion that he said was no religion. How could there be a religion without beliefs? And anyway, the guru had "entered silence," refusing to speak to his followers; so he wasn't going to be a "worker" even if his beliefs were religious.

Within a month, Niren and his orange-clad legal SWAT team had won a reversal on procedural grounds; the INS had based its ruling on information (probably informants inside the commune) it had withheld from Bhagwan's lawyers. Shortly afterward, perhaps by coincidence, Bhagwan and Sheela announced the formation of "the Religion of Rajneeshism," complete with scriptures, an academy, and a three-level clerical hierarchy.

Bhagwan also began to drive off the ranch every few days, traveling in one of his chauffeur-driven Rolls-Royce automobiles and trailed by a Jeep full of gun-toting Peace Force bodyguards. This odd group would drive the seventy miles to Madras, seat of Wasco County, where Bhagwan's driver would pull into a supermarket parking lot while an attractive young *sannyassin* ostentatiously went into the store and bought him a single can of soda. Mardo Jimenez, pastor of the Madras Conservative Baptist Church, began to greet the convoy with a sign urging Bhagwan and his followers to repent. Soon his parishioners rallied around him, and Rajneesh began bringing his own followers by the car- and then the busload. Frances FitzGerald, a writer for *The New Yorker*, began her account of the commune's life and death with a description of the daily highway standoff:

> In the days following, the double demonstration began to attract all kinds of people: curiosity seekers, families from other churches, and tough-looking guys in sweat caps hitching up their

blue jeans. Jimenez stood on top of a car holding a Bible in one hand and in the other, an American flag so big it threatened to drag him away in high winds. "I love you," he called, wind-tears streaming down his cheeks, and "Believe in Jesus." Day by day the numbers of Rajneeshee increased until there were four bus-loads of them at the weigh station. Then the truckers began coming, the drivers tooting their horns and waving V signs as they pulled their rigs off to the Jimenez side of the road.

The roadside confrontations framed the issue just as Rajneesh seemed to want it: bigoted fundamentalists rejecting anything new. That impression was deepened when a group of eastern Oregonians began circulating a ballot measure (which never ac-tually came to a vote) called the Alien Cult Bill. Under this law, the Oregon constitution's guarantee of "the natural right to wor-ship Almighty God" would apply to everyone except any "cult identified by a statewide majority vote of the people as a Jones-town, Rajneesh or similar type." The governor was "commanded to contain and repel" these religious losers. It was a classic ex-ample of Oregon's popular political theory—rights were for the majority, and only for the majority.

But Bhagwan and Sheela did not seem to understand that not everyone who opposed them was a slack-jawed yokel—and that even slack-jawed yokels resented having their ignorance publicly pointed out. Sheela had earlier raised a few hackles by sending an open letter to Governor Vic Atiyeh suggesting that "Oregon can hardly prosper if it is filled with stagnant, dilapidated little towns like Antelope—places where indolent old people go to mark time until they die." In April she published a letter warning that "we are here in Oregon to stay at whatever the cost. If that means that some of our blood is spilled . . . then this is the price we are prepared to pay." When the Oregon Legislative Assembly began its biennial session, Sheela demanded an invitation to give the opening prayer under the state's "nonsectarian" invocation program. She showed up with armed guards and intoned,

> I go to the feet of the Awakened One; I go to the feet of the commune of the Awakened One; I go to the feet of the Absolute Truth of the Awakened One.

The legislative session marked the beginning of Dave Frohnmayer's involvement with Rajneeshpuram. One legislator, besieged by constituent complaints about the Rajneesh invasion, formally requested the attorney general's opinion about whether the incorporation of Rajneeshpuram as a city violated the federal and state constitutions. In May of 1983, only a few weeks before Kirsten fell ill for the first time, Frohnmayer threw himself into the task of assessing the commune.

He sensed immediately that the issue had at least the potential to make both headlines and constitutional law; as he learned more about the patterns of land ownership on the ranch, he realized that no city in American history had been set up quite like Rajneeshpuram. Except for one narrow two-lane county road, every inch of the "city" was private land, and all of it belonged to one landlord, the Rajneesh Neo-Sannyas International Foundation, a nonprofit organ set up by the religion of Rajneeshism. No one could enter any part of the foundation's property without permission from its leaders, Bhagwan and Sheela, or from their deputies. All the construction in the city was for the use and benefit of the religious group. All public offices were filled by members of the sect.

Frohnmayer invited his old constitutional law professor, Dean Jesse Choper of Boalt Hall School of Law, to advise his office and review a draft of the opinion. Choper pointed out that the facts were reminiscent of a recent decision by the U.S. Supreme

Court called *Larkin* v. *Grendel's Den*. In *Larkin*, a restaurant in
Cambridge, Massachusetts, had been denied a liquor license because of a state law that gave veto power over new licenses to
churches within five hundred feet of the restaurants applying. A
nearby Catholic church had forced the state liquor board to turn
down the application. The restaurateur was furious—his establishment was located in the heart of Harvard Square, where wa-
tering holes abounded. Under the law, the church did not need
to give a reason for its veto.

The restaurant recruited a young Harvard law professor, Laurence Tribe, to challenge the law. Though lower courts upheld it,
when the case reached the Supreme Court, the justices held, by
a vote of eight to one, that the Massachusetts statute represented
a direct delegation of political power to a religious body; it "en-
meshe[d] churches in the exercise of substantial governmental
powers." This fusion of sacred and secular authority violated the
Constitution's ban on establishment of religion, the Court majority held.

The Rajneeshpuram opinion was the kind of task Frohnmayer
relished: complex, challenging, important, and unusual. Constitutional law was his first love, and as the months wore on, the
attorney general immersed himself more and more deeply in the
history and theory of the First Amendment's religion clauses. In
part, the work on the opinion offered a respite from the constant
fear and worry that entered his life when Kirsten fell ill. But the
work was urgent in its own right—tension in eastern Oregon was
rising by the week, as the guru and Sheela continued to show
flamboyant disdain for the opinions of the mortals who lived
around their commune.

Frohnmayer issued the opinion on October 6, 1983. It began
with a sweeping discussion of religious freedom and the demands
of a liberal, secular, democratic order. In America, Frohnmayer
wrote, "Tolerance is not merely a moral virtue; it is a matter of

constitutional policy." But tolerance could not extend to state favoritism; indeed, the government must remain strictly neutral in the marketplace of souls. "Our legal system requires that the pathway to religion be private and internal to each pilgrim's mind and soul. The state and federal constitutions do not permit the road to Damascus to be paved with public funds." After reciting the facts about land ownership and government in Rajneesh-puram, Frohnmayer concluded that "[t]he city is the functional equivalent of a religious commune." As a religious body, Raj-neeshpuram was ineligible for the payment of any state funds. There was nothing that could be done to bring the city into compliance with the law; the city of Rajneeshpuram itself was unconstitutional and must cease to exist.

With the issuance of that opinion, Dave Frohnmayer became something like Ashram Enemy Number One. "The attorney general's statement is in the long tradition of bigotry which this state has exhibited since birth," Sheela told the press. Her explanation was that Frohnmayer was insane and in need of therapy on the ranch. The commune's highly professional public-relations oper-ation swung into action against "Herr General Frohnmayer," with articles and cartoons ridiculing his family's German ethnicity and picturing Dave in a Prussian military helmet or goose-stepping in Nazi dress.

A month after issuing the opinion, Frohnmayer's office brought suit against Rajneeshpuram seeking a declaratory judg-ment that the incorporation of the city violated the Establishment Clause. The legal battle against Niren and the lawyers of Raj-neesh Legal Services was complex and slow, often turning on procedural questions such as whether the suit should be heard in federal or state court. The commune preferred federal court; it used federal statutes to "remove" the case from Oregon courts. Frohnmayer's office dismissed it and refiled in state court again. It was the kind of litigation that sets a lawyer's face alight with intellectual pleasure and the thrill of battle, and Frohnmayer still warms to the task of explaining all the details. Everyone knew the stakes were high—a victory for the state would mean an end to Bhagwan's dream for Oregon. In addition, the commune was facing other serious legal challenges—investigations by the INS into foreign *sannyassin*'s visa status, fraud and embezzlement actions brought by former disciples bilked of their assets, and defamation suits by Antelope residents whom Sheela had publicly branded racist, promiscuous, or insane.

Most people who followed the situation understood that it was dangerous. Violence could erupt between local people and the *sannyassin*; both groups were heavily armed. But what most outsiders, even those in government like Dave Frohnmayer, didn't know was that danger was rising inside Rajneeshpuram as well. Frohnmayer's challenge had created a kind of bunker mentality among Rajneesh's top lieutenants. The leaders tightened security around their perimeter and began installing wiretapping and bugging equipment in guest rooms and homes around the ranch, as if to detect betrayal from within. Inside the commune, with all "artificial" social rules and ethics removed, a vicious power struggle erupted between Sheela and her group of female lieutenants, known to the *sannyassin* as the Dowager Duchesses, and the "Hollywood Crowd," some of whom had been with the guru before the rise of Sheela. Bhagwan himself was in the middle, seemingly comfortable with his disciples' uncertainty but in reality increasingly concerned about Sheela's growing hunger for power.

The tension inside the group made it at first much more aggressive against outsiders. Facing hostility from the Wasco County government, the Rajneeshees decided to take the political offensive. They would take over the whole county (which had a population of less than twenty thousand), as they had earlier seized Antelope. In August 1984 the leaders of Rajneeshpuram announced a Share-a-Home program designed to help the urban homeless around the country. Any American citizen over eighteen was eligible for bus transportation to Rajneeshpuram, where he or she would get shelter, food, and a job. It was, they insisted, coincidental that the requirements for the program were precisely the same as the requirements to vote in Oregon. By another coincidence, the program ran from August until October 17, the last day to register to vote in the November election, in which the commune was supporting two write-in candidates for the three-member county commission.

Wasco residents were alarmed and angry. They had seen what happened when the Rajneeshees took over Antelope. But serious political analysts were puzzled. Even if the Share-a-Home program fulfilled its goals, it would still produce only about 3,500 voters, while the Rajneeshees would need more like 7,000 to swing the election. Sheela and her inner circle had a more sinister strategy for the November vote—one no one suspected, in part, because it was so bizarre. There had been early hints: in 1983 Jefferson County District Attorney Mike Sullivan, a healthy jogger, had suddenly fallen ill and come near death. Doctors never knew exactly what caused his illness, but one physician at the time reflected that—if the idea were not so absurd—he would have suspected arsenic poisoning. In 1984 two county commissioners visiting Rajneeshpuram became ill with salmonella poisoning after drinking glasses of water provided by *sannyassin*. Pharmaceutical houses in the Northwest had noticed huge orders from the Rajneeshpuram pharmacy for tranquilizers and antipsychotic medication. And then, between September 9 and 26, as the Share-a-Home program reached its peak, Wasco County was the site of an unusual public-health emergency. Nearly seven hundred county residents were incapacitated by attacks of a severe strain of salmonella poisoning. Epidemiologists traced the outbreak to salad bars at as many as ten different restaurants around The Dalles, the county seat. Oddly, the restaurants were not connected, and there was no overlap among the staff.

On September 26 a law-enforcement task force held a closed-door meeting in Frohnmayer's office. Officials at the meeting voiced a bizarre suspicion: had the Rajneesh leadership begun some kind of germ warfare to assist with a vote-fraud scheme? They did not know that *sannyassin* had in fact poisoned the salad bars as part of a dry run for Sheela's political strategy. The plan was for a repeat attack on election eve—this one so widespread that thousands of voters would be unable to make it to the polls, tipping the balance to the Rajneeshees and their legions of Share-a-Home voters.

The plan fell apart, however, when Sheela unveiled the write-in campaign in October. Oregon's secretary of state, Norma Paulus, announced that the state was taking over voter registration in Wasco County to ensure against election fraud. All new voters would be required to register in The Dalles, where state attorneys would interview them to decide whether they intended to remain in Oregon after the election, a requirement under the state's voting laws. Perhaps realizing that their streetpeople could never pass such an interview, Sheela denounced Paulus's plan as more religious bigotry and announced a boycott of the election. The voting went off smoothly on November 6. (Statewide, Dave Frohnmayer was reelected attorney general of Oregon with 66 percent of the vote. It was the most lopsided victory in a contested election in the history of the state.)

The battle now entered a quiet phase. But the danger was not past; indeed, it was just beginning. James Gordon, an American therapist who remained close to the *sannyassin* for years without joining the commune, recalled that after the election "there was a kind of madness abroad on the ranch, complete with all the traditional signs and symptoms that one might see in paranoid and schizoid patients—withdrawal and isolation; excessive preoccupation with concrete tasks or personal well-being; denial of one's own thoughts and feelings, and projection of them onto others."

Inside Rajneeshpuram, growth and optimism had come to a halt. Ordinary devotees withdrew into themselves or left the ranch; within the inner circle, both the paranoid hatred of the outside and the struggle for power within took a mortal turn. Deveraj, the guru's personal physician, fell ill after another *sannyassin* stabbed him with a needle. And Sheela convened a team of trusted *sannyassin* to carry out the new strategy—assassination of Bhagwan's "enemies." Teams were dispatched to begin planning the murder of former *sannyassin* who had "betrayed" their guru. Others began working out how to kill Leslie Zaitz, an investigative reporter for *The Oregonian* in Portland; Charles Turner, the U.S. attorney for Oregon; and Dave Frohnmayer.

The fall of 1984 was a tense time in the Frohnmayer household anyway, as Dave and Lynn struggled to understand the mysterious illness that had struck their daughter. Now, to add to the stress, they began to receive odd phone calls at two or three A.M.; Dave or Lynn would hear only breathing or the click of a receiver being replaced. Strange gifts came in the mail with no return address, and a very odd saleswoman came by the house in the afternoon when the kids were home and Dave was still in Salem. One afternoon Katie became hysterical when she found a Rajneesh anti-Frohnmayer cartoon in the driveway, smeared in the blood and entrails of a dead animal.

Perhaps because legal action was hurting them so much, the commune leadership now decided to sue their enemies—a list that began with President Ronald Reagan and Attorney General Edwin Meese and worked its way down through the federal government and then into the ranks of state officials, including the governor, the attorney general, and the secretary of state. *Sannyassin* called the lawsuit *God v. the Universe*. It is a sign of how far divorced even the lawyers had become from reality that they apparently hoped to bargain a settlement in this frivolous action for an end to the federal immigration investigation of Bhagwan and the commune.

The investigation continued, however, and by mid-1985, when Frances FitzGerald revisited Rajneeshpuram, she recorded an organization that was quietly dissolving itself. Many of the city's structures were empty, new construction had ceased, and the *sannyassin* had not bothered to water saplings they had planted the year before. Both *sannyassin* and visitors were required to follow a bizarre series of sanitary precautions, such as spraying telephone mouthpieces with alcohol, that were represented as measures against AIDS, of which Bhagwan had become mortally afraid.

It is tempting to speculate on the real roots of Bhagwan's uneasiness and concern with contamination. There was friction between him and Sheela's people. History suggests that any dictator should be nervous when those around him begin to play with poison, particularly when one of their first targets is his own personal physician. Bhagwan had used Sheela to isolate himself from the ordinary *sannyassin,* and from time to time he had been known to "go into silence," refusing to utter new discourses, and to threaten to "leave his body" if matters on the ranch did not go to his liking. Perhaps on dark nights in the high desert, the guru was troubled by visions; the *sannyassin* would be told that their leader had left his body and that his last words were to Sheela, begging her to take command of his religion and its assets.

By mid-September 1985, though, the pressure of the investigation brought an end to the internal standoff. On September 16 Bhagwan called a press conference to announce that Sheela and fourteen of her associates had fled the ranch and were in Europe. Over the next week, the guru (who loved gossip and attention) kept up a stream of revelations about Sheela's misdeeds—she had poisoned Deveraj, dosed the homeless visitors with Haldol, installed bugging devices all over the ranch, and embezzled millions. "They would even have poisoned me!" Bhagwan charged.

At Bhagwan's invitation, state and federal law enforcement moved onto the ranch to investigate his charges. Meanwhile, *sannyassin* burned Sheela's ceremonial robes and destroyed their copies of *The Book of Rajneeshism,* the bible of the new religion. Many stopped wearing their distinctive dress and reassumed the names they had been born with. Rajneesh selected a new leadership team and attempted to mend fences with the public.

But the guru had preached against rules for so many years that he had apparently forgotten that others still might apply them to him as well as to his disgraced deputy. The investigators who swarmed over the ranch found evidence that implicated Bhagwan in immigration fraud, including mass weddings designed to win green cards for foreign *sannyassin.* They also found a massive system of wiretaps and bugs, including bugged tables in the commune restaurant and voice-activated tape recorders hidden in hollowed-out library books. Underneath Sheela's cabin they found a fully equipped biological-warfare laboratory, with cultures of salmonella that matched the bacteria found in the salad bars a year before; there were also some poisons that no one could fully analyze, and evidence that the Rajneeshees had been seeking to culture the AIDS virus for use as a weapon.

Federal and state grand juries began considering the evidence produced by the search of the ranch. By late October Niren, Bhagwan's lawyer, learned that Bhagwan and seven others were about to be indicted on charges of conspiring to violate federal immigration laws. He and his legal team began to negotiate terms of a voluntary surrender of the guru. But another group of *sannyassin* had another plan. On October 27 Bhagwan and his entourage boarded two rented Lear jets at the Rajneeshpuram airstrip and disappeared into the western sky. Federal officials alerted Frohnmayer of the guru's flight. An informant inside the commune told them the planes were headed for Charlotte, North Carolina, where a *sannyassin* was supposed to meet them with larger planes for an escape to Bermuda. Federal marshals and agents of the North Carolina State Bureau of Investigation (SBI) rushed to the airport. They knew the jets could change destination if they were tipped off about the reception that awaited them. At home in Eugene, Frohnmayer waited anxiously by the phone. At 10:40 P.M., Oregon time, he heard that the marshals had secured the first jet. Half an hour later, the second jet landed and agents swarmed aboard. He awoke the next morning to a call from a gravelly Southern voice that introduced itself as Robert Morgan, a former U.S. Senator who was now the head of the SBI.

"Did you get Bhagwan?" Frohnmayer asked again.

"I don't know anything about that," Morgan drawled, "but there's a guy here who's some kind of maharajah."

Frohnmayer breathed a sigh of relief.

The capture of Bhagwan (in his plane, agents also found a .38-caliber revolver, nearly $60,000 in cash, and $1 million worth of jewelry) marked the end of the dangerous phase of the Rajneeshpuram crisis. A few hours after the arrests in Charlotte, German police arrested Sheela and two of her associates and held them for extradition on state charges of attempted murder. After his return to Portland, Rajneesh pleaded guilty to the immigration charges; under the terms of his plea bargain, he agreed to pay a hefty fine and to leave the United States for at least five years. In the spring of 1986, Sheela and her two codefendants waived extradition and pleaded guilty to federal immigration charges and to state charges of attempted murder, assault, and arson. Sheela was sentenced to two twenty-year terms in prison and was ordered to pay nearly five hundred thousand dollars in fines and restitution. The commune, by now a ghost town, went on the real-estate market.

Though the story of Rajneeshpuram was over, its effects lingered on. One of the people most affected by the crisis was Dave Frohnmayer, who had spent two or more hours a day for four years thinking about the issues it raised. Nothing he had done as attorney general attracted as much public notice as the cold war with Bhagwan; it was also exciting. For years after Bhagwan's arrest, Frohnmayer received speaking invitations from groups eager to hear the inside story of the desert commune. Two years later a reporter for *The Oregonian* wrote that the attorney general "never seems to tire of talking about the Rajneeshees." James Gordon interviewed Frohnmayer and some of his assistants for his book, *The Golden Guru: The Strange Journey of Bhagwan Shree Rajneesh*. "It became apparent that these cases got to them," Gordon wrote. "Rajneesh was not merely personally threatening or morally offensive or legally outrageous; he was also ontologically and theologically abhorrent."

It may be that Gordon brought to the interview his own preconceptions about unsophisticated Oregon officials. What most people who know Frohnmayer pick up on to this day when he talks about Bhagwan is not horror but sheer fascination. Much of what a state attorney general does is soul-numbing routine—defending against frivolous appeals by guilty prisoners, parsing turgid administrative rules, listening for hours to long-winded legislators. But Rajneeshpuram had been something new, intellectually challenging and constantly evolving. Frohnmayer himself says the experience made a deep impression on him. "It really brought home to my whole office, particularly the top professional staff, the wisdom of the religion clauses, the danger of the establishment of a religion, and the particular problems you have even if they appear to be for the most part benign."

The lessons of Rajneeshpuram loomed large for Frohnmayer for the rest of his time as attorney general. One can imagine the impact, conscious and unconscious, the experience might have on his thinking. The Rajneeshees had been adept at using the rhetoric and history of American religious freedom to serve their purposes. *We are simple pilgrims, obstructed on our road to salvation by the hostility of a bigoted society*, they had argued. *We ask only for tolerance and to be left alone.* But no one who studied the record could avoid noticing that Bhagwan's religion was constantly changing, evolving almost overnight into something different. The changes were dangerous, not just for the commune's neighbors but even for many of those who entrusted their fate to Bhagwan. The Rajneeshees wanted to be left alone, but they persisted in persecuting those around them; when they got their hands on power, they used it as a club against anyone who differed from them. They screamed that their enemies were bigots while they themselves deployed election fraud, poison, and germ warfare. No one who had been through what Dave Frohnmayer had could help but reflect that religion could be a force for evil as well for good and that, no matter what religious leaders claimed about the purity of their motives, the state might need to watch them carefully indeed.

5

THE EAGLE
FEATHER

Al Smith and Jane Farrell are a sharp contrast. Al was old when
he met Jane, who is thirty-seven years his junior. Al is Native;
Jane is an Anglo. Al is a man of the West; Jane grew up in the
East. Al is dark and stormy; Jane is fair and sunny. Al is taciturn
and skeptical; Jane is voluble and enthusiastic. But the two have
been a couple since almost the moment they met, and their love
story has given Al Smith what every man wants and so few ever
get—a second chance, a chance to do it right.

Jane Farrell was born in 1955 in Pottstown, Pennsylvania,
northwest of Philadelphia. She attended the public schools and
then got a degree in art education from Indiana University. After
college she spent a few years teaching at inner-city schools in
and around Pittsburgh. But one frigid day in the Monongahela
Valley, she found herself standing before a map of North Amer-

ica, searching for a spot completely remote from the drab industrial East. Coos Bay, on Oregon's southern coast, seemed to fit the bill. Within a few months she was there, tending bar while studying to obtain her state teaching certification.

Coos Bay nestles on the lee side of a magnificent crescent-shaped natural harbor, fifteen miles long and more than a mile wide. Though the city is small—only twenty-four thousand people lived in the metro area in 1980—it was, by the late 1970s, well on its way to becoming the largest lumber port in the world. The Coos River and the Millicoma, which flows into it a few miles east of town, were almost choked with big, old Douglas fir, Sitka spruce, and hemlock logs, drifting west to be milled into lumber for export or loaded as raw logs onto huge freighters bound for Japan. To the north of town is the mysterious solitude of the Oregon dunes, which stretch in shifting majesty nearly fifty miles, all the way to Florence at the mouth of the Siuslaw. A driver on the highway bridge across the bay could see tuna, oyster, and shark boats catching the seven-foot outgoing tide. From Coos Head on the northern lip of the harbor, watchers could spot seals and sea lions, dolphins and orcas, and great gray whales swimming south to breed off Baja.

Once or twice a week, Jane Farrell shopped for groceries at McKay's Grocery Store. The checker there was a Native woman. Debbie McClure and her husband, Charlie, almost at once began to treat Jane like a dear old friend—something that is rare indeed in Indian-white friendships. Soon Debbie was taking Jane to sweat-lodge sessions and powwows. At one of them she met a grave old Indian man named Al Smith. She didn't give him much thought, even though Debbie kept raving about what a fine guy he was. A year after their first meeting, in 1979, Al Smith came to Coos Bay. He was set to be the guest speaker at an AA meeting, and Jane went with him. When she heard Al's story—his childhood, his years on the street and in jails, his two decades of recovery—something inside her responded. Part of it was the example of his sobriety; part was his dignity. It surely is no coincidence that Al Smith and Jane's father, Thomas Farrell, were born only a few months apart.

But all the obvious explanations still leave plenty of room for mystery. Al and Jane, so different on the outside, connected somehow. And as Jane Farrell explained later, "We've been to-gether since that weekend." In July 1982, Jane gave birth to a daughter, Kaila Farrell-Smith. At the age of sixty-two, Al Smith was a father and provider again.

He took the new role seriously. This time he would not let down his family, he would be there, he would provide. Al and Jane moved in with friends in Ashland, Oregon, just north of the California line, and he looked for a job in the field he knew best: alcohol- and drug-abuse counseling. From a friend at Sweathouse Lodge, he heard that a small agency in Roseburg, forty miles east of Coos Bay, was looking for a counselor.

The agency was the Douglas County Council on Alcohol and Drug Abuse Prevention and Treatment—ADAPT for short. In January 1981 ADAPT was still small, with only four and a half full-time employees, one of whom was a trainee. Then the coun-cil hired a new young director. John Gardin was thirty-two at the time. A native of Washington, Gardin was a doctoral candidate in clinical psychology at the University of Tennessee. Gardin was dramatically handsome and ambitious, and he had caught the wave of interest and support that was surging over the drug and alcohol field in the early 1980s.

Gardin had gotten his master's in psychology at Portland State University. One semester he was assigned to a clinical rotation at the Veterans Administration hospital in Roseburg. His super-visor was John De Smet, chairman of ADAPT's board and a specialist in alcohol problems. De Smet became Gardin's mentor, and when the agency needed a new director, he recruited the younger man for the position. Once Gardin had moved to Rose-burg, the two men spent hours talking about their experiences in the burgeoning field. Talking with De Smet, Gardin mentioned a few binge-drinking episodes he had been involved with as a college student. De Smet reacted sharply. He was a believer in the AA definition of alcoholism: if your drinking ever causes any problem for you of any kind, then you're an alcoholic. Complete, teetotal abstinence is your only hope.

Gardin began to think and speak of himself as a recovering alcoholic. He did not touch alcohol in any form. In fact, he de-cided, he probably wouldn't drink Communion wine when he went to Catholic Mass; as it turned out, the parish church he joined in Roseburg didn't offer wine to the laity, so it wasn't really a problem. If they had offered it, though, he wouldn't have drunk it. According to the orthodoxy of the time, a recovering alcoholic could not use alcohol in any amount for any purpose without running the risk of creating an irresistible craving that would lead to full-scale relapse.

Gardin was good for ADAPT. By mid-1992 the agency had expanded to nearly two dozen full- or part-time employees and had opened an inpatient facility for clients who needed detoxi-fication and residential treatment. Business was booming—ADAPT got medical referrals, and some patients walked in on their own; but patients were also referred by the courts, which might send over drunk drivers or small-time criminals with substance-abuse problems. ADAPT's "catchment area" included thirteen counties in southern Oregon. In that part of the world, Native Americans were the largest single minority group, but ADAPT's staff were all Anglo. That wasn't surprising, really—even as the largest minority, Native people weren't plentiful in the area. And anyway, most groups in Roseburg, and indeed in southwestern Oregon, were (and remain today) all white, a con-dition that seems normal to most people who live there.

Roseburg is no hotbed of diversity. It is inland, separated from the sea by the Coast Range. Just south of the Willamette Valley, the city stands on the banks of the Umpqua River, one of the country's most dramatic fly-fishing streams. In the 1980s Roseburg was the largest timber-processing center in a state where forest products still dominated the economy. It was a place where three generations of one family, male and female, might work in the same plywood mill; where families lived outdoors seven months a year, hiking in the Cascades, fishing the rapids of the Umpqua, or racing motorboats and Jet Skis at the reservoir. A big night out in Roseburg was a trip to the Sizzler followed by a Babe Ruth League baseball game at the city park. Roseburgers were (and are) good-hearted people, politically moderate to conservative, but they are not possessed of a blinding curiosity about people different from them.

In fact, Gardin and his colleagues at ADAPT knew they wanted to serve their Indian clients but, beyond that, didn't know much about them. When Gardin interviewed Al Smith in the summer of 1982, he was impressed. Here was a man with twenty-five years of recovery—a path Gardin had just started to walk. Smith had a dignity and confidence that Gardin thought would appeal to Native and Anglo clients alike.

Al wasn't being hired because of his Native background, though. His job title was counselor, and his job was to provide all his clients with ADAPT's standard treatment of abstinence and Twelve Step work. And ADAPT was nothing like Sweathouse Lodge. The subject of peyote never came up. Later, when the relationship between him and ADAPT had turned sour, Al Smith admitted forthrightly that he knew that these white people wouldn't be sympathetic to peyote as a form of alcohol treatment: "When I went to work for them, did I consider ADAPT would consider peyote a drug? Yes."

There were enough bumps along the way without peyote. Al Smith's first day on the job, September 25, 1982, provided a rich illustration. Bruce Piper, ADAPT's clinical and outreach supervisor, was Al Smith's superior. On September 25 Piper, as usual, got to his office about 7:15 A.M. After a few minutes at his desk, he noticed a strong smell from the air-conditioning vents. Piper thought he recognized the smell; he picked up the phone and called the building super. "I think you've got somebody around the building here near the air intakes that's smoking a little weed," he said.

Half an hour later the super called back. "He said, 'It's your new Indian,' or something like that," Piper recalled later. Piper went straight to Al Smith's office, where the new employee was tackling his paperwork. "Hi, Al," Piper remembers saying. "What are you doing?" Smith told Piper that he had been smudging down his office. "Well," said Piper, "with what?" Al told him he was using sweet grass. Piper returned to his office, puzzled. Sweet grass is a native North American herb, relatively rare and very sacred to Native people, known for a strong, sweet odor that carries prayer to the spirit world. But Piper didn't know that. "I didn't know if 'sweet grass' meant, you know, grass or—*grass*. And so this was a pretty exciting first day of employment."

But on the whole, ADAPT was well pleased with Al Smith. For one thing, he had more sobriety than anyone else in the office. His example, his calm presence at meetings, his advice on maintaining serenity in spite of pressures to relapse, were important to the staff as well. Many of them were recovering alcoholics or users, too, and they respected what Al Smith had done with his life. Bruce Piper recalled that Al Smith's comments at staff meetings would "frequently sort of elevate a discussion to a different plane by talking about his own life and the Creator and the involvement of the Creator. He would say things that a Native American person might say from their perspective, but of course other people in the staff meeting would not think of in a million years."

With his clients in the outpatient program, Al Smith was motivated and hardworking. He spent extra time with the clients. He also set up weekly sweat-lodge programs for Anglo and Native clients alike, and he shared his spiritual views with his clients. These views were very different from what Anglo people heard in church, and Gardin found that this was a strength. Addicts and alcoholics are often angry, defiant, alienated; many long ago consigned their own religious heritage to their own personal rubbish heap. But alcohol- and drug-treatment programs usually require clients to make a strong spiritual commitment of some kind. Most treatment programs use AA's Twelve Steps, which require the recovering alcoholic or drug abuser to commit to a "higher power." If alcoholics found their way to that power blocked by childhood anger, their recovery might fail. But when Al Smith talked about the Creator, the Indian concept of the spirit that had made and moved the world, many clients found the talk less threatening than ordinary Jesus language.

One person who responded to Al Smith's talk about Native religion was Galen Black. Black is an important character in the story of the *Smith* case in much the way a catalyst is in a chemical reaction. Had Galen Black never met Al Smith, there would most likely never have been a case.

Black is not an Indian, though later in the case a number of judges and commentators would make him into one. It's easy to see why—two Native Americans seeking to practice an ancient religion make a tidier picture than does a white man who has just discovered Native spirituality and a Native man dragged into the case almost against his will. But Galen Black is not a tidy figure; he is, in his way, an American original, a spiritual seeker who is also a genuine rolling stone, careening around the western half of the continent without seeming to stop long enough to draw breath.

By the time he sobered up, Galen Black had taken on the weather-beaten look of a man who has spent a lot of time on lonely roads. He is lean and hungry-looking, with a solemn expression. He wears large plastic eyeglass frames of a kind that were fashionable in the 1970s. He wears his gray hair slicked back, and his lantern jaw is covered with a neat salt-and-pepper beard. The overall look is like a WPA Depression-era photo come to life. This is a man who has had some hard traveling to get where he is.

Black was born in Russell, Kansas, on October 1, 1947. He grew up in and around Wichita, where his father worked at a Boeing aircraft plant. After high school Galen entered the navy, where he served as a food handler on an aircraft carrier off the coast of Vietnam. After four months at sea, he became depressed and had to be taken ashore; eventually the navy gave him a medical discharge. He went back to Wichita, married a local girl, and went to work at the local Big Boy restaurant. He and his wife had a child, Shane, but the marriage quickly dissolved, leaving Galen with custody of Shane.

Four years later Galen married Lindy, his second wife. Their stormy relationship would define most of the next two decades of his life. In about 1975, the Blacks were divorced. Each quickly remarried, then as quickly divorced their new mates and remarried each other. Galen worked as an auto mechanic and a general Mr. Fixit. A good mechanic can always find work, which was good, because Lindy and Galen Black began rattling around the country like ball bearings in a pinball machine—moving west to California, east back to Kansas, and eventually north to Oregon. Galen could work when he wasn't drinking, but that was less and less often as the years went on. He and Lindy tried to start a family, but when she miscarried three times, that dream seemed closed to them. The open road and the bottle took its place.

In fact, Galen Black had his bottom—the same turning point that Al Smith found in an alley in Sacramento—on the road. He was coming north on Interstate 5, on his way back home to Sutherlin, Oregon, after his father's funeral. He had started drinking at Kingman, Arizona, with three hundred dollars in his pocket. By the time he pulled into a gas station in Roseburg, he had eighty-seven cents left; he traded the station attendant his pocket knife for enough gas to get to Sutherlin. Over those last few miles, he thought about his life and concluded that it was out of control. Within a month he had checked himself into the Rogue Recovery House Treatment Center in Grants Pass, Oregon. He successfully completed the program and began a new life as a recovering alcoholic. He helped start two AA meetings and decided that he liked working with other recovering alcoholics. He could, he concluded, begin a new career as well as a new life. He applied to ADAPT; two weeks before Al Smith started at the agency, Galen Black started as a resident assistant at the inpatient treatment facility.

A few weeks later Galen Black met Al Smith. He was impressed with Smith's story; when he first tried the sweat lodge Al was running for ADAPT clients, he was more than impressed—he was transformed, he was energized. In the sweat lodge, he found a way to rid himself, body and mind, of a lifetime's worth of toxins; in Native religion, he thought, he had found a way to cure his own spiritual malaise and reach out to others. Like Saul of Tarsus after his vision on the Damascus Road, Galen Black adopted Indian religion with the zeal of a classic convert.

Unlike Al Smith, Galen Black had less than two years' sobriety at this point. That did nothing to quench his enthusiasm; alcoholics in the early stages of recovery often feel energized, almost messianic, to pursue the new route to salvation they have found. And it didn't hurt, either, that Galen saw this new spirituality as a ticket up in his new career. The proposal by which ADAPT had gotten state funding for the residential unit clearly promised that the agency would "attempt to reach special need populations by providing culturally appropriate outreach and treatment" to "women, American Indian, Spanish-American, and black" clients. Only a few of the residential clients were Indians—Galen estimates today that, during his time at ADAPT, about eight Natives came through out of four hundred clients—but, as Galen saw it, "we were obligated to provide those people their culturally specific treatment." Galen Black saw his new knowledge of Native spirituality as a professional credential that would make him more valuable to his employers. "So I took on that role," he recalled. He began to attend Indian ceremonials and collect Indian artifacts—which caused some friction at home. Lindy called his Native objects his "wannabe Indian kit." But Galen was determined; he had found a new way and he was going to stick with it.

As Al Smith remembers, one day Galen came to him with a question. He had heard about a ritual involving peyote and the group called the Native American Church. Did Al know anything about it? Did he think Galen should try it? The truth was, Al later recalled, at that point he wasn't too clear on who Galen Black was. Counselors in the outpatient program didn't have that much contact with the residential staff. Al had seen Galen at sweat lodges, but in his mind Galen was a client, not a staff member—a client seeking spiritual strength to help him with his recovery. Al answered honestly: If you want to know about peyote, go talk to Stanley Smart, he said. Black asked whether he should take peyote during the ceremonial. Al Smith wasn't an adviser. That's up to you, he said. It's your personal choice.

Al and Galen planned to go to a ceremony together; at the last minute, though, Al got sick and couldn't go. So on September 10, 1983, Galen Black went up to Sweathouse Lodge to meet Stanley Smart. He took his son, Shane, then thirteen, along with him, as a chance to see something about Native spirituality. Father and son drove up to Sweathouse Lodge in the afternoon. Galen talked to Smart for a few hours, trying to assure himself that peyote was not a drug, not a stimulant that would threaten his sobriety. Stanley Smart assured Galen that peyote was a sacrament, not a drug, and that its only effect would be to bring him closer to the Creator, to strengthen him in his new life. That night Galen and Shane sat in the meeting, and when the dried peyote was passed around, Galen ate a small amount.

Soon, he recalled, he began to feel "a real close bond" with the other participants in the ceremony. "It became real intense, almost to the point that you could feel what the other person was thinking." After an hour or so, he began to look inside himself, to see the parts of his life that needed attention and change: "I was looking at the bare facts of me." The effects were subtle, but real, and Galen felt excited at the discoveries he had made.

Galen's excitement—his conviction that he had found a new spiritual home, that he had found a way to transform alcohol- and drug-abuse treatment, that he had found a way to change his life—led him astray. That wouldn't surprise AA old-timers; they warn newly sober members to be very careful of strong emotions—joy, fear, anger, anxiety. Serenity, not intensity, is the aim of the Twelve Steps; many newly sober alcoholics—"white-knucklers" in AA parlance—find themselves craving the highs and even the lows that alcohol brought into their lives. Sometimes they find new ways to produce them without drinking; AA veterans refer to these intense but nonalcoholic experiences as "dry drunks."

On the way back home, Black was so elated by his experience

that he stopped by ADAPT, even though he wasn't on duty. He told the counselor on duty what had happened, that he had gone through "this really super Native American Church meeting." But her reaction brought him up short. *Are you taking drugs?* she asked at once. *Who are these Indians; why are they holding these ceremonies? Isn't peyote illegal?* Galen suddenly realized that not everyone would see what he had done as a positive thing. "So I didn't say anything to anyone else."

But it was too late. Galen had set off a crisis; he had also, without knowing it, walked into one of the bitterest controversies in the alcohol- and drug-abuse field in the early 1980s.

The genesis of alcohol treatment in America was religious. Early American physicians like Benjamin Rush, who lived in Philadelphia about the time of the Revolution, first began to see alcoholism as a disease, but a disease with a moral component. Eighteenth-century reformers called for temperance—meaning moderation in use of alcohol. But in the early nineteenth century, Protestant clergy like the Reverend Lyman Beecher transformed the conventional wisdom. Alcoholism became more than a disease—it was a spiritual failing, and even a trap set by Satan in the guise of "demon rum." And though the anti-liquor crusade called itself the temperance movement, the new goal was not moderation but abstinence—complete renunciation of alcohol in any form or amount. The concept and the word itself arose straight out of Christian beliefs in fasting as a means of penance and spiritual cleansing.

Abstinence, with all its religious overtones, became the central concept of Alcoholics Anonymous, in part because it fit in with AA's own roots in Christian thought. AA dates its founding as June 10, 1935. That was the day when Bill Wilson, a former stockbroker who had drunk away his career and nearly died of drinking, told another "hopeless alcoholic," Dr. Robert Holbrook Smith, how God had helped him attain sobriety after medicine had given him up. Bill W., who became a legend within AA, had drawn his inspiration from an aggressive evangelical Christian movement called the Oxford Group, which later became known as the militantly anticommunist Moral Rearmament. AA's Twelve Steps emphasize surrender of the will to a higher power (in the early days of the movement, "HP" was pretty clearly the Christian God), prayer, meditation, and spiritual renewal as means to relieve the compulsion to drink.

Upon this religious foundation grew a secular alcohol-treatment industry that never quite lost its underlying evangelical fervor—in large part because so many alcohol- and drug-abuse counselors were themselves alcoholics who had found recovery through AA. Giving up alcohol had become, for recovering drinkers and those who treated them, something akin to the experience of "conversion" that American Christians have pursued since the days of the Puritans—an overwhelming experience that remakes the life of a sinner, reordering all desires and relationships and providing an inner meaning that enables the convert to live successfully in the world. The goal of alcohol treatment was to bring the alcoholic to this moment by piercing the psychological mechanism called denial—the alcoholic's insistence that (in James Thurber's famous phrase) "I can take it or I can leave it alone." Alcoholics beginning treatment are often emphatic—*I don't drink all that much; I'm in control of my own drinking; it isn't really a problem for me or my family.*

But during the 1970s, the quasi-religion of abstinence spawned its own heresy, which went under the name "controlled drinking." As early as 1962, some well-known clinicians observed that some patients with drinking problems are able to stop drinking on their own and even to return to social drinking for a sustained period of time. In 1971 the National Institute on Alcohol Abuse and Alcoholism (NIAAA) contracted with the RAND Corporation, a semi-official think tank, to do a massive study to de-

termine the effectiveness of NIAAA-funded alcoholism programs. The result, published in June 1976 as *Alcoholism and
Treatment*, hit like a bombshell, because it suggested that significant numbers of recovering alcoholics were able to return to
social drinking without suffering relapse.

The findings made a huge splash in the press; in response,
the treatment community went into a defensive crouch. Counselors feared that if left unchallenged, the RAND study would
provide a new layer of denial for their clients. They attacked the
study's methodology, arguing that the sample of patients studied
was too small and that the six-month follow-up was too short for
meaningful results. Many critics also suggested that the "controlled drinkers" in the study were not "real" alcoholics. The logic
was seamless and was also an example of the almost hermetic
mind-set of much of the alcoholism-treatment community: alcoholics cannot return to social drinking; if the study found some
who could, it simply proved that they were never alcoholics.

Outside observers sometimes found themselves at a loss to
understand the bitterness of the "controlled drinking" dispute.
After all, the question was one of scientific fact, and scientists
like to picture their work as a dispassionate process of forming
hypotheses, testing them by measurement and then reforming
them to explain experimental results. The attack on the RAND
study was not dispassionate; it had all the heat of a dispute
among seminarians about the nature of the Trinity.

The religious roots of alcoholism treatment aren't the only
explanation for this reaction. For those in the field, proper treatment for alcoholism was not a scientific puzzle but a daily battle
against death. The statistics studied by RAND researchers represented patients' lives, their families' solvency and safety, the
sanity of millions of people. Like physicists whose measurements
change the state of a subatomic particle, the RAND researchers
were not only measuring but changing the equation. The "con-

trolled drinking" theory would simply strengthen denial, many professionals feared; if the study suggested that a small percentage of alcoholics could go back to drinking safely, every client would insist that he or she was one of that small number.

In 1980 RAND issued a follow-up report using a longer time horizon than it had for the first study. *The Course of Alcoholism: Four Years After Treatment* confirmed the earlier findings but added that for most patients abstinence was the safest method of preventing a relapse. Younger alcoholics, who had not yet developed certain symptoms of physical dependency, did better as controlled drinkers; older drinkers, who had already developed blackouts, tremors and shakes, and continuous binges of twelve hours or more, tended to do better if they abstained altogether. Critics of the first report insisted that the new one was a "retraction" and assured their clients that abstinence was the only treatment for their drinking problem.

But the battle wasn't over. Beginning in 1970, Mark and Linda Sobell, behavioral researchers in California, had been trying to use behavior modification to teach alcoholics to return to social drinking. In research results published between 1973 and 1978, the Sobells reported that they had divided patients at a state hospital into two groups. One group received standard in-patient treatment—AA meetings, group therapy, and drugs like Antabuse designed to produce an aversion to alcohol. The other cohort was given behavior-modification training to teach controlled-drinking skills. After following the patients for two years, the Sobells reported that controlled-drinking training not only worked but produced a better outcome than did standard abstinence.

The Sobells' results enraged advocates of abstinence. First the RAND researchers had questioned the treatment community's basic understanding of the disease; now the Sobells were proposing an alternative treatment that many counselors thought would lead to fatal results. In 1982 three alcohol researchers, Mary Pendery, Irving Maltzman, and John West, submitted a draft article to *Science*, one of America's most prestigious scientific journals. In its original form, the article accused the Sobells of producing results that were not just flawed but consciously fraudulent. *Science* refused the original draft, fearing a libel suit; the authors revised it for publication, toning down the accusations of fraud. But they circulated the original draft to reporters, and the ensuing publicity created a widespread impression that the Sobells had been caught faking their results. Two formal investigations—one by the Addiction Research Foundation and the other by the NIAAA—found no evidence of fraud, but these sober conclusions never caught up with the original charges.

The fight over abstinence was more than a scientific dispute; it was seen by many participants as a life-and-death struggle. The difference in part was between the perspective of the research scientist and that of the clinician. To a scientist, there could be little question that some drinkers did return to social or controlled drinking; but to some of those who spent their days trying to pierce the cocoon of alcoholic denial, this "fact" was so dangerous that it was easy to consider it morally indistinguishable from a lie. Many people in the treatment community were themselves in recovery, maintaining their own sobriety only by abstinence and strenuous spiritual practice, so perhaps it's not surprising that the controlled-drinking controversy took on some of the aspects of a holy war.

This was the background against which the management at ADAPT would have seen Galen Black's visit to the peyote meeting. Under the leadership of John De Smet and John Gardin, the agency was squarely in the abstinence camp. Neither man knew much about peyote, but they knew it was classified as a Schedule I substance by the federal Drug Enforcement Administration.

That classification meant that the agency considered it a drug with a "high potential for abuse and no accepted therapeutic use," dangerous even if used under medical supervision. For Galen Black, a low-level employee with only a few years' sobriety, to use peyote was, to them, a clear-cut violation of the agency's policy against "misuse" of drugs.

On September 19, 1983, Gardin called Black into his office and suspended him from his job. He ordered him to report to Mike Hendricks, a counselor at the Veterans Administration hospital nearby, for a psychological evaluation to determine whether he had relapsed. Next, he called Al Smith into his office. Gardin thought Al Smith had also been at the peyote meeting. He confronted Smith aggressively. Al said he would go to a meeting if invited, but he hadn't gone. Gardin then curtly told him that he was forbidden by ADAPT policy to use peyote at any time. If he violated the policy, he would be terminated. Gardin later testified that Al Smith became furious; he jumped to his feet and stomped over to the door. Al does not remember becoming enraged; he said later Gardin's words had shocked him. But no one disputes that the meeting was tense.

Here was a cultural miscommunication more serious than the difference between sweet grass and grass. Gardin believed he was simply defending the integrity of ADAPT'S treatment program. But to this day, Al Smith remembers the message differently. *I can't go to church?* he remembers asking himself. Jane Farrell-Smith said later, "If you know Al's personality, you know first of all you don't just get in his face and point a finger—particularly if you're a white man thirty years younger and reek of dominant culture. You're messing with the wrong man." To Al Smith, Gardin's ultimatum seemed like a gauntlet flung down. Al Smith had never walked away from a fight.

He went home that night and talked the situation over with Jane. Their family had a lot to lose. On one level, it wasn't

much—a little green house that fronted a gravel driveway, right
in the middle of Roseburg. There was no yard: Kaila played with
the neighbors' children in an old refrigerator box Jane had dec-
orated with crayons. The house was barely furnished. They would
buy one piece at a time at thrift shops; Al often stained them
on the front porch, drawing upon his days as a furniture refin-
isher. Roseburg, Jane recalled, seemed like a cultural void. But
they could swim in the Umpqua on summer afternoons, and their
next-door neighbor was a Native woman who took them to sweats
and powwows in the hills around town. Besides, they were only
a few hours from Ashland, a glorious, sunny resort town where
old friends had a house overlooking Lithia Park. Al might be
sixty-three, but they were newlyweds with a beautiful new baby,
and the days were sweet. Al's paycheck was what kept them in
their home. But there was a lot to lose the other way, too. He
hadn't looked for this fight, but it had come to him; if he walked
away, he might be betraying himself and his lifelong fight for
spiritual autonomy.

Meanwhile, Mike Hendricks of the VA hospital was preparing
his report on Galen Black. Hendricks met with Galen and Lindy
Black and their son, Shane, and submitted a five-page, single-
spaced report. It wasn't the clean bill of health that Galen had
hoped for, but it wasn't the clear-cut finding of "relapse" Gardin
had expected, either. Hendricks wrote that Galen had made "a
crucial error in judgment" by ingesting peyote. But that in itself
did not constitute a relapse. In fact, Galen's problems were more
generalized: "Mr. Black has been in relapse (in terms of thinking
and behavior) for most all of his 'clean and sober' time." His life
was unmanageable on many levels. He attended AA meetings
and worked to support the meetings he had helped start, but his
involvement with Native religion seemed "extreme" to Hendricks,
"indicating a tendency towards obsessive-compulsiveness."
Black's justification of his decision to use peyote "clearly points

out stinking thinking"—an AA term for the distorted and self-serving thought pattern of an alcoholic.

Hendricks added a warning to Gardin and the ADAPT board:

> I feel this is going to be a "political" issue in the local community
> and controversy may eventually be involved. There are those in-
> dividuals who are going to support Mr. Black's decision to use
> peyote in the way he did and these include some recovering
> individuals. I have heard an argument about "freedom of religion"
> and that there has been some talk about possibly filing a legal
> suit in terms of some of these areas by Native American indi-
> viduals.

On October 3 Gardin met with Black again and offered him a choice: report for inpatient treatment at a residential facility, with the prospect of returning to a lower-level job; resign; or be fired. Black rejected all three. "I said, 'No, there's another option, Mr. Gardin.' And I told him, 'There's a court option, because what you're doing is simply racist discrimination.' " Gardin fired Black on the spot.

Hendricks's report had pointed up a dilemma faced by all the participants. Word of what had happened to Galen was out, both inside ADAPT and in the larger community it served. *Respect* is an important word to Native people. Native ways, Native elders, and Native religion are worthy of respect even by those who do not follow them, and the white man has never shown the respect these ways are entitled to. Now ADAPT had shown disrespect to a Native religion and to Al Smith, by now an elder and a man with more sobriety than anyone else in the building. Native people in the area saw Gardin's actions as a challenge, not just to Al Smith but to all of them. They began to let Al know that they were watching to see what he would do.

To make the challenge clearer, the ADAPT board now adopted

a new personnel policy that made its conditions perfectly clear: "Use of an illegal drug or use of prescription drugs in a nonprescribed manner is grounds for immediate termination from employment."

For the next six months, Al pondered the challenge. He carried on at ADAPT, but the honeymoon was over. Many times Gardin would call him into his office and question details of his performance. To Gardin, Smith seemed more passive than he had been, troublesome about paperwork. Some other ADAPT staff reported that he had begun blowing off sweat-lodge sessions and generally taking a light approach to his job.

In January 1984 Al asked Gardin to allow him to go to Salem for a training session aimed at Native counselors from around the state. Gardin refused. Al went anyway. ADAPT records showed him as having requested sick leave; Smith insists that he had called in to take a personal day of unpaid leave. Gardin found him at the meeting, and the two men had an ugly scene. Al Smith began to suspect that he was being set up to be fired.

Meanwhile, Native friends were talking to Al Smith. Everyone knew that Galen Black was not going to let the matter drop. He was planning some kind of court challenge to his firing. But some of the Native people thought this was dangerous—Galen was an Anglo, and in truth he knew very little about Native ways. If the case went forward with only a white man as plaintiff, Indian people wouldn't be represented, even though the result might affect their religious freedom. The implication was that Al needed to get involved, regardless of the cost to him and his family.

Al asked Jane for advice, and she told him—she was a fighter too, in her way, as spirited as Al—to follow his heart. It was a lonely time for him, the more so as he knew both white and Native people were watching him. In March of 1984, he got an invitation. Stanley Smart was to lead a ceremony at Coos Bay.

People would be coming from all over the state. Al hadn't decided what to do when he went to the office one morning that week. In his interoffice mailbox he found a large manila envelope. There was no return address, just his name. When he opened it, he found the full tail feathers of an eagle—one of the most sacred symbols in Native spirituality. "I interpreted that as an invite to the meeting," he recalled. "If I accept these feathers, how can I not go?"

That Friday Al Smith walked into Gardin's office and told him he would be going to a meeting that weekend. That weekend, when the buttons were passed, Al ate and prayed for strength. In the morning, when the congregation emerged from the ceremony for a communal breakfast, the others present began ribbing Al—"Well, now you're unemployed like us."

On Monday Gardin called Al in and asked him if he had gone to the meeting. Yes, Al said. Did you take peyote? Gardin asked. "I said, 'Well, I took the sacred sacrament and prayed for you and the rest of you sick mothers,'" Al recalled. "Well, I got fired. He said, 'Have your desk cleaned out and let your clients know you'll be leaving at the end of the day.'"

That was that. Al Smith had fought the good fight once again. Now there was nothing for it but to go down to the county building and get his unemployment check while he looked for a new job.

But the county building is where the real fight began—the fight that would go to the U.S. Supreme Court not once but twice and would rewrite the American law of free exercise—because the Employment Division, which in Oregon oversees the unemployment-insurance program, sent Al Smith a letter on March 22 denying him unemployment compensation. His employer opposed the award of benefits, the letter said, because Smith had committed a "willful violation of the standards of behavior that an employer has the right to expect of an employee."

Now Al Smith realized there would be no walking away. "You go to church, and then you get terminated," he said. "It is a continuation of being put down, of my people and our religion not being recognized by you newcomers. They just riled me up to the point where I'm ready for a fight. Do you want to fight? Okay."

6

FREEDOM OF
"RELIGEON"

Dave Frohnmayer doesn't remember the exact date he first heard the names Al Smith and Galen Black. It was probably early in 1984, as Black's challenge to his denial of unemployment compensation began its journey through the administrative labyrinth of Oregon's Employment Division. He does remember the circumstances, though: it was an advisory from the Attorney General's Office of General Counsel, which provided legal advice to state agencies. The Employment Division of the Department of Human Resources had an interesting pair of cases down in Roseburg—alcohol- and drug-abuse counselors who had been fired for attending peyote ceremonies. The division had asked what law governed a case like this, and the office reported the advice it had given. Frohnmayer agreed with what the office had said, which was "there was something wrong with the notion that a person who uses a controlled substance, the use of which would be illegal for everyone else, should be able to receive an unemployment benefit when that person engaged in voluntary conduct that was contrary to the work rules of an employer. Especially a drug rehabilitation center."

That advice seemed at first to conflict with the leading cases on the issue under the U.S. Constitution. When it discusses religion, the First Amendment puts limits on what government can do to advance or hinder religious beliefs; those limits come from the Establishment Clause, which says that Congress (and, under the Supreme Court's reading of the Fourteenth Amendment, the state governments as well) shall "make no law respecting an establishment of religion," meaning no official government-sponsored religion. Americans who are not lawyers—and who aren't members of minority religious groups—often tend to think of the Establishment Clause as the primary guarantee of religious freedom in America. Until very recently, the widely publicized constitutional cases about religion tended to be Establishment cases—whether the state government could require Christian prayers in public schools or put up publicly owned Nativity scenes to honor Christmas.

But the second of the twin religion clauses is designed to protect individuals rather than restrain government. It guarantees "the free exercise" of religion against state and federal infringement. Cases brought under this clause almost always concern individuals or small groups whose beliefs differ from those of their neighbors. The most important case decided under the Free Exercise Clause had arisen in the precise context that Smith and Black's case arose—unemployment compensation. The Supreme Court's decision in *Sherbert* v. *Verner* was seen by most lawyers as a solidly established part of the liberal legacy of the Warren and Burger Courts, and as the cornerstone of federal free-exercise law.

Adell Sherbert was an employee in a South Carolina textile mill. She was also a member of the Seventh-Day Adventist Church, a homegrown Christian sect that religious scholar Paul K. Conkin lists as one of the "American originals," the peculiarly American contributions to the history of Christianity. The Adventists arose in the early nineteenth century, when a self-educated prophet named William Miller studied Old Testament prophecy and proclaimed that Judgment Day would come during late 1843 or early 1844. By 1844, the year Adventists remember as "the Great Disappointment," Miller had fifty thousand disciples. Many drifted away when the Apocalypse tarried, but a hard core of followers reorganized themselves under a strict reading of the Bible. Adventists observe Saturday, not Sunday, as their Sabbath, and follow a strict dietary code—no meat, no alcohol, no tobacco—that has made them one of the healthiest subcultures in the country. Adventists founded hospitals across the country and relocated their headquarters to Battle Creek, Michigan. There, in the early twentieth century, a pair of lapsed Adventist brothers named Kellogg adapted Adventist dietary doctrine to produce the nation's first packaged breakfast cereal.

By the late 1950s Adventists had spread to all parts of the country. They maintain a strict separation from other Christian bodies, and "mainstream" Protestants often disdain them for their insistence on Saturday worship—called Sabbatarianism.

None of this, however, made Adell Sherbert a bad worker. Five days a week she spun cotton in the Spartan Mill in Beaumont, South Carolina. On Saturdays she worshiped with her fellow believers. But then in 1959 her employer extended the work week to six days, requiring Saturday shifts for all workers. Adell Sherbert asked to be allowed to work her old schedule, but the company fired her. She was offered other jobs, but all required Saturday work; when she applied for unemployment compensation, the state unemployment office denied her benefits on the grounds that she had refused suitable work without "good cause."

Mrs. Sherbert challenged the refusal before South Carolina's courts, which summarily rejected her claim. Some states chose to include religious reasons as "good cause" for declining work; South Carolina had not, and that was that. As far as the state courts were concerned, Mrs. Sherbert had no grounds to complain that her religious freedom had been abridged; she was simply being treated like anyone else. A minority religion like Adventism was still free to believe in its eccentric view of the Sabbath, but the state and federal constitutions did not obligate the government to create special privilege for her that others did not enjoy.

In 1963 Mrs. Sherbert went to the Supreme Court. During the heyday of the Warren Court, minority groups all over the country had come to regard the Court as the special guardian of their place at the American table. The liberal New Deal justices named by Presidents Roosevelt and Truman had been bolstered unexpectedly during the 1950s by two Eisenhower appointees— Chief Justice Earl Warren, a genial former politician adept at procuring majorities for his favored positions, and Associate Justice William Brennan, a jovial Irish American imp with a brilliant legal mind and a ready sympathy for the ordinary American facing the coercive power of the state. Warren, Brennan, and "the brethren" (as the all-male Court then referred to itself) did not disappoint Adell Sherbert. In a groundbreaking opinion by Justice Brennan, the Court held that denying her unemployment payments violated the Free Exercise Clause. The denial forced Mrs. Sherbert to choose between following her faith on the one hand and receiving a government benefit on the other. Brennan wrote for a six-to-three majority: "Government imposition of such a choice puts the same kind of burden upon the free exercise of religion as would a fine imposed against appellant for her Saturday worship."

But the Court did not hold that such a burden on free exercise was flatly forbidden. Instead, it measured the denial of benefits by a test it imported from its cases on freedom of speech: the state could impose such a burden only if it was pursuing "some compelling state interest" and if it could show that "no alternative forms of regulations" would achieve the same end. Here, the only interest the Court would recognize was the state's desire to prevent false claims; granting an exception would not destroy its ability to protect the fund from fraud.

Adell Sherbert got her benefits, and constitutional lawyers came to consider the "compelling interest test"—now known as the *Sherbert* test—as the basic template for deciding questions under the Free Exercise Clause. But the Court was not unanimous in *Sherbert*; Justice John Marshall Harlan, joined by Justice Byron White, dissented. The Court had decided that the Constitution required states to "single out for financial assistance those whose conduct is religiously motivated," Harlan wrote. This went too far; the Free Exercise Clause, he argued, meant only that the state *could* choose to accommodate religious believers, not that it was *required* to. By treating nonreligious and religious claimants equally, he said, the state had fulfilled its constitutional duty.

But despite Harlan's dissent, Brennan's *Sherbert* test seemed to become the law of free exercise. Nearly twenty years after *Sherbert* v. *Verner*, in fact, the Burger Court reaffirmed and even extended the rule in a case called *Thomas* v. *Review Board*. In that case, a Jehovah's Witness had quit a job producing tank turrets because he objected to working directly on weapons. His church did not require him to quit; other Witnesses were content to build parts for tanks. It was his own interpretation of the Bible that led to his resignation. That didn't matter, said the Court; he, like Mrs. Sherbert, was entitled to unemployment checks.

Sherbert certainly suggested that Oregon was obligated to pay Al Smith and Galen Black if they had been fired for exercising their religious beliefs. There were only a few differences between their actions and Mrs. Sherbert's. First, Mrs. Sherbert wasn't claiming the right to engage in religious behavior on the job, such as stitching Adventist messages into the textiles she helped weave; ADAPT argued that Smith and Black's use of peyote actually changed their ability to counsel clients. That was the issue that ADAPT focused on. The attorney general's office, however, from the beginning focused on another distinction. Resting and worshiping on Saturday doesn't violate any law, and no state could constitutionally pass a law against it. Use of peyote, however, was illegal in Oregon.

One of a state attorney general's duties is to defend the law of the state as set out by the legislature and the courts. Most AGs believe that, in most cases, it is not their duty to decide whether they agree with the law; for an attorney general's office to refuse to defend a statute simply because the AG doesn't approve of it, they argue, would be malpractice—just as it would be malpractice for a private lawyer who disapproved of a state statute to refuse to plead that statute when it supported a client's cause. Attorneys general are often confronted with state statutes or state court decisions that may seem erroneous, even ridiculous; but ethically, the only time it would be proper to refuse to defend such rules would be if no reasonable lawyer could consider the law constitutional.

In the case of peyote, the law of Oregon was clear enough. In fact, Oregon was the only state in the Union whose courts had recently rejected a religious defense to its peyote statutes. The case, *State* v. *Soto*, arose almost by accident in 1973. Reginald Soto, a Native American peyotist, was driving in Tualatin, Oregon, when a state police car pulled him over. When the officer shone his flashlight into the car, he found something more than a lapsed license: Soto, like a number of Native peyotists, liked to drive with a "medicine bundle" dangling from his rearview mirror. Soto's bundle included a dried peyote button; peyotists don't carry them around in order to ingest them but rather because they believe peyote is literally God, and like others who carry statutettes of the Virgin on their dashboards, they want their God near them at all times.

What the officer saw, however, was a drug that was illegal under the state controlled-substances law. He arrested Soto and charged him with possession of "mescaline" (one of the psychoactive ingredients in peyote).

So far there was nothing unusual; many states during the sixties and seventies had tried to enforce their state drug laws against religious use of peyote. In California and many other states, the defendants would come to court to argue that their religious beliefs merited protection under the state and federal constitutions. Beginning in 1964 with a California case called *People* v. *Woody*, peyote worshipers had won most of these cases.

What was unusual about *Soto* was what happened at trial. The Oregon trial judge refused even to hear Soto's evidence and arguments about religious freedom. Under Oregon law, religious motivation was irrelevant, the court said. The legislature hadn't provided any exemption, and the courts had no business even considering one. In language that echoed Harlan's dissent in *Sherbert*, the Oregon Court of Appeals agreed that Soto's free-exercise arguments were irrelevant once the Oregon legislature decided not to consider them:

Peyote and mescaline have been declared by the legislature to be dangerous drugs as a matter of law. The preservation of the

health and safety of the people is the presumed purpose behind
that legislative declaration and a valid and reasonable application
of the criminal laws of the state. There is, thus, a compelling
state interest.

Like Harlan, the Oregon court seemed to deny the Free Exercise Clause any mandatory force against the government. Free
exercise was a license for government to aid religion when it
chose, but the choice made by a legislature would be final.

It's not likely that all this background went through Frohnmayer's mind when he was first briefed on the unemployment-
compensation challenge by Al Smith and Galen Black. It wasn't
a high-profile case at that point, and the attorney general's office
wasn't directly involved. In Oregon, as in most of the fifty states,
unemployment insurance is a state program funded by federal
dollars and by premiums paid by private employers. It is designed
to provide transitional aid for employees who find themselves out
of work. In early 1984 the dispute was still between Al Smith
and Galen Black on the one hand and ADAPT on the other.
ADAPT was opposing the award of benefits, and the Employment Division was in essence the referee. The AG's office was
advising the state agency.

That was a responsibility that Frohnmayer took very seriously.
From the day he was elected, Dave Frohnmayer had insisted that
state agencies regard his office as *the* law firm for the state. The
state should speak with one legal voice, he said. That was because the issue in any given case was not simply what would be
best for the state agency involved but what would be best for the
state of Oregon as a whole. Legal positions taken by one agency
could compromise the state's interests down the road, and so
they needed to be reviewed by the AG, who was trying to think
ahead of all the pending and possible issues that could be affected by a given case. The AG's role, if he or she plays it prop-

erly, is a bit like that of a chess master, who must not be distracted by a current threat or opportunity and thus neglect the possibility of a strategic disaster many moves away.

One question that recurs in the story of the *Smith* case is why the state of Oregon, in the person of Dave Frohnmayer, fought so long and so hard against allowing unemployment benefits to two obscure former alcohol- and drug-abuse counselors. Commentators and outsiders often remarked on the tenacity with which both sides pursued a dispute over a small amount of money. The answer is complex. Much of the reason for Frohnmayer's obstinate defense of Oregon's position arose simply out of his own nature. Lawyers—all lawyers—like to win their cases; they are a self-selected and carefully trained group of gladiators who fight for their clients' rights as if their own lives depend on it. Lawyers also come, by the workings of human nature, to believe in the absolute rightness of their cause. And even among lawyers, Dave Frohnmayer was an unusually determined advocate. The same determination he brought to the fight against Fanconi anemia found its way into even routine cases under his official jurisdiction.

Another reason was the attorney general's own disapproval of illegal drug use. Oregonians, by and large, are a libertarian group. The state had been the first in the nation to "decriminalize" possession of small amounts of marijuana; a person caught smoking a joint or holding a small stash was not arrested. Instead, police wrote a citation, like a traffic ticket, carrying a small fine. But Frohnmayer was out of step on the issue. Through Lynn's experience with abusive families, he had become convinced that even "harmless" drugs like marijuana could be gateways to serious drug addiction and other lawless and destructive behavior. And besides, there was something about the whole drug scene— about voluntarily losing control of oneself—that grated against Frohnmayer's faith in reason and order. One of his assistants once remembered asking the attorney general whether he would try marijuana—just once, just to see what it was like—if he found himself in a place where it was legal. Absolutely not, Frohnmayer answered. End of discussion. Frohnmayer pushed for stricter drug enforcement. On Frohnmayer's office wall he had once posted an ambiguous headline hastily written by a newspaper deskman over an account of one of Frohnmayer's anti-drug speeches: FROHNMAYER ON DRUGS: PEOPLE ARE FED UP. Peyote might be "harmless," as its adherents argued; but, like marijuana, something about a religious group that took hallucinogens bothered him.

But Frohnmayer's obstinacy in *Smith* was not just reflexive rigidity or even anti-drug orthodoxy. Though the amount of money at stake was small, the case raised issues under Oregon's constitution that had the potential to disrupt state government in a number of ways if the decision came out the wrong way. One reason was the peculiarity of Oregon's state constitution. Frohnmayer worried that a slip in his handling of this small case could open the door to a flood of religious claims by devotees of drugs he saw as far more harmful than peyote.

Though lawyers sometimes speak of "constitutional law" as if it concerned only the workings of the federal constitution, every state in the Union also has a state constitution that can affect the outcome of cases—particularly cases involving civil liberties—that come before the state's courts. During the Warren Court years, federal courts were eager to recognize new federal constitutional rights, and state courts in general were in disfavor, tainted by the insistence of Southern jurists that "states' rights" should protect such local customs as segregation and lynching.

But during the 1970s a reaction set in. Judicial appointments by Richard Nixon brought judges to the bench who did not eagerly embrace new federal constitutional rights. In 1986 Associate Justice William Brennan, the intellectual spark plug of

Warren-era liberalism, publicly warned lawyers that the golden age of federal civil-liberties litigation was over. In the new climate, he suggested, activist lawyers should look first to their state constitutions. That was because the increasingly conservative federal courts had no jurisdiction to contradict state court rulings interpreting state constitutions. In lawyers' language, these did not present a "federal question," and so federal courts could not intervene. Federal constitutional law, and federal law in general, took precedence over state law, of course; in the language of the Constitution, the Constitution and laws passed by its authority were "the supreme law of the land" and overruled any state law, constitutional or statutory. Thus, for example, when the Supreme Court ruled that criminal suspects had the right to see a lawyer before answering questions—the famous *Miranda* rule—it didn't matter that the state of Arizona, where Miranda had been arrested, didn't recognize such a right in its own constitution. A state constitution couldn't contradict the U.S. Constitution.

But there was a paradox: a state constitution couldn't grant fewer rights than the federal constitution, but it could grant *more*. If a state chose to recognize a broader right to counsel for criminal suspects than the federal courts did, then defendants in state courts could win new trials when that right was violated, even though the police might have acted perfectly properly under federal constitutional law. Brennan pointed out that lawyers in state court systems could easily add a claim under the state constitution to lawsuits filed on behalf of criminal defendants, civil-rights plaintiffs, and others. If a state court decided that the federal and state constitutions protected the client, then a federal court could not overturn that holding.

Brennan's suggestion was particularly welcome in Oregon, which has an active civil-liberties bar. It also has the second-oldest state constitution in the country; Oregon's statehood constitution was written in 1857. Since then, every other state except Massachusetts had revised its constitution, some of them several times. Oregonians didn't want to replace their constitution (a measure to produce a new, more modern constitution had failed by one vote in the state legislature in 1963); they did amend it often, until it had come to resemble the kind of rural farmhouse a driver sometimes spots in western Oregon's river valleys: a nineteenth-century frame house joined to a ramshackle garage at one end, with a vinyl-sided 1950s-style addition at the other and a brand-new deck jutting over the stream. But just as the house never completely loses its Victorian character, the Oregon constitution remains, at its heart, a product of nineteenth-century frontier liberalism, a political construct that was very different from the political thought of the Enlightenment that produced the federal Constitution and the Bill of Rights. The history of Oregon's constitution provided lawyers with a rich source of arguments for independent interpretation of the document. And during the 1970s state constitutional activists found a receptive ear on Oregon's bench; in fact, Oregon led the rest of the country in what lawyers had started to call the revival of state constitutional law. The revival in Oregon was largely the creation of one judge, Justice Hans Linde of the Oregon Supreme Court.

Hans Linde was born in 1924 in Berlin. As a child, he could look down from the window of his family's apartment on the Kurfürstendam and watch Nazi brownshirts battling communists while the police stood by. In 1933 his parents fled the Nazis to Copenhagen, Denmark—then five years later they fled again, to the United States. Linde and his family came to Portland, where Hans attended public high school and then Reed College. Despite his American education, Linde never lost his German accent—and he never forgot the sight of brownshirts swaggering down the Ku-dam. Linde obtained a law degree from the Uni-

versity of California at Berkeley's Boalt Hall School of Law and
then served a year as law clerk for Supreme Court Justice William
O. Douglas, a Pacific Northwesterner who kept a ranch in
Oregon and shared Linde's passion for a genuinely free society.
At night the law clerks gathered for an endless poker game; one
of Linde's card partners was a young Stanford-educated lawyer
named William H. Rehnquist, who would become an associate
justice, and then chief justice, of the U.S. Supreme Court.

After a stint in Washington, D.C., Linde returned to Oregon
in 1959 to teach at the University of Oregon Law School in Eugene.
He kept up a high profile as a scholar and political activist.
His chosen field was state constitutional law—the proper
interpretation of state constitutions generally and Oregon's constitution
in particular. In an influential series of articles in the
1970s, Linde argued that state courts had become too passive;
because the federal courts were turning out a large and complex
body of case law about the federal constitution, too many state
judges were content to decide constitutional cases on the basis
of what the federal constitution said, making the assumption
that the state charter should simply be read as an echo of the
federal document. This was backward, Linde suggested; state
courts have a responsibility to turn to their own constitutions
first and to do independent legal and historical research to find
a state rule of decision. Only if this inquiry fails, he said, should
judges turn to federal case law. State judges are first and foremost
state officials, he argued; they should put their state responsibilities
first.

In 1977 Oregon governor Bob Straub elevated Linde to the
state supreme court. Self-assured, eloquent, and persuasive,
Linde quickly emerged as the intellectual leader of the court,
and his influence inspired a series of decisions breathing new
life into the Oregon constitution. The court held that the state
charter provides far more protection against search and seizure

than does the federal constitution; it held that, unlike the First Amendment, Oregon's guarantee of free expression means that books and movies cannot be banned even if they are obscene. And in a case known as *Salem College & Academy* v. *Employment Division*, the court found that the Oregon constitution's guarantees of religious freedom are quite different from those provided by the federal First Amendment.

Oregon's constitution and bill of rights were written in 1857 by a convention that gathered in Salem in preparation for statehood. It was a much different kind of group than the high-minded assembly in Philadelphia that framed the U.S. Constitution. Oregon's delegates, on the whole, were less educated and less idealistic than the federal framers; their chief concerns were keeping Oregon all white and all Protestant, and their political philosophy could be summed up as "majority rules." They believed in religious freedom, to be sure, but they also feared the influence of organized church bodies, which they tended to see as sinister shadow governments that sought to subvert free religion and free government. Accordingly, they phrased the state's guarantees of religious freedom somewhat differently than did the First Amendment (one difference, though far from the most important one, is that the frontiersmen who framed the Oregon charter were not strong spellers, and consistently misspelled *religious* as *religeous*). Instead of "the free exercise of religion," which is the guarantee of the First Amendment, the Oregon constitution protected the freedom "to worship Almighty God," "the free exercise and enjoyment of religeous opinions," and "the rights of conscience." Instead of a general prohibition against government "establishment of religion," the Oregon constitution says that "no money shall be drawn from the Treasury for the benefit of any religeous, or theological institution."

Even before Linde became a judge, the Oregon courts had found a different, stricter meaning in these provisions than federal courts have derived from the First Amendment. From the early days of the Republic, for example, Congress and many state legislatures have hired chaplains to lead their members in prayer before each daily session; in 1983 the U.S. Supreme Court found that this practice didn't violate the Establishment Clause of the First Amendment. In Oregon, though, paying chaplains would be a clear violation, so the legislators rely on volunteers to invoke God's blessing on their meetings.

Under federal case law, state governments were free to pay for textbooks and other class materials to be used by students in religious schools; the Supreme Court reasoned that since the aid was going to the students and not to the church that ran the school, the Establishment Clause would not be violated. The Oregon courts saw it differently; in 1962, in a case called *Dickman* v. *School District 62C*, they held that such a textbook program would be paying money for the benefit of a "religeous" institution. In some ways, the "religeon" clauses of the Oregon constitution were the strictest in the nation.

Linde's decision in *Salem College*, if anything, made them even stricter. Salem College and Academy was a small, evangelical private school. Unlike traditional parochial schools, Salem College had no affiliation with a church or with any organized religious body. It was run by its own board of trustees and had no denominational ties. Under Oregon's unemployment-compensation program, Salem College was required to pay a payroll tax to fund future unemployment claims. Other religious schools, however, were exempted from the tax under the terms of a state statute that exempted schools "operated by a church." To Salem College, this was rank discrimination; it asked the state courts to order the state to exempt it as well.

Oregon's statute had been written to follow federal law. The U.S. government pays most of the cost of state unemployment-insurance programs, but Congress has put strict conditions on how the money can be used. One requirement was that state unemployment-insurance programs exempt church-affiliated schools; Oregon's legislature adopted an identical exemption.

When the case came before the Oregon Supreme Court in 1985, Linde crafted a decision that emphasized his "first things first" approach to state constitutional law. Oregon's constitution required strict neutrality on the part of the state. Therefore, he reasoned, exempting some religious schools and taxing others "contravenes the equality among pluralistic faiths and kinds of religious organizations embodied in the Oregon Constitution's guarantees of religious freedom."

But Linde went further. The case could have been dealt with by holding that whatever Oregon's constitution said, the federal statute displaced it under the terms of the Constitution's "supremacy clause." That was the kind of servile thinking Linde despised, however. He did not question that Congress could, if it wanted, pass a law requiring Oregon to violate its constitution. But Congress hadn't done that here. All the statute did was offer Oregon federal dollars for its insurance program if the state administered the plan according to federal criteria. In theory, at least, the state was free to refuse the federal funds and run its own program with its own money. To be sure, this would be impractical—but it wouldn't be forbidden by Congress. Therefore, Linde wrote, Oregon officials were bound by their oaths as state officials to administer the program in a way that did not violate the state constitution.

Salem College didn't win, however; the snapper in Linde's opinion was his conclusion that the court did not have the power to order the state to exempt independent religious schools. Crafting exemptions to tax laws is something only a legislature can do; therefore, Linde ordered the Employment Division to stop exempting any religious school.

The decision in *Salem College* threw Oregon's unemployment

system at least briefly into chaos until the legislature could assemble and write a statute that satisfied both the Oregon constitution and the federal law. But even after the statute had been written, the decision remained in the background, seeming to embody a particularly sweeping principle: under the Oregon "religeon" clauses, the state could not make exemptions for some religions and not others; the law probably could not distinguish even between religious groups that differed in structure, behavior, and belief. All groups were equal; if one group got a special deal, then all had to get the same deal. Like an indulgent parent with a large family, the state of Oregon could easily find itself drawn into something it didn't want by making one seemingly harmless exception to its laws.

And there was another reason that Frohnmayer's Justice Department took a hard-nosed approach to this obscure unemployment claim: they smelled a trap. Oregon's civil-liberties lawyers knew about the Oregon religion clauses just as surely as did the Department of Justice. Al Smith and Galen Black were sympathetic plaintiffs: two sober and productive former alcoholics seeking equality for an ancient religious tradition. Maybe too sympathetic, Frohnmayer and his aides thought. Maybe the case was a Trojan horse, designed to open a small exception in the state's drug laws that other users of other drugs would try to force their way through.

"When the case went forward for what was a fairly small amount of money, we thought, as it later turned out in error, that this was a test case," Frohnmayer recalled later. "That in fact it was deliberately set up by the petitioner, or by Black and Smith and whomever was supporting them as a test." Frohnmayer recalled being struck by the persistence and determination on the other side and wondering why two outsiders like Al Smith and Galen Black would stick with their quest over long and expensive months. "In fact, I believed that until only a few months before the case went to the U.S. Supreme Court the second time, that it was a test case. I actually thought the ACLU was behind it."

It was an easy mistake to make. Many others, over the years, had underestimated Al Smith.

THE WISDOM OF

SOLOMON

Great cases should flow from great courtroom confrontations. The images of our legal history are of evidence and argument before judges and juries, in the light of day—John Adams defending British soldiers in the Boston Massacre trial; Clarence Darrow cross-examining William Jennings Bryan on the story of Jonah in the Scopes "monkey trial"; Kenneth Clark explaining how black children threw down their black dolls and cried for white ones; O.J. Simpson trying on the bloody glove and saying, "It doesn't fit."

But constitutional law rarely affords such electrifying tableaux. The issues are often cerebral or elusive, and the arguments are about theory rather than the stuff of daily life. *Marbury* v. *Madison*, the first great case in American constitutional history, never came to trial at all, and James Madison, the nominal defendant, took no notice of the action against him by his political enemies. Dred Scott never made it to court; neither did Homer Plessy. Their cases were decided on preliminary motions, what the lawyers call dilatory pleas.

Employment Division v. *Smith*, as the case of Al Smith and Galen Black would come to be known later, never came to open court, either. Its drama was offstage, in the lives of the participants or the hidden deliberations of the judges. The nearest the case came to trial was in two short hearings, closed to the public, held in a dusty hearing room in the back room of the Oregon Employment Division's Roseburg office.

That is where Al Smith and Galen Black amassed the evidence behind their challenge to the state's refusal to pay them unemployment compensation. By the time the case went to the U.S. Supreme Court twice, Al Smith and Galen Black, working only with such help as they could pick up from legal aid lawyers, had managed to fight a respected state attorney general's office to a standstill. That part of the story seems a bit like the biblical story of David and Goliath.

But in the beginning the story more closely resembled David against David, because ADAPT, which was responsible for the early decisions in the case, was not particularly well funded, either. A nonprofit agency, it relied on a volunteer board of directors to set policy and on a local Roseburg lawyer, Eldon Caley, to represent its interests in court. ADAPT carried an insurance policy designed to protect its directors from liability and to pay Caley's legal fees in case the agency was sued. But beyond the protection of the policy and the devotion of its patrons in the community, ADAPT had few resources with which to meet the threat of prolonged litigation.

But the agency was determined to win its point. From ADAPT's point of view, there was a principle at stake: the right of a private health agency, funded by a mixture of private and

public funds, to base its policies on what it considered valid clinical concepts. And as far as ADAPT was concerned, it didn't
really matter whether Galen Black had "relapsed" or not, or even
that peyote had been part of Al Smith's unbroken twenty-five
years of sobriety. What mattered was the impact on ADAPT's
clients, who would learn of the counselors' use of peyote and
conclude that they, too, could use alcohol or drugs on an occa-
sional basis.

Ten years later Bruce Piper, Al Smith's former supervisor and
now the chief executive officer of ADAPT, explained the agency's
perspective in a short essay he wrote to be published in a newspaper:

> Imagine, as a patient, seeing your "recovering" counselor sidle
> up to the bar and order a scotch on the rocks. Or listening to a
> lecture on how relapse can only be avoided with total abstinence
> only to find out later that the counselor likes to use a hallucin-
> ogenic drug (peyote) on weekends. Would you enroll in such a
> program? Would you encourage your son or other family member
> to enroll?

In this analysis, it wouldn't really matter whether Al Smith
and Galen Black could incorporate peyote into their programs
for staying sober. The mere fact that counselors used peyote, an
"illegal drug," would be enough to undermine and even destroy
ADAPT's entire program of treatment.

Piper's argument alone doesn't explain why ADAPT opposed
Smith and Black so ferociously in the early days of the case. If
the agency had been willing to come to some kind of compromise
in 1984, when it still had control of the case, it might have made
the entire matter go away. Instead, ADAPT dug in its heels until
the case turned into a moving train that it could not stop even
when it realized it wanted to. But compromise was not in the air

at ADAPT. John Gardin remembered discussing the case with John De Smet, then his board chairman and his professional mentor. "John's a very black-and-white guy," Gardin recalled. "He felt that the grounds for their being fired were that they screwed up, that he was not going to support their messing up. So it was on his direction that we opposed the applications." Gardin remembered asking De Smet, *Why don't we just let it go, what difference does it make?* De Smet rejected that option out of hand, he said. "It would just go against his entire temperament to let them get away with it—that's the way he viewed it."

Of course, De Smet was not the only participant with a black-and-white view. Galen Black, newly sober, pursued his case against ADAPT with the zeal of a convert—even if it wasn't clear what he had been converted to. In his mind, his dismissal had been an act of disrespect to Indian people and Indian culture, and it didn't matter that he wasn't an Indian and didn't know much about Indians. Galen had begun attending meetings of state boards dealing with Native Americans to complain about his treatment at ADAPT; he wrote to the federal Equal Employment Opportunity Commission and to the Civil Rights Division of the Oregon Bureau of Labor and Industries to complain that his dismissal constituted "racist discrimination," that he was being punished because he associated with Native Americans. Neither agency bought the argument.

Black also called the Native American program of Oregon's legal-services agency to ask it to assign him a lawyer. The lawyer who took the call was named Sande Schmidt; she recalled having to explain to Black that the program could not represent him. It was set up with federal funds earmarked to help Indian people with their legal problems. Galen Black was not an Indian, and his attendance at a peyote ceremony didn't make him eligible for Indian services.

But it wasn't just the racial issue that troubled Galen Black.

Why should it matter whether he was an Indian or not? he wondered. To Black, he had been fired for doing what he was hired
to do. One of the most important aspects of ADAPT's residential
program, he argued to anyone who would listen, was its charter,
supported by earmarked state funds—to offer counseling in a
multicultural manner so as to make it effective for people of
different backgrounds. That, Black argued, was just what he had
been doing. For Native American clients, peyote might be just
as therapeutic and helpful as Antabuse, the chemical the program
used to cause nausea when patients drank. Galen had been fired,
he argued, just for doing his job and doing it well.

To this day, Black sees that as the primary issue in the case:
a dedicated drug counselor was fired for doing his job in a creative and conscientious way. The slow transformation of the dispute into an argument about Indians, about religious freedom,
and finally about Al Smith and Dave Frohnmayer has left him
frustrated and confused.

But to lawyers who heard his story, then and now, the decision
to frame the case as one of religious discrimination was obvious.
Courts are reluctant to step in and tell employers that their way
of doing business is mistaken. Employees are expected to carry
out their work assignments in the way the employer directs—
even if the employee thinks those directions are stupid and
wrong. Whatever was written on the paper, "multicultural services" meant, for ADAPT, whatever its leadership decided it
meant, and Galen Black would have a hard time getting anyone
even to listen to the issue he thought of as central to the case.

So, on December 5, 1983, Galen Black showed up alone at
the Employment Division office in downtown Roseburg to argue
that he should receive unemployment. His opponent was John
Gardin, who also came without a lawyer. The judge—actually his
title was "referee"—was a Roseburg lawyer named Robert
Gruber, a full-time hearings officer with the state of Oregon,

whose job involved listening to challenges to state agencies' decisions.

Gruber died a few years after the hearing; locals remember him as a thoughtful, scholarly man who realized almost at once that the case in front of him had the potential to become a landmark constitutional dispute. Gruber would have needed an incisive mind to cut through the arguments presented to him that day in December; if ever two people were talking past each other, John Gardin and Galen Black were. To Gardin, the issue was treatment philosophy and the seeds of the "controlled-drinking heresy"; to Black, on this day at least, it was his freedom of religion, his freedom to pursue the "Native American way."

Gardin went first. He explained the agency's treatment philosophy: "Any use by a recovering person is misuse. . . . Within the treatment field there is a small group of people that believe in controlled drinking or controlled use for addicts and alcoholics. There had consistently been no literature or research to show that that's valid." For most people in the alcohol-treatment field, "Abstinence is the accepted lifestyle for an addict or alcoholic."

Gardin fretted that a layperson could not understand the importance of complete abstinence by a recovering alcoholic. It wasn't the amount, it wasn't the context, it wasn't even what substance it was. "It's very difficult to understand how one taste, we can see that as relapse if you're not in the substance field," he said. "We would have taken the same action had Galen consumed wine at a Catholic ceremony or any drug anywhere. It would be that same result. I'm concerned that that is a difficult concept to convey."

To Galen, the issue was much simpler. He was a member of the Native American Church. He had a First Amendment right to use peyote at a ceremony.

There were problems with this argument. The Church and local congregations often don't keep formal membership records, but it's hard to imagine that any peyote Road man—or any Native peyotist—would have called Galen a "member" of the Church because he had attended one ceremony. Black explained that all his ventures into Native spirituality were signs of his membership in this specific church:

> I started pursuing the Native American way in that the sweat-lodge was a part of our treatment here at ADAPT, and I started choosing as I was participating as part of my job, taking residents to that ceremony, the sweat, and there are not drugs or anything used at that particular ceremony. . . . I also attended, on the outside, pow-wows, a Sun Dance. I've read many books, such as *The Sacred Pipes, The Seven Arrows, Black Elk Speaks*. And I've really pursued this as a way of life, a spiritual way of life for myself.

Gardin tried to shed some doubt on this claim. In cross-examining Black, he pointed out that sweat lodges and Sun Dances had nothing to do with the Native American Church. But the question just lay there. In religious-freedom litigation, very few advocates like to try to argue that someone isn't really an adherent of the religion he claims; it smacks of the Inquisition. So Galen Black's claim to Church "membership" entered the record of the case.

Black also argued that ADAPT had no business trying to regulate religious observance, because religion was a part of the agency's philosophy of recovery. "[W]e try and help people learn a spiritual way of life, and in that spiritual way of life the actual use of a communion the body and the blood is up to an individual and their higher power. It shouldn't be mandated by any laws."

Gardin, though, honed in on the issue of laws. Peyote was an illegal drug, he said. From one of his board members, Gardin had gotten the erroneous idea that Native American Church ceremonies were illegal unless the congregation had a specific permit from the federal Drug Enforcement Administration. He kept asking Black whether Stanley Smart had shown him a permit for the ceremony he attended. Black flared back, "That's like going to the Catholic Church and saying, 'Pope, do you have the legal right to practice this here?' "

This was the first time the issue of the law entered the case; it would never go away, although there was no way ever to settle it. Whenever ADAPT and the state of Oregon were pressed, they returned to the issue of the law, that peyote was illegal in Oregon. But ADAPT at the same time insisted over and over that the issue wasn't really whether peyote was legal—Communion wine would be treated the same way, they said. In closing before Gruber, Gardin said, "The issue again is the ingestion of a drug, an illegal drug. Even if Galen believed it was legal, by a recovering person, in any amount, we consider unacceptable from a treatment perspective."

Al Smith's "trial" came six months later, on June 6, 1984. Unlike Galen Black, Al had found counsel—David Morrison, a young lawyer in the Roseburg office of Oregon Legal Services. Smith and Morrison had been busy in the weeks before his case came up, contacting experts in Native religion and alcoholism treatment. The evidence they submitted to the referee is as close as the case has to a real "record." Al Smith's affidavits discussed his own spiritual development, the history of peyote religion, and the role of peyote in the treatment of Indian alcoholism. Al's own affidavit told the court that his "spiritual needs as an Indian person" had led him to "become a member of the Church and . . . participate regularly, perhaps twice a year, in church ceremonies involving the ingestion of peyote." Stanley Smart signed a statement vouching that Al was "a sincere member of the church." Emerson Jackson, head of the Native American Church of North America, vouched for Stanley Smart; so did Omer Stewart, the

Anglo historian from Colorado University who had devoted his life to the study of peyote religion.

Al Smith had also found experts in alcohol treatment to state that peyote religion was a valid and useful part of treatment and sobriety for Native American alcoholics. Robert Bergman, the former chief of mental-health programs for the federal Indian Health Service who had first studied peyote among the Navajo, wrote a detailed defense of peyotism:

> The Native American Church, and its ceremony involving the use of peyote, is the single most effective manner of treatment for Indian alcoholism and other drug abuse. It is not the best treatment for everyone, but it is the best treatment for Indians. Thousands of Indian people have gained control of a drinking problem through the Native American Church. The use of peyote is essential to the Church and its practices, analogous to the sacramental offerings in the Roman Catholic Church.
>
> There is no positive correlation between alcoholism and the use of peyote in a Native American Church ceremony. On the contrary, there is a great deal of evidence pointing the opposite way—that the use of peyote in ceremonies of the Native American Church helps the participants to control and overcome a problem with alcohol. Whereas the abuse of alcohol leads to terrible effects upon the mental and physical health of the individual and upon surrounding friends and family, it is extremely rare for the use of peyote in a Native American Church ceremony to lead to any such negative effects. The hallucinogenic effect of the drug has generally been exhausted by the time the religious ceremony is complete.
>
> Although a general theory in alcohol and drug abuse treatment is that the use of any mind-altering drug or alcohol is likely to result in relapse, an important exception is the use of peyote by Indians in ceremonies of the Native American Church.

Not only is the use of peyote in a Native American Church ceremony helpful in maintaining sobriety; if a church member were not allowed to practice his or her religion or to use peyote in the ceremony, that denial would itself threaten the individual's sobriety.

ADAPT responded with affidavits of its own; its arguments demonstrate the ways that alcoholism treatment had become a closed system, like Freudian psychoanalysis or fundamentalist religion. These systems have the ability to repel any challenge by explaining that even the desire to question orthodoxy is a symptom proving its truth. A patient who challenges his psychoanalyst's interpretation is "resisting" because of inner conflicts; a convert who questions biblical inerrancy may be possessed by Satan; a recovering alcoholic who questions the dogma of abstinence is in relapse and denial. So John De Smet took the definition of relapse—that it produces "psychological, behavioral, social, occupational, or health problems as a direct consequence of use"—and demonstrated that Al Smith must already be in one because ADAPT would not have fired him otherwise: "If an individual uses such drugs knowing full well that the ingestion of such a drug is against the personnel policy of the organization to which he or she belongs, then such use must be interpreted as having severe occupational and vocational consequences. This use despite severe occupational consequences constitutes relapse."

The transcript of Smith's referee hearing hasn't survived, so the affidavits are all we have. But David Morrison, Al Smith's young legal aid lawyer, remembers the scene in the dusty hearing room vividly. "There were very powerful emotions at play in that hearing," he said. "What I remember about [Gardin] was that he was so rigid and so unbending and so completely set about this question of sobriety, this no-substance use, being a precondition of employment. I don't think it was a real-world position."

Gruber's written decisions in the appeals represent a milestone in the case. In Black's case, Gruber wrote that "[w]hile the referee agrees that the claimant's use of peyote was cause for great concern by the employer, that action was nonetheless an isolated instance of poor judgment. Such incidents do not constitute misconduct under [Oregon administrative rules]."

The opinion seemed to split the difference neatly. Black got his benefits; ADAPT got a ruling that participation by any of its staff in peyote ceremonies would constitute misuse. Gruber's opinion in Al Smith's case was similarly Solomonic. Gruber concluded that Smith's discharge was caused by "misconduct in connection with his employment" but that he should receive benefits. "In view of the employer's clearly stated philosophy of total abstinence from alcohol and drug use as the only road to recovery from substance dependence and in view of claimant's position as a role model for clients enrolled in the employer's program, the total abstinence standard was reasonable. Claimant['s] ingestion of peyote was, therefore, a willful violation of reasonable standards of behavior which the employer had a right to expect," Gruber wrote.

But Smith had been dischargeᵤ for obeying the dictates of his religion, he continued; the state had no "compelling interest" that would allow it to deny him unemployment compensation. "In this case, as in *Sherbert* and *Thomas*, the State's interest is limited to protecting the undue depletion of the unemployment insurance fund by payment of benefits to those who would otherwise be disqualified." The evidence in the hearing had not suggested that false claims of peyotism were a widespread problem; therefore, "it cannot be held that the alleged State interests warrant interference with the claimant's freedom of religion. Thus, while claimant's activities constitute 'misconduct' . . . the First Amendment of the U.S. Constitution prevents disqualifying claimant from benefits in this case."

The *Smith* case would last four more years, consuming thousands of hours of briefing and argument, and dozens of hearings before exalted and mighty judges. But none of them coming after would approach the practical wisdom of Robert Gruber. All the parties got some of what they wanted: Galen Black and Al Smith could collect their unemployment and get on with their lives; ADAPT could require its new employees to refrain from peyote use, even in worship. The case could have rested there, an obscure footnote in the administrative annals of a small Western state.

But ADAPT would not let the matter rest. Gardin and De Smet hungered for full vindication. To begin with, the theology of alcoholism treatment seemed to demand it. Abstinence was not simply one valid way to treat recovering clients; it was the only way, and it was offensive for heretics like Black and Smith to profit from apostasy. But there were practical reasons to be obdurate as well. Black and Smith showed no sign of moving on with their lives; they were suing the agency for firing them.

Galen Black had been unable to get anyone to represent him as a victim of discrimination. But Eric Roost, a lawyer in Eugene, agreed to take him on as a client in a wrongful-discharge action. This kind of lawsuit does not argue that the employer discriminated but that the employee's contractual rights were violated. Black's argument was that because the written policy did not clearly spell out the definition of "misuse," the agency had not had proper grounds to fire him.

Black's lawsuit was a long shot; it was hard to imagine convincing an Oregon jury that an alcoholism-treatment agency lacked authority to fire a recovering alcoholic for using illegal drugs, ceremony or no ceremony. But ADAPT was facing a dou-

ble whammy: Al Smith's case had been accepted by the federal
Equal Employment Opportunity Commission (EEOC), which
filed suit accusing the agency of racism in its treatment of its
only Native employee. This meant that Smith would be represented by government lawyers, backed by the power and the bud-
get of the federal government—a power that can humble mighty
multinational corporations, let alone small local nonprofits.

Nevertheless, De Smet and Gardin were determined to fight
on. Accepting the referee's decision in the unemployment case
might have implied an admission of fault, even though partial.
So, by the middle of 1984, ADAPT appealed Gruber's rulings to
the Oregon Employment Appeals Board, the administrative body
that reviews all decisions by hearings officers. The board found
against Black and Smith. In Galen Black's case, it reasoned that
Black had ingested peyote even though "the use of an illegal drug
was optional during the religious ceremony" and "he was advised
by others that such a choice would perhaps be incorrect or im-
proper." Because of "the seriousness of the claimant's conduct in
violating the employer's rules," Black's actions could not be considered an "isolated act of poor judgment," as Gruber had found.
He had committed "misconduct" and could not receive benefits.

In Al Smith's case, the board reasoned that "the use of mescaline is illegal in Oregon." The religious context was simply irrelevant: "The claimant's ingestiun of peyote was illegal, was
contrary to the employer's legitimate interest and reasonable
rules and disqualifies the claimant from benefits."

Even though the appeals decisions seem like victories for
ADAPT, they also mark the moment at which the agency lost
control of the litigation for good. If ADAPT had accepted
Gruber's decisions, Smith and Black could not have appealed.
Even though Gruber did not affirm their freedom of religion in
ringing terms, they had won. But now, with the board's order
denying them benefits, they were "aggrieved parties" and had the

right to appeal directly to the Oregon Court of Appeals. Proceedings in this court were public, and ADAPT was no longer the only party opposing them. The names of the cases changed—they were now *Black v. Employment Division* and *Smith v. Employment Division*. Because the appeal was a challenge to the decision of a state agency, the attorney general's office now entered the case, representing the Employment Appeals Board. The AG's office was not primarily concerned with the effect of the case on ADAPT or its philosophy of treatment; its concerns were the state's unemployment system, its constitution, and its drug laws.

At first, the state's interests and ADAPT's seemed similar—to fight tooth and nail. But before the case could reach the Oregon Supreme Court, ADAPT suddenly switched. In August 1985 John Gardin left ADAPT to begin private practice as a psychologist in Southern California. The agency entered a period of financial uncertainty. And it got word from its insurance company that the insurer would no longer pay for legal fees or damages if ADAPT didn't settle the case as soon as possible.

The insurance company's decision cut ADAPT off at the knees. Insurance was paying Eldon Caley's fees; though the lawyer was willing to donate his time to offer routine legal advice, he couldn't afford to represent the agency in four cases—two unemployment appeals, a state wrongful-discharge action, and a federal discrimination suit—without recouping his expenses. Beyond that, if ADAPT carried the cases forward and lost, it—not the insurer—would now be liable for the damages, which might be prohibitively high. Very suddenly, just as the cases were headed for the Oregon Supreme Court, ADAPT's board clenched its teeth and authorized Caley to negotiate a settlement with Black's lawyer and Smith's representatives from the EEOC.

On March 5, 1986, the EEOC lawyers and Caley signed a consent decree under which ADAPT promised never again to fire or discipline an employee for "non-drug sacramental use of peyote during a bona fide ceremony of the Native American Church." In return, the agency agreed that ADAPT could require any future peyotist employees not to discuss the details of their worship with clients. In addition, Al Smith accepted $15,552 in back pay and released his claims against ADAPT. A few weeks later Caley and Eric Roost signed a similar settlement granting Black back pay for the period since his discharge. By overplaying its hand, ADAPT had lost what it had won in front of the referee.

But the settlement marked a change in the case for Al Smith and Galen Black as well. Now that the wrongful-discharge and federal discrimination suits were settled, the issue was no longer their personal rights, but religious freedom. They now had to rely solely on their legal aid attorneys, because the EEOC and Black's lawyer had no more reason to be involved. And the adversary was no longer a small-town drug agency with volunteer counsel and limited resources. Now they were facing Dave Frohnmayer and the brainpower and resources of the attorney general's office, which was determined to fight to the end.

Goliath had entered the field.

8

FIVE SMOOTH
STONES

Ordinary Americans sometimes think of the U.S. Supreme
Court as a guardian of their rights, a marble palace of justice
where even the humblest suitor can hope for a sympathetic ear.
The reality is colder. The justices have made clear over the years
that, except in unusual cases, the wrongs suffered by any individual hold no interest for them. No ordinary citizen has a "right"
to have the Court consider his or her case. The Court's jurisdiction is discretionary, meaning that almost every case it hears is
there because the Court chose to review it. Losers in lower courts
who want the Court's attention must file what is called a petition
for a writ of certiorari—a cert. petition, in lawyers' slang. Most
such petitions go nowhere, regardless of any unfairness committed to the losing party; each year the justices leave in place
thousands of lower-court decisions that are almost certainly

wrong and unquestionably unfair. The justices—and their clerks, the smooth-faced, elite-law-school meritocrats who set much of the Court's agenda—are more concerned with cases that present an opportunity to make law: to resolve a disagreement among the lower federal courts; to interpret a new federal statute; to reexamine an old constitutional doctrine; to deal with what lawyers call cases of first impression, new areas of doctrine and theory.

Many private parties do not weigh the odds against them; if they have the money (even to petition the Court for cert. can be costly, involving printing dozens of specially colored petitions and preparation of a documentary record of the case) and the inclination (an unsatisfied plaintiff, a defendant facing financial ruin, imprisonment, or death), they enter the Court's lottery in hope that they will beat the odds. Government lawyers, on the other hand, must deal with the Court on a regular basis. Each day, the federal Department of Justice and the attorneys general of the states are named as defendants in cert. petitions filed by death-row inmates, prisoners challenging prison regulations, corporations attacking regulatory schemes, and angry crackpots convinced that the Internal Revenue Service is unconstitutional. Government lawyers often hesitate to seek cert. themselves when they have lost a case below. They sometimes prefer to suffer an individual loss or leave a questionable precedent in place rather than annoy the Court by asking it either to reexamine a settled area of law or to involve itself in a dispute the justices might consider unworthy of their notice.

Beyond the credibility concerns, there is always the possibility of miscalculating. For a lawyer, no failure is more public than a loss in front of the Supreme Court.

In late 1986 Dave Frohnmayer faced a decision. In June the Oregon Supreme Court had decided against the Employment Division. In its opinion on Al Smith's claim, the court began by holding that the religious-freedom clauses of the Oregon constitution offered Smith no protection. *Salem College* said that state laws must simply be neutral, neither favoring nor disfavoring religious claims. This statute was neutral—the state had not denied benefits because Smith engaged in *religious* conduct but because he did something against ADAPT's rules. If the rules infringed his freedom to worship, the court wrote, "that interference was committed by his employer, not by the unemployment statutes."

But the Oregon court then held that the denial of benefits violated Smith's rights under the federal Free Exercise Clause. Under *Sherbert*, the burden on free exercise had to be necessary to achieve a "compelling state interest." The fact that peyote was illegal in Oregon was irrelevant: "The state's interest in denying unemployment benefits to a claimant discharged for religiously motivated misconduct must be found in the unemployment compensation statutes, not in the criminal statutes proscribing the use of peyote." As the court read *Sherbert*, the only "state interest" it could consider was the state's desire to save money by denying religious claims to unemployment compensation. But that interest wasn't good enough: "the state has not shown that the financial stability of the fund will be imperiled" if it recognized religious claims. "Therefore, under the federal test, Smith is entitled to receive unemployment benefits."

The opinion in *Black* was shorter but relied on the same reasoning: denial of benefits "did not violate [the Oregon religious clauses] but did violate the free exercise clause of the First Amendment to the United States Constitution."

As Frohnmayer saw it, the opinions in both cases seemed to beg for Supreme Court review. The Oregon Supreme Court was the guardian of the Oregon constitution. But in this case, it had turned down the chance to find for Smith and Black as a matter of state constitutional law. If the court had done that, the Supreme Court would have been irrelevant. The federal high court will not hear cases decided on state-law grounds—even if the state law is only one of several reasons for the result. Supreme Court lawyers call this the doctrine of adequate and independent grounds, meaning that state-law grounds, being beyond the Court's jurisdiction, insulate the decision from federal review.

But the Oregon court didn't do that; instead, it seemed to be saying that Oregon law did not protect religious use of peyote at all. Only federal First Amendment law—the doctrine of *Sherbert* v. *Verner*—required payment of benefits to Al Smith and Galen Black.

Frohnmayer faced a difficult choice. He could appeal the case to the Supreme Court, possibly provoking the Court by asking it to overturn an established precedent, or he could accept the Oregon court's ruling. If that meant only that Smith and Black would get their money, then the attorney general's office would not have had a problem living with the result. But it might mean more than that, because the "neutrality" rule of the Oregon constitution might be interpreted to require the state to accept other religious claims as well. At a minimum, it would spark challenges from employees dismissed for using other drugs; at a maximum, it might form a wedge with which proponents of drug liberalization could try to split open state law to allow broad exemptions for religious use of marijuana and hallucinogens.

And Frohnmayer was still convinced that someone must be behind this challenge—that it was a test case being brought by civil libertarians or drug reformers. That's what convinced him to seek cert., he recalled: "a sense of what the state's interest was. It really was a concern about the spillover effects into other controlled substances and other religions."

In December 1986 the attorney general's office filed a petition for certiorari with the clerk of the Supreme Court. According to the state's petition, the question posed by the case was, "Does the Free Exercise Clause compel a state to award unemployment benefits to a drug rehabilitation counselor who agrees to refrain from using illegal drugs as a condition of his employment and is fired for misconduct after illegally ingesting peyote as part of a religious ceremony?" The petition made a potentially radical suggestion: that the Court discard *Sherbert* v. *Verner* and adopt something much closer to the Oregon rule of "neutrality": "It may be that the 'compelling state interest' test . . . is not a correct analysis, and that *Sherbert* and *Thomas* were a false step."

But Frohnmayer quickly learned that the real "false step" was his suggestion of scrapping *Sherbert*. On February 25, 1987, the Court released a decision called *Hobbie* v. *Unemployment Appeals Commission*, in which it explicitly reaffirmed *Sherbert* and extended it. *Hobbie* dealt with an unemployment claimant who was not a member of any church. He had begun reading the Bible, however, and had decided on his own that it forbade Saturday work. The Court held that his lack of membership in a historic Sabbatarian church was irrelevant; all that mattered was his sincere religious belief.

The next month the Court granted cert. in the two Oregon cases; it consolidated them into one case, *Employment Division, Oregon Department of Human Resources* v. *Smith and Black*. A few days after the Court's order, Dave Frohnmayer convened a daylong session in Portland to consider what arguments the state might make. The guest of honor was Dean Jesse Choper of Berkeley's Boalt Hall School of Law, Frohnmayer's old constitutional-law professor and a leading authority on church-state issues.

Sitting before the assembled lawyers, Choper told them flatly to forget any thought of challenging *Sherbert*. The Court was wedded to it; Choper himself counted at least five explicit votes to affirm the doctrine in almost any situation. In his handwritten notes of the meeting, Frohnmayer set down Choper's advice: "Start w[ith the] premise that [we] don't want to fight *Sherbert, Thomas*, [and] *Hobbie. Hobbie* shows 5 solid votes for continuation of basic principle. Brennan, Marshall, Blackmun, O'Connor, White—Scalia may not know approach on relig[ion] cases yet." Frohnmayer later recalled that "Choper just said there is no way that they are going to overrule *Sherbert*. And so, therefore, any theory you have about the case has to be argued in the context that either it is an exception to *Sherbert* or it is a different case than *Sherbert*." From then on, until the day the opinion was handed down in *Smith*'s second appearance in front of the Court, Frohnmayer and his subordinates worked on the assumption that *Sherbert* would be the framework under which the case would be decided.

The Portland meeting was a formidable assembly of brainpower: a distinguished constitutional analyst, a former Rhodes scholar, and half a dozen highly trained appellate lawyers. It exemplified the resources that Frohnmayer's office could bring to bear on *Smith* now that the case had firmly caught his attention. Against this legal war machine, Al Smith and Galen Black were now truly in the position of David, the shepherd boy armed with only a slingshot and five smooth stones who went forth to fight a ten-foot-tall giant.

Now, as the battle began in earnest, the two men lost their champion. David Morrison, who had guided their cases from the administrative appeals through the Oregon Supreme Court, decided to leave legal aid and go into private practice. He had represented Smith and Black well and could have taken their cases with him when he left. Morrison was tempted. He had known since he first met Al Smith that this case had the potential to go to the big leagues, and like most other idealistic legal aid attorneys, he yearned to speak for his clients at the pinnacle of the judicial system. But starting a private practice is a demanding task. Because Smith and Black were indigent, they would not have to pay the filing fees and printing costs of their appeal, but they couldn't offer Morrison anything for his time, either. And the case would take everything he had for the next year or longer. If they won before the Supreme Court, there was a chance that their lawyer could win legal fees from the Department of Justice. But such an award was uncertain; it might not come at all, and even if it did, it would not mean cash in the bank until months after the case was decided. Morrison decided it would be unfair to his clients to keep them if he could not give them his very best, and so he reluctantly bowed out as counsel.

This sort of imbalance is common in American law. In almost every litigation, one side has more money, more legal talent, and more time at its disposal than the other. This inequality is a blot on the implied promise of "equal justice under law" Americans believe in. And it does not always cut against the less powerful party, particularly in civil-liberties litigation. Anthony Lewis of *The New York Times* wrote a memorable account of *Gideon* v. *Wainwright*, the landmark case that established that an indigent person facing a possible prison sentence has a right to a lawyer before his case is heard. One of the most poignant characters in Lewis's book, *Gideon's Trumpet*, is Bruce R. Jacob, a twenty-six-year-old assistant attorney general for the state of Florida charged with opposing Clarence Gideon's claim. In the middle of the case, Jacob left the AG's office and went into private practice in the small town of Bartow, Florida. Every weekend he drove two hundred fifty miles to the law library in Tallahassee to research the state's brief. Meanwhile, the Court appointed counsel for Gideon—Abe Fortas, a top Washington appellate lawyer who later became a justice himself. Jacob did his best, but he was no match for Fortas and his firm, Fortas, Arnold & Porter. The state of Florida lost.

In this case, however, the state was Goliath. And Al Smith and Galen Black got another lawyer from the legal aid office in Roseburg, a young woman named Suanne Lovendahl. Lovendahl had been a member of the bar for less than three years. She had never argued a case in front of the Supreme Court; in fact, she had never had a case before any federal appellate court. She had argued only two appeals of any kind; both of them had been unemployment-compensation cases heard by the Oregon Court of Appeals. Young lawyers sometimes make history on their maiden voyages: Sara Weddington and Linda Coffee, two recent law-school graduates, convinced the Court in 1973 to recognize a woman's constitutional right to seek an abortion. But the Supreme Court is a conservative institution, and the justices often prefer to see advocates they know and who understand their ways. Lovendahl was badly overmatched.

She had resources available to her. Oregon Legal Services had a special office in Portland that provided advice and representation in cases involving Native American issues. Craig Dorsay, the head of that office, was a former assistant attorney general of the Navajo nation and a nationally recognized authority on federal Indian law. But Dorsay and others who remember the months of preparation leading up to oral argument got the impression that Lovendahl didn't want their help. This was her case, and she was possessive of it and suspicious of more experienced advocates who might try to take it from her.

But we remember David because he slew Goliath with his smooth stones from the river. And Lovendahl, inexperienced as she was, almost outflanked the attorney general's office and destroyed the state's case singlehandedly.

Lovendahl's analysis of the record centered on something everybody knew: federal law did not explicitly exempt peyote from its criminal prohibitions on possessing "controlled substances." Instead, the federal statute delegated the listing of controlled substances to an administrative agency, the Drug Enforcement Administration. The DEA had issued a regulation listing peyote on Schedule I—its list of the most dangerous illegal drugs—but exempting its use by members of the Native American Church. If an administrative agency could legalize peyote religion nationally, Lovendahl reasoned, why couldn't a state agency do the same thing in Oregon?

The state lists of controlled substances were maintained by the Oregon Board of Pharmacy, a panel of volunteers appointed by the governor, with a small staff to handle the administrative details of publishing its regulations. Why shouldn't Al Smith—a Native American, a peyotist of long standing, and an impressive witness—ask the board to adopt an exemption like the federal one? When Al agreed to do it, Lovendahl asked Sande Schmidt, an experienced lawyer with the Legal Services Native American program, to represent him.

Schmidt proceeded openly; her first call was to an assistant attorney general who handled the board's procedures. The assistant helpfully sent her a summary of how ordinary citizens could ask the board to change its rules and even advised her on the best way to word Al Smith's petition. Apparently the board never formally requested an opinion from the Department of Justice about the proposed rule change; possibly that was because the AG's office billed state agencies by the hour for the time it spent working on their business.

On February 25, 1987, Schmidt and Smith appeared before a board meeting in Portland to argue for the change. Stanley Smart came with them, as did several Native people who worked for the state in one capacity or another. Despite having had notice, Frohnmayer's office sent no representative.

Sande Schmidt remembers the atmosphere as surreal. The pharmacy board was used to hearing from drug companies, pharmacists, physicians, and law-enforcement personnel. No one there could remember the precedent for a parade of Indian people asking for protection for their religion. They listened in silence as Schmidt told them, truthfully, that "we're not aware of any arrest or attempts to enforce Oregon's law presently. So we have no awareness or knowledge that this is in fact a law enforcement problem in Oregon." Al Smith reminded the board that "we were the first citizens here. So I'm here before you today to ask you to go ahead and adopt this rule so we can feel, as citizens of the state, an equal right to attend a religion. That's why I'm here." Stanley Smart told them that "Al Smith had a problem with the State of Oregon. We have gained through the peyote medicine rather than lost, which was called the relapse and to me it's the other way around. We gain by going to a ceremony."

The members of the board sat in utter silence throughout this unusual presentation. "They were just stunned," Sande Schmidt recalled. Afterward, the board went into closed session and amended its controlled-substance rules to exempt "the non-drug use of peyote by members of the Native American Church."

Before the board meeting, Schmidt had warned Al Smith that getting the rule change might not affect his case. But Dave Frohnmayer's office reacted like Goliath struck by surprise by a stone between the eyes. The rule change could compromise their case; when they got before the Supreme Court, they would have to argue that the state had an interest in restricting peyotists even though the agency that regulated drugs in Oregon didn't see a danger in religious use of the drug. And there was the danger that other religions might use the Oregon constitution to try to get courts to order exemptions for them. That, by now, was no longer a hypothetical possibility.

On July 23, 1987—less than a month before the Board of Pharmacy took its action—a policeman wandered onto a farm near Grants Pass. His mission was to confirm something that had been spotted from the air. It wasn't hard—on Alan Venet's commune, twenty-eight marijuana plants were growing openly. Venet wasn't particularly defensive when the officer questioned him. He explained that he was an ordained minister, or Boo Hoo, in the Universal Industrial Church of the New World Comforter.

The Church was founded by a Californian named Allen Michaels, who in 1947 announced that he had received a revelation from space aliens who had taken him aboard their flying saucer. Michaels set out the aliens' teaching in a book called *The Everlasting Gospel*. Alan Venet, a genial sixties dropout from New Jersey, had met Michaels and received his ordination in 1977. In recent years, however, Venet had drifted away from the outerspace theology of the mother church. He and friends had founded a commune near Grants Pass inspired in large part by a passage in *The Everlasting Gospel* that commended "the herbs of the field" to humans as a source of health and spiritual enlightenment. Marijuana was an herb of the field, and it had come to occupy a central role in the life of the Grants Pass commune. There was no special ritual, and the church maintained no membership list. But where two or three were gathered together, they would worship the sacred herb.

Any second-year law student could find important distinctions between peyote religion and the Universal Industrial Church. Peyotists used only small amounts of peyote, and only during ceremonies. The sacrament was usually not available to strangers and newcomers, while in Venet's commune simple good manners impelled the worshipers to invite visitors and friends to join. But the problem was that under Oregon's constitution, those differences might be irrelevant. If an exemption was granted for peyotism, it was not out of the question to think that some court— maybe even the state supreme court—would hold that under *Salem College & Academy,* the Universal Industrials were entitled to an exemption, too. *Salem College* seemed to say that the government could not differentiate among religions based on their belief, ritual, or organization: whatever privilege was granted to one must be granted to all. And if that happened, how long before drug worshipers would form the Church of Acid, the Temple of Speed, the Cathedral of Crack?

It was, perhaps, a far-fetched worry, but not an imaginary one. Alan Venet, for one thing, was a bit dreamy but not a fraud or a troublemaker. No one who talked to him doubted that he believed in his divine herb. At his trial, in fact, the judge complimented him on his eloquence, just before finding him guilty and sentencing him to probation. But there was another part of it that was not far-fetched at all. Much of the work of any state attorney general's office involves reading and responding to meritless appeals: petitions from inmates arguing their convictions were illegal because the courtroom flag had a fringe on it; writs of mandamus seeking to force local officials to reveal their contacts with the Bavarian Illuminati; criminal appeals arguing that the tax laws are unconstitutional and can not be enforced against "Sovereign American Citizens." It is tedious, stultifying work; each paper in each proceeding must be read by a lawyer, who must draft a reply and sometimes must appear in court to argue against the challenger. Lawyer time does not come cheap, even in a state government; more frivolous appeals mean more funds used for unproductive work. The state might win every time, but at what cost? A religious exemption for any drug would give drug defendants another weapon to deploy in this unending paper war. Frohnmayer and his aides foresaw thousands of hours every year responding to phony or at least outlandish religious-freedom claims.

So when Frohnmayer realized what the pharmacy board had done, he reacted as if it were a live grenade flung into his foxhole. "It would have made us look silly," he said later, "as though state government not only couldn't speak with a single voice but didn't even know what it was composed of." At his urgent request, the

Board of Pharmacy scheduled an emergency conference call to hear from Bill Gary, Frohnmayer's deputy.

In the days before the conference, Sande Schmidt called the Justice Department repeatedly. Al Smith had not been thinking primarily of his own case, she explained. It wasn't clear that the new rule would affect his case at all. It might, in fact, just underscore that when he and Galen Black had gone to their ceremonials, Oregon law made no exception for religion. But Al wanted to make sure that no one else would ever get in trouble for ritual peyote use; he wanted something good to come out of this dispute.

Schmidt found no interest in settling the case. "They absolutely stonewalled us," she said later. "They all said, 'There's absolutely no language you can send us that is acceptable.' Whether accurately or not, I felt that the case was more important to them than at this stage getting this religious practice to be legal. And they just wouldn't look."

When the board met on October 8, the justice department took the same hard line. The new rule was "unconstitutional in Oregon," they said; it was an establishment of religion. Cowed by the vehemence of the lawyers' disagreement, the board immediately withdrew its rule. Peyote was still illegal in Oregon as the case went national.

9

APPEAL TO
CAESAR

The Court to which the case now went was in the midst of a rapid and unpredictable process of change. Since the early days of the Warren Court in the fifties, American conservatives had made "capturing" the Court a top priority. Beginning in the New Deal and gathering force in the civil rights era, the Supreme Court had been a liberalizing force in American society: upholding economic experimentation by the government, challenging the states' rights to enforce segregation, erecting a complex shield of protections between citizens and police. Conservatives despised Chief Justice Warren and his intellectual second-in-command, William Brennan; and their hatred was increased by knowing that both men—more "liberal," in many ways, than New Deal liberal justices like Felix Frankfurter and Hugo Black—had been appointed by a Republican president, Dwight Eisenhower.

In 1968 Richard Nixon promised the party and the nation that he would reclaim the Court, appointing justices who would be "strict constructionists" and would recognize that safe streets were "the first civil right of every American." Nixon appointed conservatives to the bench, but their behavior disappointed him. Beginning with Warren Burger, the gruff Minnesotan who replaced Chief Justice Warren, Nixon's nominees led what one law professor christened "the counter-revolution that wasn't." Instead of rolling back the Warren Court's broad reading of constitutional rights, the Burger Court tended to qualify them slightly—or even to find new ones, as it did in 1973, when (in an opinion by another Nixon appointee, Harry Blackmun) it held for the first time that pregnant women had a constitutional right to an abortion.

This failure was galling to many on the right; and when they swept to power in 1980, they vowed not to let it happen again. It was 1986, however, before the Reagan counterrevolution on the Court began in earnest. In May of that year, Chief Justice Burger announced that he was resigning in order to spend his full time preparing for the bicentennial celebration of the U.S. Constitution. In the vacuum left by his departure, the administration moved to capture the Court decisively. To replace Burger, President Reagan named Associate Justice William H. Rehnquist. Rehnquist had been a Justice Department lawyer when Richard Nixon plucked him out of obscurity and named him to the Court. Nixon himself knew little about Rehnquist when he named him—the transcripts of the Nixon tapes show the President speaking dismissively of "Renchberg" as one of "that group of clowns we had around here." But Rehnquist had been the one reliably conservative vote to come out of the Nixon years. For a decade and a half, he had been a lonely figure on the Court's right fringe, dissenting from almost every opinion that expanded constitutional guarantees, protected the rights of criminal sus-

pects, or upheld programs like affirmative action and school desegregation.

Rehnquist is a genial Westerner whose gentle, almost shy
manner contrasts sharply with the ferocity of his views. In May
1986 he finally got his chance to lead the Court and shape a
conservative majority for a generation to come. But Court watchers agreed that he would need some help. Bill Rehnquist's core
beliefs were so strong that sometimes he had trouble explaining
why his side of a case should win. Many commentators called
his opinions "result-oriented," a cutting insult among lawyers that
suggested the new chief justice was willing to distort precedent
to make the case come out his way. If the counterrevolution was
to succeed this time, Rehnquist would need an ally with a grand
theory—a thinker and persuader who could play the role William
Brennan had played as top ideologist to Chief Justice Warren.
By moving Rehnquist to the top spot, Reagan opened up an associate justiceship to be filled by a conservative playmaker.

Since Reagan's election, it had been assumed that the president and his legal advisers had a name in mind for this job—
Robert H. Bork, the brilliant, voluble former solicitor general who
had become the leading spokesman for hard-right judicial con-
servatism. Bork had first become famous for his role in the "Saturday Night Massacre" during the waning days of the Nixon
administration. When Special Prosecutor Archibald Cox pressed
a subpoena for secret White House tapes, Nixon had ordered
Attorney General Elliott Richardson to fire Cox. Richardson, who
had promised Cox independence, refused and resigned; so did
his deputy, William Ruckelshaus. Bork, the solicitor general, was
the number-three man in the Justice Department. He agreed to
fire Cox and become acting attorney general.

In the years since Nixon left office, Bork had become a prominent spokesman for the philosophy of "originalism," which held
that the only role of a judge in constitutional cases was to de-

termine what the framers of the Constitution intended its words to mean. Originalists scorn liberal justices like Brennan and Thurgood Marshall, who sought to give constitutional guarantees a meaning in the changed circumstances of the twentieth century. These partisans of the Constitution as a "living document" were lawless, Bork and others argued—using their life tenure to write their own policy views into law.

Reagan had placed Bork on the U.S. Court of Appeals for the D.C. Circuit—often a training ground for Supreme Court justices—in 1982. He told friends that Bork was his favorite member of the judiciary. So it came as something of a surprise when, instead of Bork, the President named another D.C. Circuit judge, Antonin Scalia, to the vacancy left by Rehnquist's elevation.

Those familiar with Scalia's career pointed out, however, that he was as well equipped to be the Court's conservative spark plug as Bork. In 1986 Scalia (friends called him by his childhood nickname, Nino) was fifty years old. He had grown up in Trenton, New Jersey, and Queens, New York, the son of a Sicilian immigrant. But Eugene Scalia was no fish peddler or carpenter; he had been a professor of Romance languages who saw to it that his only child received a rigorous Catholic education. Nino attended Xavier High School, an elite Church-run military prep school in Manhattan. At Xavier, and later at Georgetown, Scalia impressed teachers and classmates alike with his intelligence (he was number one in both his high-school and college classes), his self-assurance, and his devotion to Catholic orthodoxy. One of his classmates later told a reporter that even at the age of seventeen, Scalia was "an archconservative Catholic. He could have been a member of the Curia."

Scalia graduated high in his class at Harvard Law School, then gravitated toward law teaching. After four years at the University of Virginia, he entered the Nixon administration. In 1974, just as Nixon was leaving office, Scalia became head of the Justice

Department's Office of Legal Counsel (OLC)—the office that issues legal and constitutional advice to the president and the attorney general. Because President Gerald Ford was attempting to govern with a hostile Democratic Congress, many of the questions that came before the OLC during Scalia's tenure involved the power of the executive to act without congressional authorization—or even in the face of congressional disapproval. Like most Republican legal thinkers in the seventies, Scalia quickly became a hawk on presidential powers. Properly interpreted, these thinkers argued, the Constitution gave the president wide powers in both domestic and foreign policy, with Congress playing a distinctly secondary role.

After Ford left office, Scalia went to teach at the University of Chicago Law School, where he fit in well with the predominantly conservative, cerebral faculty. His specialty was administrative law—the arcane system of rules and precedents that govern regulatory agencies in areas like consumer protection, environmental quality, transportation, health, and safety. Scalia also wrote conservative commentary on constitutional law; he attacked affirmative-action programs and ridiculed *Roe* v. *Wade*.

His attacks on affirmative action, in particular, revealed a bitter and resentful side of Scalia's character that surprised observers who had seen only the smoothness of his ascent in the firmament of American law. Friends reported that despite his middle-class origins and elite private education, Scalia saw himself as an outsider and a self-made man who had pulled himself up by his own efforts. He was privately scornful of anyone who needed help from society. Sometimes the scorn spilled over in public.

One of his best-known law-review articles was an attack on affirmative action and the white judges who supported it. As his central metaphor, Scalia appropriated the old joke in which the Lone Ranger and Tonto find themselves surrounded by hostile Indians.

"Looks like we're in trouble, Tonto," the masked man says. Replies his Indian sidekick, "What do you mean 'we,' white man?"

Scalia saw himself and other white children of immigrants as Tonto. He felt no responsibility for the disadvantages suffered by black Americans. "My father not only never lived off the sweat of a black man's brow, he never saw a black man until he was twenty-one years old," Scalia wrote. It was Southern liberal whites who owed their privilege and eminence to slavery and racism, he said; he singled out Justice Lewis Powell, an aristocratic Virginian, and Judge John Minor Wisdom, a Louisiana jurist who broke new ground in desegregation rulings during the early 1960s. But these liberal whites were now proposing to give black Americans jobs and educational opportunities that Scalia felt belonged, on grounds of pure merit, to white ethnics like himself.

It was a bold and eloquent statement of the case for white backlash against affirmative action, and almost certainly played a role in moving Scalia into line for a judicial appointment under Reagan. It was in vain that critics argued that Scalia's discussion asked the wrong question. Affirmative action, they said, was not about ancestral guilt but about present racism. These critics would not have asked whether Scalia's father had benefited from racism—they would have suggested that Scalia himself had been accorded educational and social privilege based at least in part on the color of his skin. Critics—particularly those interested in Native American rights—might have pointed out another irony. Scalia's manifesto disclaiming responsibility for America's racial divide began with a joke about one of our culture's most enduring racial stereotypes, the comic Indian sidekick. Apparently unaware of or simply indifferent to the fact that his language might give offense to Native people who read it, Scalia had liberally larded his discussion of racism with stage-Indian dialect, complete with broken syntax and pidgin phrases like "ugh" and "ride-um west."

In 1982 Reagan named Scalia, too, to the D.C. Circuit Court. There, some observers felt, he simply leapfrogged ahead of Bork by a display of energy and self-assurance. Scalia's opinions were sweeping and quotable. He took a narrow view of the role of courts; they had no legitimacy to decide important social questions or to reflect changing social conditions. Their major role was to decide disputes between individual parties and to decide them, moreover, on narrow grounds drawn from within the law itself. For courts to do otherwise—to extend constitutional guarantees in light of perceived new threats to liberty—would make courts a legislative, not a legal, arm of the government. At the time of Scalia's elevation, one scholar summed up his judicial opinions as follows:

> Though frequently set forth in "conservative" terms, Justice Scalia's jurisprudence in administrative and first amendment law calls for substantial change in existing legal doctrines. The impetus for this change stems from his tendency to view the substantive issues in a given case through the prism of the institutional constraints on courts within the scheme of representative government.
>
> For Justice Scalia, the Constitution does not give a mandate to the judiciary to ensure perfect government. That responsibility rests with the formal mechanisms of the representative process. As his tenure on the Supreme Court begins, Justice Scalia stands as a lawyer skeptical of the transformative power of law, a jurist uneasy with judicial authority.

Despite his hard-edged views, Scalia breezed to confirmation in 1986 by a Senate vote of 98 to 0. In part, this was because Senate liberals like Edward Kennedy and Howard Metzenbaum were concentrating their fire on Rehnquist. But it was also due in no small part to the fact that Scalia was the first Italian American ever named to the highest court; in his community, even liberals rallied to his cause. New York governor Mario Cuomo, for example, warned members of Congress that they would face his wrath if they voted against Scalia. ("I don't think it hurt Mario Cuomo," Scalia later remarked dryly.)

Once on the Court, Scalia quickly showed that his distrust of courts generally did not translate into diffidence about his own abilities. Having been first in his class in school seems to have convinced him that he would inevitably be number one on the bench. Rarely has a new justice made such an assertive debut: at his very first oral argument, Scalia peppered the lawyers with so many combative questions that Justice Lewis Powell finally leaned over to Justice Thurgood Marshall and declaimed in a stage whisper, "Do you think he knows that the rest of us are here?"

Powell, a reserved, aristocratic Virginian, had an almost visceral negative reaction to the voluble, aggressive Scalia. But his was a minority view in the late 1980s. Scalia is a small, trim, solidly built man with dark hair and round features that give him the look of a younger version of the Italian American actor Paul Sorvino. He and his wife, Maureen, have nine children—five boys and four daughters. He was known in legal circles, left and right, for his charm and drive. Whether it was competing fiercely on the tennis court or relaxing over cocktails, Scalia seemed comfortable trading views with lawyers and judges from across the spectrum. Many observers expected him to cement and extend the Court's emerging conservative majority by convincing waverers with the force of his arguments and the power of his personality. In 1987 the *American Lawyer*, an influential trade magazine, proclaimed that the Supreme Court was "Scalia's Court." Scalia's "vibrancy," the author said, had created an atmosphere on the Court that was "much more amiable than it has been in recent years." All signs indicated that "Scalia could have a far more fundamental impact on the next 20 years of constitutional interpretation than any other justice."

By 1988, then, when the *Smith* case first reached the Supreme Court, there was every reason to expect Scalia's influence to grow. Political observers believed that the Republican Party had established an unbreakable hold on the White House. The Democrats were divided and disheartened. They could slow the march rightward (one casualty of this rear-guard action was Robert Bork himself, who was nominated for the Court only after the Republicans had lost the Senate in November 1986; had he been nominated when Scalia was, he would surely have been confirmed); but they could not change the general direction. Scalia had every reason to consider himself the leader of a growing army of reliably conservative judges who would set constitutional policy for a generation to come.

No one knew what the accession of the right on the Court might mean for First Amendment protection of religious freedom, though—or whether it meant any change at all. In general, conservatives tend to be friendly toward religious belief and to admire small religious groups that cling to their faith against the secular tide of contemporary society. Chief Justice Burger had written one of the most famous examples: in a case called *Wisconsin* v. *Yoder*, the Court voided the convictions of an Old Order Amish couple who refused to send their children to public school beyond the eighth grade. Amish parents believed that the secular curriculum and social atmosphere of public high school would turn their children into competitive individualists, unfit—or unwilling—to carry on the Amish traditions of cooperation and separation from the world. The state had argued that the law was valid because free public education was an important governmental priority, or "state interest," and because the law was neutral—it treated the Amish no differently from any other family.

Burger cited *Sherbert* v. *Verner* as holding that such a "neutral" law "may offend the constitutional requirements for governmental neutrality if it unduly burdens the free exercise of religion." Then Burger, who had a strong sentimental reverence for images of a simpler time, appended a kind of love letter to the Amish, with their biblical values, their horse-drawn carts, and their farming ways:

> When Thomas Jefferson emphasized the need for education as a bulwark of a free people against tyranny, there is nothing to indicate he had in mind compulsory education through any fixed age beyond a basic education. Indeed, the Amish communities singularly parallel and reflect many of the virtues of Jefferson's ideal of the "sturdy yeoman" who would form the basis of what he considered as the ideal of a democratic society. Even their idiosyncratic separateness exemplifies the diversity we profess to admire and encourage.

The *Yoder* opinion seemed at first to offer a good way for Al Smith and Galen Black to appeal to conservative judges; peyotists, like the Amish, are a small subculture that keeps itself separate and emphasizes similar values. But many conservatives had long felt a nagging embarrassment about *Yoder*. They did not quarrel with the result: parents, they would have argued, had a right to direct the education of their children within very broad limits. But the way Burger reached this conclusion suggested that the Free Exercise Clause existed to protect "traditional" American minorities, the kinds of "sturdy yeomen" that middle-aged white judges could be expected to admire. This embarrassment was heightened by Burger's language, in which he warned that the Amish case should not be viewed as precedent by unworthy minorities, such as "a group claiming to have recently discovered some 'progressive' or more enlightened process for rearing children for modern life."

And there was the larger embarrassment conservatives had come to feel about courts as instruments to "find" rights not mentioned explicitly in the Constitution. Liberals argued that "unenumerated rights" were specifically envisioned in the Ninth Amendment, which warned that "[t]he enumeration in the Constitution, of certain rights, shall not be construed to deny or disparage others retained by the people." In addition, they said, some rights—such as the right to direct children's education—were implied by other "enumerated" rights, such as free exercise. But to conservatives, the spectacle of unelected judges "creating" rights not mentioned in the Constitution was judicial legislation. Since 1973 they had fashioned an angry and powerful critique of one such right in particular—the right to privacy, which the Court had used in *Roe* v. *Wade* to proclaim a woman's right to choose abortion over childbirth.

No one knew how Scalia would come down between these competing values. He was a rigid conservative who had argued before and after his appointment that courts should defer to legislative majorities in the name of democracy; but he was also a faithful Catholic, and thus a member of a religious group that had known its share of persecution in American history, including an attempt during the 1920s by the state of Oregon itself to close the Church's schools. Court watchers thought this case would give some hint of how he would resolve this tension. But more likely not; *Employment Division* v. *Smith* was just another unemployment case, almost exactly like *Sherbert* and the others. There was no reason to expect fireworks.

In fact, Dave Frohnmayer had decided early in 1987 that he himself would not argue the case. It was a tough decision: there was nothing Frohnmayer enjoyed more than a chance to argue before the Supreme Court. He was a star at oral argument, and a constitutional case was a welcome refuge from the daily details of politics and routine legal work. But Frohnmayer was not one to hog the limelight at the expense of his staff. His deputy, William Gary, was a talented appellate lawyer who had become a close friend of the whole family. Gary had never argued before the Supreme Court. One night in 1986, the two men found themselves drinking in the Red Dog Saloon in Juneau, Alaska. Nicholas Spaeth, the attorney general of North Dakota, began teasing Frohnmayer, asking him when he would finally let Bill Gary argue before the Supreme Court. Frohnmayer idly replied that he would let his deputy take the next case. Gary, who was nothing if not ambitious, picked up a cocktail napkin, wrote down the promise, and had Frohnmayer sign it.

A few days later, the Court granted cert. in a case, *Coos Bay Care Center* v. *Department of Human Resources*, involving Oregon's rates of Medicaid and Medicare reimbursement to nursing homes and hospitals. Frohnmayer was excited about another trip to Washington. But Gary pulled out his signed napkin and demanded the case. Frohnmayer protested in true lawyer's fashion: the promise had been made under duress, it was unenforceable. But he yielded with good grace, and Bill Gary prepared for his first outing in the major leagues. Then the Court decided another case, *Wilder* v. *Virginia Hospital Association*, that settled the Medicare issue. Bill Gary's case was remanded to the U.S. Court of Appeals. "But in the meantime the *Black* and *Smith* decision had gone up," Gary recalled. "When the *Coos Bay* case went away, Dave took pity on me and said, 'Well, since you didn't get to argue *Coos Bay*, why don't you argue *Black* and *Smith*?' "

Dave Frohnmayer had other things on his mind in the months before oral argument. Amy Frohnmayer had been born in February 1987, and her birth had brought the family face-to-face with the realization that there would not be a sibling donor for any of the three daughters stricken with FA. Transplants between unrelated donors were still, in 1987, all but impossible for FA patients. The family's only hope lay in finding a related donor somewhere in the family tree. By 1987 all the close relatives had been tested; Dave and Lynn Frohnmayer began to look for relatives they had never known.

The quest was for bone-marrow donors who could match one of the girls in a specific gene form, or haplotype. In their testing of their close relations, the Frohnmayers had found that Dave's mother, MarAbel, had a genetic pattern that was tantalizingly close to that of the girls; their genetics advisers concluded that the necessary haplotype had probably come down to Dave from his mother, and to her from her Braden ancestors in Ohio and Minnesota. So they began to look for Minnesota cousins. At first, the news was promising; MarAbel's father was one of twelve children, of whom nine had survived to adulthood. There were hundreds of cousins around the Midwest. Dave called each one he could find, reaching them out of the blue and saying, in so many words, " 'I'm David Braden Frohnmayer, and you don't know me, but I'm your cousin and I'd like your blood.' I coated it with, 'I have two daughters who are affected with Fanconi anemia, and we are looking for a related donor. You might be that person; would you be willing to submit to a blood test?' And to their enormous credit, everyone said yes." The Frohnmayers paid for the blood testing; the money came from fifty thousand dollars raised for them by retired Admiral Elmo Zumwalt. Zumwalt was an early and ardent supporter of the National Bone Marrow Donor Registry; he had become involved in the program because his son, Elmo, suffered from lymphoma and had required a sibling transplant.

Like a quest in a fairy tale, the search for donors was arduous and frustrating. At every turn, they found signs of the elusive haplotype—but not a full match. By the fall of 1987, they had decided to move back a generation, to Nova Scotia, where the Bradens had lived before MarAbel's father emigrated to Minnesota. The family found a team of amateur genealogists—eighteen in all—who pointed them to communities where Braden blood might still be flowing in living veins; and in October 1987 the Frohnmayers arrived to test all willing comers.

Canadian TV and radio followed their quest breathlessly; even the *CBS Evening News with Dan Rather* did a segment—although it had to be delayed when the New York Stock Exchange crashed on the Monday the item was scheduled to run. The genealogists had traced the Bradens to a village called Middle Musquodoboit, some forty miles outside Halifax. The principal of the local high school sent flyers home with students asking their parents to dig out family Bibles and to come to a meeting if they thought there was any chance they were related to the Frohnmayers. More than a hundred fifty people showed up; they heard appeals from Katie and Kirsten for the tissue that might save their lives. Then they were tested.

There was hope and laughter and the warmth of strangers' good wishes on the trip, but there was no match. "In retrospect, that's really sad," Frohnmayer says mildly, "because the strategy was right, the search strategy, rather than looking to a pool of unknown donors for a rare tissue type. It should have been possible to find someone who matched my rare haplotype that the kids had gotten and the fairly more common ones that they shared on Lynn's side." One genealogist pointed out to Frohnmayer that two Braden cousins, inspired by the struggle against slavery, had left Nova Scotia and died fighting for the Union. "Maybe that's where that family lineage died out," he said to Dave.

The family returned to Eugene, resigned to the likelihood that they would never find a related donor. Bone-marrow transplants could be done using nonrelatives' marrow if the genetic types were similar. Transplants like that had helped some patients who had leukemia and immune disorders. But Fanconi anemia made an unrelated transplant too dangerous—an FA patient's cells are so fragile that any bad reaction to donated marrow would lead to catastrophic illness within hours. The family's real hope lay in a medical breakthrough; they turned their efforts to getting funds for FA research. "At this point," Dave said, "we had decided that, in addition to our family support group and in addition to raising money for scientists, we ought to attempt to take charge of bringing the scientists together." The girls were stable so far; perhaps a miracle could be arranged before it was too late.

Also in the fall of 1987, Suanne Lovendahl was preparing for her first appearance before the U.S. Supreme Court. It's difficult to reconstruct her strategy; she died in 1991 and had not let other lawyers into her thinking. But at some point in the fall, she apparently had a bright idea. Lovendahl's experience as a lawyer had been all but exclusively concerned with the Oregon unemployment-compensation statute. She must have reread the Oregon Supreme Court's opinions in the Black and Smith cases and suddenly seen them through the lens of unemployment law. It was a worthwhile insight to pursue—if she could convince the Court that the Oregon decision rested upon the interpretation of state law, the case would simply go away and Smith and Black's victory would stand. Lovendahl thought she had found a winning argument.

Her new contention centered on the language used by the Oregon Supreme Court in deciding that Smith and Black were entitled to benefits under the "compelling interest" test:

> [T]he legality of ingesting peyote does not affect our analysis of
> the state's interest. The state's interest in denying unemployment
> benefits to a claimant discharged for religiously motivated mis-

conduct must be found in the unemployment compensation statutes, not in the criminal statutes proscribing the use of peyote. . . .
[T]he state's interest is simply the financial interest in the payment of benefits from the unemployment insurance fund to this
claimant and other claimants similarly situated.

This was an ambiguous passage. It could have simply represented the Oregon court's interpretation of previous federal case
law. In *Sherbert* and other cases since then, the Supreme Court
had said that the state governments were not just free to make
up "state interests" to balance against claimants' free-exercise
rights, they had to point to something in their own statutes. But,
Lovendahl now apparently thought, the Oregon court *might* have
been saying something slightly but vitally different—it might
have been saying that, as the court in charge of construing
Oregon's own laws, it had concluded that Oregon's state unemployment statutes just did not assert any "state interest" except
the fear of false claims.

If the U.S. Supreme Court accepted that interpretation of the
Oregon decision, it would have to ignore any claims the attorney
general made about Oregon's drug laws—the state's own supreme court had ruled them irrelevant. Lovendahl found some
case law to support her argument—including a case in which
the Oregon courts had ordered Portland State University to pay
unemployment compensation to a professor the university had
fired for plotting to bomb the federal office building in downtown
Pioneer Square. The misconduct that led to his dismissal, the
Oregon court had concluded, was not "work-related"; therefore,
the employer had to pay.

For good measure, Lovendahl threw in an additional statutory
argument for the Court to consider if it did not buy into her
argument about the unemployment statutes. The state argued
that peyote use and possession was illegal in Oregon. The main

authority for this argument, she noted, was *State* v. *Soto*. But since *Soto* was decided, the state had changed its drug statutes. The old law had forbidden both "use" and "possession"; the new statute outlawed only possession. Lovendahl suggested that in a typical peyote ceremony, ordinary worshipers like Black and Smith did not *possess* the peyote, which was in the custody of the Road man. They only ingested, or *used*, the buttons the Road man gave them. Thus, she argued, there was no unambiguous evidence that Smith and Black had violated Oregon law at all.

These weren't frivolous arguments, but there were two problems with them. First, even if Lovendahl was right and the Oregon Supreme Court had been reading Oregon state law, the "state interest" involved was still being used in a *federal* balancing test. The Oregon Supreme Court had refused to find grounds of decision in the state constitution, so the judgment turned on the *Sherbert* test, a Supreme Court formulation that had no counterpart in Oregon law. Under Supreme Court precedent, the state grounds below might not be held to be "adequate and independent." Lovendahl's argument was certainly the kind of reason the Court liked to consider for not hearing a given case— whether it had a federal issue at its heart or not, a decision that also turned on one state's law would obviously not be a crucial national precedent.

But that was the second problem: Lovendahl had waited too long to raise the argument. The Court grants cert. to most cases on the basis of a petition by the loser below, but before the cert. decision is granted, the Court allows the winner to file a Brief in Opposition—a thirty-printed-page argument why the Court should not consider the judgment below worthy of its time and attention. Because the party opposing cert. is the winner below, it is in that party's interest to argue that the victory was not important—that the case turned on special facts unlikely to occur again or that it involved specialized questions of state law.

The Court's rules are stern in commanding litigants to raise those arguments *before* cert. is granted, or to lose them.

Two years before the *Smith* petition came before it, the Court, in a case named *Oklahoma City* v. *Tuttle*, had warned litigants that the party opposing cert. should raise this sort of argument in the Brief in Opposition: "Our decision to grant certiorari represents a commitment of scarce judicial resources with a view to deciding the merits of one or more of the questions presented in the petition. Nonjurisdictional defects of this sort should be brought to our attention *no later* than in respondent's brief in opposition to the petition for certiorari; if not, we consider it within our discretion to deem the defect waived." By raising the issue now, in a brief filed only eight days before oral argument, Lovendahl was running the risk of irritating the justices to no good effect. (In 1990, too late to help Lovendahl, the Court added this warning to its official rules; in 1987 it would have required an experienced Supreme Court litigator to warn her of the danger.)

Lovendahl and Gary traveled to Washington to argue before the Court. In its first trip to the Supreme Court, *Smith* attracted little notice from the press or Court watchers. It seemed to be a routine unemployment-compensation case, with the slightly exotic addition of Native religion. It was not the most important Indian law case the Court heard that week, much less that year. The high-profile case, heard a few days after *Smith*, was called *Lyng* v. *Northwest Indian Cemetery Protective Association*. *Lyng* was a challenge by three Indian tribes in Northern California to a plan by the Forest Service to run a logging road through lands that were, to them, the center of the world. It had attracted the notice of most of the Native American legal groups and the press. By contrast, *Smith* received virtually no mention in *The New York Times* and *The Washington Post*, the national newspapers that follow the Court most closely.

The oral argument was held on December 8, 1987. Bill Gary's presentation was straightforward: the Oregon Supreme Court had not construed state law but had simply engaged in a "wooden application" of *Sherbert*. And it had gotten *Sherbert* wrong, he said. "If the conduct is criminal, the state cannot be required to provide benefits to these claimants because the claimants had no right to engage in the conduct in the first place."

Justice John Paul Stevens commented that "it seems to me you're suggesting that really the critical issue in the case that has to be decided is whether the conduct of using peyote in a Native American religious ceremony is constitutionally protected or not." Gary replied, "Yes. It is critical to our case that there is no constitutional protection."

The case turned entirely upon federal constitutional issues, Gary said. Oregon's constitution forbade the state from granting exemptions to one religious body. "Oregon . . . as a matter of constitutional law, is foreclosed from granting that kind of an exemption for its criminal law, unless it is compelled by the [federal] Free Exercise Clause."

When Lovendahl got up to argue, she quickly ran into heavy weather because she had not included her statutory arguments in her Brief in Opposition. One justice read to her from her own brief:

> You had two points. Reason for denying the writ: (1) the federal question raised by Petitioner has been clearly settled, (2) the decision of the Oregon Supreme Court is consistent with applicable decisions of this Court. One would have expected (3) this case represents nothing but a question of state law. . . . [All] of a sudden, in your reply brief, we find that this case has just been decided under state law. Had we known that, we wouldn't have granted cert. in the case.

Under this intense questioning, Lovendahl appeared to concede that the case had not been decided on a state-law issue: "I mean that there's not a federal distinction between this case and *Sherbert, Thomas,* and *Hobbie.*"

Much of the rest of the argument circled around the interpretation of Oregon's criminal and unemployment-compensation law. One justice asked whether the respondents conceded, as the state had contended, that job-related drug use would be automatically disqualifying. Lovendahl responded that under Oregon law "[j]ob-related drug use would be protected if it was a product of an illness. In other words, not willful, which I think is the same situation when you're talking about a religious impulse, and so that's why we feel that they're in the same position in *Sherbert, Thomas,* and *Hobbie.*" Chief Justice Rehnquist broke in, "[A]re you saying that they didn't smoke the stuff or whatever you do with it voluntarily?"

Though Lovendahl attempted to turn the argument to the history and safety of religious peyote use, the state-law question continued to dog her. Was her argument that religious peyote use was *not illegal* under Oregon law, that the legality was *irrelevant* as a matter of state law, or that legality was irrelevant as a matter of *federal* free-exercise doctrine? Her reply seemed to suggest that the irrelevancy arose under the free-exercise cases. "And if we disagree with you," one justice said, "I would think we could disagree with the Oregon Supreme Court's conclusion that it is irrelevant and send it back. They may end up saying that, well, it's—so it's relevant, but in this case, there's no criminal conduct."

In rebuttal, Gary quickly asserted that the entitlement to benefits found by the Oregon Supreme Court arose solely under federal case law. Oregon's strict establishment provisions made an accommodation for one religion unconstitutional "unless it is

required by the Free Exercise Clause [of the U.S. Constitution]."
He concluded,

> This Court has never held that a state must accommodate pro-
> hibited conduct. Therefore, the criminal law issue must be ad-
> dressed as a matter of federal law in order for the claimants to
> prevail, and at a minimum, this case must be sent back to the
> Oregon Supreme Court with instruction to do so.

When oral argument ended, the case disappeared into the
bowels of the Court. Few processes in American government are
more mysterious than the deliberations of the justices. The Court
jealously guards its privacy, and observers must often guess at
what has transpired in the period between argument and the
appearance, much later, of an opinion. What is well known is
what Justice Brennan used to call "the rule of five"—it takes five
votes to "make a Court," that is, to support an opinion that will
have the force of law. The justices take an initial vote at their
weekly conference, held the Friday after they hear oral argument.
Each justice briefly discusses his or her reasoning and votes for
the result he or she favors.

Then the hard work begins. One justice is given the task of
writing the opinion. If the chief justice votes with the majority,
assigning the opinion is his prerogative. If the chief justice is in
the minority, the senior justice in the majority assigns the writing
of the opinion. The justice who receives the assignment then
draws up a draft opinion setting out reasons for the result. Copies
are sent to every justice, and a process of negotiation may begin.
Sometimes a justice who voted with the majority at conference
may object to the wording of the opinion. The writer may then
offer changes in wording or rationale in an effort to keep the
majority. If these negotiations fail, the writer may "lose the Court"

and end up writing in dissent what started out as the Court's decision.

In 1993 the Court's veil of secrecy was pierced. Associate Justice Thurgood Marshall, who had retired in 1991, died in 1992. He left his papers to the Library of Congress with instructions to open them to researchers. The Marshall Papers are a treasure trove of draft opinions and memoranda between the justices as they fine-tune their opinions. And the papers show a complex process of refinement going on in the consideration of *Smith* during 1988.

On December 11, 1988, before a majority opinion had been circulated, Justice William J. Brennan Jr. wrote to Justices Thurgood Marshall and Harry Blackmun, reflecting the vote at conference: "We three are in dissent. I'll take it on." On February 20, 1988, Justice John Paul Stevens circulated a first draft of a majority opinion in the case. The opinion resembles the final opinion issued two months later. But there are a few significant changes, which show that Justice Scalia was taking a keen interest in the precise wording of the opinion. Stevens's draft opinion contains this draft footnote:

> Efforts to exempt the religious use of marijuana from laws punishing its possession and sale have been unsuccessful. Even state and federal courts in jurisdictions that have exempted peyote use from the reach of their criminal laws have rejected claims that the First Amendment requires a similar exemption for religious use of marijuana.

At its conclusion, Stevens's draft also states that if, on remand, the Oregon Supreme Court were to hold that the ceremonial use of peyote was not illegal, that decision "would almost certainly preclude any further review by this Court."

On April 14, 1988, Scalia responded to the February 20 draft. The letter, signed "Nino," tells Stevens that Scalia "thinks" he is able to "join your thoughtful opinion" but that he has "two relatively minor problems that I hope you can remedy."

First, . . . I think footnote 15 too strongly hints to the Oregon Supreme Court that it should find [ceremonial peyote] use lawful as a matter of state law *because* of federal constitutional concerns. The footnote not only contains extensive parentheticals making the First Amendment argument, but also tells the state court why recognizing a peyote exemption may not require it to recognize similar exemptions for other drugs such as marijuana. I would hope that you could strike everything except the statutory references directly supporting the point made in text.

Second, I am unwilling to suggest that if Oregon does not make religious use of peyote illegal, the federal constitutional inquiry is at an end. . . . I think it far from clear that *Sherbert, Thomas* and *Hobbie* control where the state has an interest in prohibiting, discouraging or regulating the conduct for which the employee was dismissed even though it does not make the conduct illegal. For this reason, I have difficulty with the next to last sentence of the opinion. I would not say that if Oregon holds religious use of peyote is legal then further review in this Court is "precluded." Some of us may be unwilling to grant certiorari in such a case, but that does not justify the implication that the federal constitutional problem would no longer exist.

If you could make these changes, I would be pleased to join.

Five days later Justice Stevens wrote Scalia back, "[c]onfirming our telephone conversation." Stevens wrote that he was "happy" to make the changes in footnote fifteen Scalia had requested. He said that he "still would prefer not to change the next to last sentence" but then proposed four alternative wordings for Scalia's approval. One of the alternatives read that a holding that the ceremonial peyote use did not violate Oregon law "would make it more difficult to distinguish our holdings in *Sherbert, Thomas,* and *Hobbie.*"

The Court's opinion was announced on April 20, 1988. Justice Stevens's opinion, joined by Chief Justice Rehnquist and Justices White, O'Connor, and Scalia, remanded the case to the Oregon Supreme Court for an opinion on Oregon law:

> The state court appears to have assumed, without specifically deciding, that respondents' conduct was unlawful. That assumption did not influence the court's disposition of the cases because, as a matter of state law, the commission of an illegal act is not itself a ground for disqualifying a discharged employee from benefits. It does not necessarily follow, however, that the illegality of an employee's misconduct is irrelevant to the analysis of the federal constitutional claim. For if a State has prohibited through its criminal laws certain kinds of religiously motivated conduct without violating the First Amendment, it certainly follows that it may impose the lesser burden of denying unemployment compensation benefits to persons who engage in that conduct.

Though *Sherbert, Thomas,* and *Hobbie* appeared to control the result, the Court's decision in those earlier cases "might well have been different if the employees had been discharged for engaging in criminal conduct." Thus, the crucial issue was "the status of [peyotism] as a matter of Oregon law." Some states and the federal government did exempt religious peyote use from their drug statutes, the opinion noted; the footnote questioned by Justice Scalia here appeared in a much-scaled-down version, including no case citations and no discussion of the differences between religious peyote use and marijuana. Oregon law might contain an implicit exemption:

> [o]n the other hand, if Oregon does prohibit the religious use of peyote, and if that prohibition is consistent with the Federal Constitution, there is no federal right to engage in that conduct in Oregon. If that is the case, the State is free to withhold unemployment compensation from respondents for engaging in work-related misconduct, despite its religious motivation.

The Supreme Court, the opinion stated, would not decide the federal constitutional issue prematurely. However, the criminality issue made the Court reluctant to affirm the Oregon court's opinion without a full understanding of its basis:

> If the Oregon Supreme Court's holding rests on the unstated premise that respondents' conduct is entitled to the same measure of federal constitutional protection regardless of its criminality, that holding is erroneous. If, on the other hand, it rests on the unstated premise that the conduct is not unlawful in Oregon, the explanation of that premise would make it more difficult to distinguish our holdings in *Sherbert, Thomas,* and *Hobbie.*

Justice Brennan, as he promised, produced a dissent, joined by Justices Marshall and Blackmun. The only material difference between *Smith* and the *Sherbert* line, Brennan wrote, was the state's asserted interest in drug enforcement as well as in the fiscal integrity of its unemployment-compensation fund. Brennan's dissent reasoned that the Oregon Supreme Court had refused to use drug control as a state interest because that interest was not mentioned in the statute. It concluded that "the Court has tacitly left the Oregon Supreme Court the option to dispose of these cases by simply reiterating its initial opinion and appending, 'and we really mean it,' or words to that effect."

The case was headed back to Oregon for a discussion of Oregon drug and unemployment law. It seemed likely to end there, in a decision construing the state's constitution or statutes. Such a decision would have little national or constitutional importance. But it was still important to Al Smith.

Al had been uneasy ever since the Supreme Court ordered his case and Galen's consolidated into one. To the justices and their clerks, it must have seemed eminently logical to move the two cases—presenting almost identical issues and almost identical facts—into one package for briefing or argument. But to Al Smith, the consolidation was a kind of theft: *Smith* v. *Employment Division* was *his* case, his fight against the insensitivity of white culture; now the case had been taken away from him and put together with Black's. Black was not a Native American, nor did he have a long history of involvement with the Native American Church. Joining the two together had the effect of blurring the facts, of subtly changing a dispute among real people into the kind of hypothetical law professors use to torment students: *A and B join a religious body making sacramental use of hallucinogens.* . . . Smith perceived the consolidation as something that had been done to him; he associated it with the emergence of Frohnmayer as the state's leading advocate and his chief adversary. "The whole thing changed when he got involved and when they started bringing Galen and putting us together or setting this case up as a drug case," he recalled. "I realized that the state—Frohnmayer—was pushing us."

10

SINS OF THE
FATHERS

John Echohawk and Dave Frohnmayer were friends. Something in them was alike, though to all outside appearances, they were as different as two men could be. Echohawk is athletically built—a former high-school football and baseball star—and plainly Native. The son of a Pawnee father and a white mother, he has broad features and long gray-black hair. Where Frohnmayer is merry, Echohawk is grave; where Frohnmayer is garrulous, Echohawk is reserved, almost shy. But the two men share the bonds of high achievement, self-confidence, and curiosity. And they share the law. John Echohawk is among the most stellar of the first generation of Native people to carve out a presence in American law. Raised as a Mormon, he graduated from public school in Farmington, New Mexico, and entered the University of New Mexico in Albuquerque in 1963. In 1970 he became the first Native American to graduate from the University of New Mexico School of Law.

John's achievements are part of the story of a remarkable family, which has become known over the past quarter century as "the Kennedys of Indian country." The Echohawks have a proud heritage—the name is said to have been given to an ancestor who refused to boast of his prowess in battle, leaving others to echo his praises. John's younger brother Larry became the first Native American to be elected attorney general of an American state. In 1994 Larry Echohawk ran for governor of Idaho, the first Native to receive a major-party gubernatorial nomination anywhere in the United States. He lost in the Republican landslide that year and joined the faculty of the Brigham Young University law school in Provo, Utah. John's youngest brother, Tom, also became a lawyer, as did a cousin, Walter Echo-hawk. (John's mother, tired of being called "Mrs. Hawk," had insisted that her husband spell the name as one word.) John's sister, Lucille, is chief executive officer of the George Bird Grinnell American Indian Children's Fund.

After law school, John and a group of friends won a grant from the Ford Foundation to begin what has become his life's work—the Native American Rights Fund (NARF) in Boulder, Colorado. NARF has become a powerhouse in the world of federal Indian law. It represents tribal governments and Native organizations around the country; it has helped win tribal status for unrecognized or terminated tribes, fought to preserve reservation water rights against the pressure of white industry and development, advocated for Alaskan Native fishing rights, and even challenged the Washington Redskins' mascot. In 1988 the *National Law Journal* included Echohawk on its list of the "100 most powerful attorneys in America."

Echohawk was disturbed by reports of what his friend Frohnmayer was doing in Oregon. The two men had met during meetings sponsored by the Western Conference of Attorneys General.
Relations between most tribes and most state governments in the
West are wretched. State governments tend to view Native reservations, with their claims of sovereignty, as obstacles in the
face of "inevitable" progress. For their part, tribal governments
are often more comfortable dealing with the federal government,
with which they have a longer history and more influence, than
with states. When Frohnmayer headed the group of attorneys
general, he sought a formal dialogue with Native officials and
lawyers. John Echohawk responded to the invitation. The two
men did not always agree, but Frohnmayer was willing to listen,
and that created the basis for a professional friendship.

But now Frohnmayer was pursuing a case that had the potential to harm one of NARF's clients, the Native American
Church of North America. NACNA is one of the largest of the
dozens of NAC denominations. Headquartered on the Navajo
Reservation in Arizona, it is headed by a Navajo, Emerson Jackson. NACNA likes to claim that it is the NAC, but there are
frequent disagreements between the many offshoots of the original "mother church," the Native American Church of Oklahoma. One of the bitterest quarrels is whether non-Indian
people can join the church. Jackson and NACNA say no—
Grandfather Peyote is for Native people only. Emerson Jackson
has gone so far as to report non-Native peyotists to police and
urge their arrest. Many of the smaller NAC groups follow the
lead of the mother church, which had white members on its executive board and believed that peyote came to earth for all who
want its help.

By early 1989 NACNA had become alarmed at what was
happening in Oregon. Before it was remanded, the *Smith* case
had not seemed terribly important: an unemployment dispute

that, however it came out, would affect relatively few peyotists. Oregon is a small state; in 1989 there was no organized chapter of the NAC anywhere in the state. But then the Supreme Court had remanded the case for a state-court decision about whether peyote was legal in Oregon.

That was an issue the state court had tried to dodge. Now the U.S. Supreme Court wanted an answer. The lawyers geared up for another oral argument, which took place in Salem on September 6, 1988—four months after the Court in Washington announced its decision. Once again, Lovendahl and Bill Gary tangled over the meaning of Oregon's drug-possession statutes. This time Bill Gary told the Oregon judges that the Oregon legislature had decided that "peyote has no place in society." In October 1988, less than six weeks after hearing argument, the Oregon court produced another decision—one that, in barely civil terms, told the U.S. Supreme Court to take a flying leap.

The opinion was a skimpy, oddly truculent document. To begin with, it was issued per curiam, meaning that no individual justice took credit for writing it. This form of opinion is usually reserved for decisions that raise few interesting issues or have been made necessary by the obstinacy of the parties rather than the legal requirements of the case. In its 2,300 words, the opinion recited its holding that, under *Sherbert*, the state's interest was limited to the financial health of the unemployment-compensation fund. It then answered the Supreme Court's first question—whether the Oregon law could be applied to Smith and Black:

> [T]he Oregon statute against possession of controlled substances, which include peyote, makes no exception for the sacramental use of peyote, but . . . outright prohibition of good faith religious use of peyote by adult members of the Native American Church would violate the First Amendment. . . . We therefore

reaffirm our holding that the First Amendment entitles petition-
ers to unemployment compensation.

The Supreme Court had also asked whether peyote religion
was protected under the Oregon constitution. In a terse footnote,
the Oregon court explained why it would not give an answer:

> Because no criminal case is before us, we do not give an advisory
> opinion on the circumstances under which prosecuting members
> of the Native American Church under [the state statute] for
> sacramental use of peyote would violate the Oregon Consti-
> tution.

The opinion had an impatient tone, as if the court was asking
what *Smith* was doing in front of it again. The opinion might be
read as retorting to the U.S. Supreme Court that the First
Amendment case law was its invention, not that of the Oregon
Supreme Court; it is *your* doctrine, the opinion can be read to
say; if you want to scrap it, then *you* do it.

So far so good, from the point of view of Al Smith and Galen
Black, and from the Church's point of view as well. But then,
on January 16, 1989, the attorney general's office filed for certiorari again. In its petition, the state argued that the case now
presented the federal issue of whether "the federal constitution
protects religious use of dangerous drugs." The state argued that
the Oregon court's opinion had settled the matter of Oregon law:
the petition claimed that the lower court had "unequivocally concluded that religious peyote ingestion is criminal under Oregon
law and not protected." Now, Oregon argued, the Supreme Court
must decide whether peyote was entitled to protection under the
First Amendment. The petition now went beyond the issue of
Oregon's law; it suggested that even the federal exemption for
religious peyote use was constitutionally suspect. Citing recent

opinions by the Office of Legal Counsel of the Reagan Justice Department, the petition argued that

> the [federal] exemption for peyote was merely a product of the [Drug Enforcement Administration's] perception of congressional will; that in fact the agency lacks authority to create such exemptions; and that, in any event, congressional members were wrong: The Free Exercise Clause does not require government to exempt religious peyote or other drug use from valid and neutral criminal laws of general applicability.

In Oregon many people were surprised that the AG's office was asking the Supreme Court to get involved again. Editorials at the state's two largest newspapers, the *Oregonian* in Portland and the *Register-Guard* in Dave Frohnmayer's hometown of Eugene, ran hostile editorials. A group of professors from the University of Oregon law school had written the attorney general asking him not to seek cert. The wrong result in Washington might harm Indian religions around the country. Why couldn't Frohnmayer just let it drop?

But to Dave Frohnmayer, the issue wasn't even close. The state supreme court opinion was wrong on the merits, he believed: by favoring peyote religion, it "established" this one sect as a favored government church. And besides, it was going to open the door to a flood of religious drug-use litigation—which would begin with Allen Venet's appeal and keep going until the end of time. "If we couldn't take that case off the books," he said later, "we were in a major world of hurt."

On March 19, 1989, the Court once again granted cert. Suddenly NARF's client—and every peyote congregation nationwide—saw a dagger pointing at its very heart. If the federal exemption was not valid, and not required by the First Amendment, then the DEA, or any state government, would be free to

ban peyote and jail peyote worshipers. The obscure unemployment dispute had turned into a deadly quarrel, which would be
decided by a Court that had begun to show little sympathy for
Native people and their rights.

Only the year before, in 1988, the Court had delivered a stunning rebuke to those who thought that Native religion deserved
the same level of government solicitude as established Anglo
faith. The case, *Lyng* v. *Northwest Indian Cemetery Protective
Association*, involved a claim by three small California tribes that
the U.S. Forest Service was planning to quite literally destroy
their religion forever. The Court had agreed that the government's
plans would devastate the traditional belief systems of the Yurok,
Karok, and Tolowa tribes; but it had, in effect, said that the
government could carry out its plan—even though the reasons
would clearly not have passed the "compelling interest" test.

At stake was the pristine beauty of a mountainous region between the small logging towns of Gasquet and Orleans, California. Since time out of mind, the three tribes had viewed this
"high country" as the home of the spirits who lived on earth
before the emergence of humans and who lingered on, hidden
in rock formations, streams, and stands of virgin forest, to watch
over the earth and its people. All three bands believed that regular rituals in the high country were what kept the earth in har-
mony—not just for Indian people, they would hasten to point
out, but for everyone. In addition, Indian shamans and curing
doctors used the high country as a retreat where they could receive power from the spirit world. Old people hiked laboriously
into its high recesses to pray for renewal of their health. Young
people went there to acquire power and see visions. For these
three bands, the high country was the Wailing Wall, the Basilica
of Guadelupe, and Mecca rolled into one.

The Indians had signed a treaty in 1851 giving them a reservation that included the high country. But the U.S. Senate,

under pressure from white settlers, refused to ratify the deal. Years of massacres and raids had forced the Indians into a smaller reservation. Eventually, the federal government took the sacred heights as part of the Six Rivers National Forest. Though they did not own the land, Indian people continued to visit the inaccessible forests and peaks and to focus their tribal life around it.

In the early 1970s, though, the Forest Service began to take an interest in the economic potential of the high country. The area held nearly a billion board feet of virgin Douglas fir— valuable old growth that would enrich private loggers and help fund Forest Service operations. Logging would require a road between Gasquet and Orleans, which would help economic development in the two isolated mountain towns.

So the service came forward with a proposal for what they called "the G-O road." There were routes that would have completely avoided the Indians' sacred grounds, but they would have cost somewhat more—and besides, much of the timber the government wanted to sell lay within view of the Indians' holy places. The Forest Service hired a consultant to determine whether a road through the high country would really burden the Indians' religion; this expert, picked by the government, concluded that the G-O road would "cause serious and irreparable damage to the sacred areas which are an integral and necessary part of the belief systems and lifeway of Northwest California Indian peoples." The road should not be built, he wrote.

The Forest Service thanked its consultant, paid his bill, and prepared to build the road anyway. The Indian tribes, joined by the state of California, went to federal court. Lower-court judges granted an injunction under the Free Exercise Clause. The service's reasons, they held, did not satisfy the "compelling interest" test.

But when the issue reached the Court, the justices brushed aside the Native people's concerns. In an opinion by Justice

Sandra Day O'Connor, the majority agreed that "the logging and road-building projects at issue in this case could have devastating effects on traditional Indian religious practices." But the land was government land, the Court said, and Indians had no right to tell the federal government what to do with "what is, after all, its own land." In fact, O'Connor wrote, the "compelling interest" test did not apply at all in this kind of case, which concerned only "incidental effects of government programs, which may make it more difficult to practice certain religions."

NARF had been heavily involved in *Lyng*, which had been the highest-profile Indian case in the Court's 1988 term; in fact, *Lyng* had been argued just a few days before the Court heard arguments the first time in *Smith*. The *Lyng* decision brought howls of protest from Native Americans and those allied with them. They bitterly pointed out that the land "belonged" to the government only because the Indians had been kicked off it by trickery and force. They further asked whether the Court would have been so cavalier if the project had been a highway through Temple Square in Salt Lake City, sacred to the Mormons, or a Spanish mission on the West Coast or the colonial-era Anglican church at Bruton Parish in Virginia. This place was as holy to the Indians as any of those could be to Christians, yet these claims could be brushed aside for the mere convenience of a federal agency, without even a judicial balancing of harms.

Most of the outcry treated *Lyng*, understandably, as a case about Indian tribes and Indian religion. At the time, few observers noted that O'Connor's language suggested that the "compelling interest" test no longer applied (if it ever had) in *most* religious-freedom cases. "[G]overnment simply could not operate if it were required to satisfy every citizen's religious needs and desires," she wrote. "The Constitution does not, and courts cannot, offer to reconcile the various competing demands on government, many of them rooted in sincere religious belief, that inevitably arise in so diverse a society as ours. That task, to the extent that it is feasible, is for the legislatures and other institutions."

During the 1930s the Yale law scholar Felix Cohen had almost single-handedly created the field of federal Indian law. In his handbook of the subject, Cohen memorably compared Native Americans to the canaries that coal miners carried in cages into underground mine shafts to warn them of a buildup of explosive gas. Because their lungs were delicate, the birds keeled over at the first whiff of impure air, giving the miners a chance to scramble for safety. Similarly, Cohen wrote, democratic government sometimes turned toxic, poisoned by the impatience of the majority with any group that got in its way; the first sign that freedom was in trouble was often an assault on Native people. After the decision in *Smith*, it would become possible for scholars to look at *Lyng* and see in it the outlines of a new legal attitude toward freedom of religion—one that left minority faiths, Native or otherwise, at the mercy of the majority.

But in the fall on 1989, all that could be said for certain was that this Court did not seem likely to extend protection to peyote religion.

The Native American Church of North America turned to its lawyer, John Echohawk, for help. Echohawk knew Dave Frohnmayer; indeed, they had talked about the case once before, when the Oregon attorney general and his deputy, Bill Gary, had visited Boulder for a convention. Frohnmayer had been adamant then about the need for neutrality under the Oregon constitution. The state could not pick and choose among religions. If one got an exemption, then all would get them.

John Echohawk's cousin, Walter, had been there. Walter Echo-hawk, or Bunky as he is universally known in Indian-law circles, had tried to educate Frohnmayer about the history of peyote worship and the importance of the sacrament to members of the Church. Frohnmayer recalls that Bunky invited him to come to a ceremonial—fully legal under federal and Colorado law—but that he declined. "There would have been something untoward about law enforcement engaging in a ritual," Frohnmayer said later. Sande Schmidt, who sat in on the meeting, recalled that Bunky told Dave that Oregon was probably the only state in the Union where the peyote ritual was outlawed. "Dave and Bill both said, 'Yes, we know.' End of discussion," she said later.

But still, John Echohawk thought there was a chance that NARF could do something to avert the threat of an adverse decision. Frohnmayer would at least listen to him. Echohawk was not naive, however. He knew that sweet reason alone is often not enough to change the mind of a government bureaucracy once it has chosen a course of action. So he devised a dual strategy. As Frohnmayer's friend, he was Mr. Inside. He would keep the lines of communication open. But there was to be an outside strategy as well. NARF would put pressure on the attorney general by appealing to Oregon religious leaders on behalf of the Native American Church and Al Smith.

To run the outside strategy, Echohawk turned to Steve Moore, an Anglo staff attorney with NARF in Boulder whose work was largely concerned with Indian religious rights. Moore threw himself into the *Smith* case. He prepared a circular letter to Northwest religious leaders alerting them of the dangers to religious freedom lurking in the state's position.

The letter conspicuously omitted any mention of Galen Black, a non-Indian who might have muddied the issue. Instead, it asked for "your moral support for [Al] Smith." Recipients were asked to write or call Frohnmayer and ask him to drop the case. "We are asking him to be compassionate and not seek to destroy this 10,000-year-old religion," Moore wrote. Along with the letter, Moore sent a four-page summary and analysis of the case, which said:

> Reasonable minds are loathe [sic] to understand Mr. Frohn-mayer's motives. Whose law or policy is he attempting to exercise here? Given the decisions of the Oregon Supreme Court and the Pharmacy Board, his actions represent, at best, a usurpation of authority through the exercise of law and policy decision-making rightfully vested in other branches and agencies of Oregon government.
>
> Moreover, in order to catch the interest of the U.S. Supreme Court the second time, Mr. Frohnmayer has deliberately mis-represented the interests of the State of Oregon respecting religious use of peyote. Mr. Frohnmayer's briefs to the Court irresponsibly portray the Native American Church as a thin veneer of religiosity fronting drug abuse. . . .
>
> We ask our rabbis, priests and ministers, many of whom have already expressed condemnation of any further harassment of Mr. Smith and the efforts of Mr. Frohnmayer to destroy the Native American Church, to stand together in seeking an end to this harassment.

Steve Moore was not Dave Frohnmayer's friend. As far as he was concerned, Frohnmayer was just another politician, who would respond best to a direct threat of public criticism and adverse consequences at the polls. "We knew he had political aspirations," Moore said later. "The whole idea was to shock Frohnmayer from a moral standpoint into agreeing to dismiss the appeal." Moore pushed that line, too, in op-ed articles for Oregon newspapers. Frohnmayer's office began to get letters and calls. And in liberal Eugene, a group of local clergy approached Paul Olum. Olum, the president of the University of Oregon, was an old friend and colleague of Dave Frohnmayer's. He agreed to ask Frohnmayer to meet with the religious leaders at a conference room in a downtown Eugene hotel to listen to their side of the case.

The group convened in October of 1989. Frohnmayer brought along Marla Rae, his executive assistant. She recalled that the meeting turned ugly almost at once. "There were times when it was extraordinarily heated. Screaming, screaming, about cultural genocide, screaming about 'You have no understanding of my religious tenets! How dare you!'" she recalled. "And then people began taking off after Dave for being a racist and a bigot and generally evil person."

At this point Paul Olum stopped the meeting. Dave Frohnmayer was a friend and a valued colleague, he explained. He had known him for more than ten years. There was no question of his being a racist; he had always spoken up for equal opportunity for all. The meeting calmed down. And then John Echohawk began to speak. "John Echohawk in this very quiet, very forceful, absolutely sincere tone, almost with tears in his eyes, says, 'This is my religion, this is my religion you're attacking,'" Marla Rae recalled. "You could have heard a pin drop in there."

The meeting broke up inconclusively. But afterward, Frohnmayer remembers, John Echohawk sought him out privately to press his plea for a settlement. "He's not a man of great public emotion or temper," Frohnmayer recalled. "But one could tell the steeliness of his resolve. Something like 'This is the wrong thing, Dave' or 'Make it go away, Dave' or 'Get rid of this case, Dave.' I mean, it was a very direct kind of statement. I didn't need to know that he felt strongly about the case, but I do remember the intensity of his conviction that this should not be allowed to proceed."

Moved by his friend's appeal, Frohnmayer agreed to sit down and talk with NARF's lawyers about a possible settlement. Echohawk and Moore were encouraged. But first they needed to get permission from Al Smith and his lawyer. NARF didn't represent a party to the case; the Church was not formally involved. In fact, the Church was somewhat skeptical of Al Smith. Steve Moore recalls that "the Native American Church was incensed at Al Smith because no one regarded him as a member of the Church. They knew who Stanley [Smart] was but they didn't know he was running meetings up in Oregon and that he was inviting non-Indians into the meetings and that whole thing. When all of that became known to the leadership of the Church, they were absolutely incensed."

This difference of viewpoint complicated Al Smith's relationship with NARF. John Echohawk was what Al called a "national Indian"—educated, affluent, well traveled. Al had worked with national Indians, but he did not feel like one of them. In fact, he had called NARF for help early in his dispute with ADAPT. Whoever he had talked to told him the fund couldn't get involved in his dispute; NARF represented tribes and Indian organizations.

NARF was there to negotiate with Frohnmayer—but not exactly on Smith's behalf. It's easy for confusion to arise when Native groups deal with the government. Since the first days of white settlement in America, white groups have sat down and cut deals with "representatives" of Native people. Often these representatives spoke for no one but themselves. Later, during the reservation era, federal officials would sometimes choose white attorneys to speak for tribes, then sign agreements to suit themselves without consulting the nominal clients. It was somewhat easy now for Indian public-interest groups to be taken as "spokesmen" for all Indians. But nobody spoke for Al except Al.

Al Smith had appreciated NARF's efforts to build support for him. Smith had dinner with Moore and Echohawk and told them to go ahead. He had a new lawyer, Craig Dorsay, who agreed.

Dorsay was a graduate of the University of Oregon and a specialist in Indian law who knew John Echohawk well. Dorsay had been an assistant attorney general of the huge Navajo nation in the Four Corners area of the Southwest before returning to Oregon as head of the Native American Law Program of Oregon Legal Services (OLS). He had been asked by OLS to help Suanne Lovendahl with the remanded case in front of the Oregon Supreme Court. He remembered her as not wanting much help, however; in fact, he only found out about the argument of the case when he read it in *The Oregonian*. But once Frohnmayer displayed his determination to petition for cert. again, Lovendahl apparently decided she was outgunned; she passed Al Smith and Galen Black along to Dorsay to prepare for the second round before the justices in Washington.

John Echohawk and Steve Moore arrived in Salem on October 24, 1989. The NARF lawyers gathered in the attorney general's second-floor conference room. Frohnmayer was there with his key staffers: Oregon Solicitor General James Mountain, Assistant Attorney General Virginia Linder, and Marla Rae.

It was an unusual settlement conference. For one thing, oral argument was just two weeks away. It's very rare for a case to settle after the Supreme Court has agreed to hear it, and besides, the meeting was interrupting Frohnmayer's preparations for argument. But Echohawk and Moore didn't have the same pressures on them—they weren't arguing the case. Steve Moore, in fact, was hoping that the meeting would throw the attorney general off his game, even if no settlement was reached. Frohnmayer was feeling other pressures as well. Two weeks earlier he had announced that he was running for the Republican nomination for governor of Oregon. And on the day of the meeting, Katie was back at Sacred Heart, undergoing bone-marrow biopsies to monitor the course of her Fanconi anemia.

When the meeting began, Steve Moore made it clear that, to

him at least, this was no friendly chat: "I was very confrontational because I went in almost like on a crusade," he said later. "We came in and just immediately demanded the moral high ground here. Personally, I felt very offended by the state's unwillingness to do anything but just withdraw the appeal *sua sponte*, and [I] pretty much took that attitude in the meetings, that you don't have a right to do anything but withdraw your appeal."

Moore's attitude offended Frohnmayer and his staff. The attorney general didn't want to send state troopers sweeping through the woods looking for tipi ceremonies. But they were worried about the prospect of other religious drug-use cases. And beyond that, there was the issue of credibility: the case had been accepted for review. Both sides had filed briefs, and now argument was only days away. The Oregon attorney general's office cared about its reputation with the justices. Yanking the case from the docket so late would make them seem feckless, even frivolous.

Moore brushed off these concerns; he remembers saying that "your concerns about precedent in Oregon and your reputation in the Supreme Court and Dave's political future—all of that is bullshit." After he had repeated this a few times, Virginia Linder, a soft-spoken appellate lawyer, exploded: "I don't remember even what I said except it was something to the effect of 'Listen, you're there arguing for your side of the case. We've tried to explain ours. But don't tell us what our interests are.'" After the meeting, Linder found herself with Marla Rae, a hard-bitten survivor of Oregon's political wars. "By God, Linder," Rae said admiringly, "you really *are* a bitch."

By now the meeting had turned into a confrontation. So Dave Frohnmayer asked John Echohawk to step into his private office to tell him that he had heard his concern and that of the religious leaders. If they could work out a compromise, he would be willing to pull the case from the Court's docket. But probably it would have to be Echohawk and Frohnmayer who worked it out; unless Echohawk could muzzle Moore, nothing was going to happen.

But one player was missing. NARF did not represent Al Smith or Galen Black and had no formal authority to agree to a settlement. As afternoon turned into evening, Frohnmayer sent out for pizza and the NARF representatives adjourned to another room to call Craig Dorsay, Smith and Black's counsel of record. Dorsay drove down from Portland, and the negotiations continued until the early-morning hours of October 25.

By about one-thirty A.M., the participants had worked out a fairly complex compromise. The meeting adjourned at about three A.M. Frohnmayer had the agreement typed up, and the next morning they met again to sign the deal. The settlement document set out the following terms:

- Black and Smith would repay the unemployment compensation they had received to date as a result of the Supreme Court's order, which the agreement estimates to be no more than eight thousand dollars.
- Black and Smith would file statements with the U.S. Supreme Court withdrawing their federal constitutional claims and asking the Court to vacate the Oregon court's judgment and remand to the Oregon court for entry of a new order.
- The attorney general's office would notify the Court that it support vacating and remanding the case.
- After remand, the parties would stipulate before the Oregon Supreme Court that the appropriate disposition of the case would be reversal of the Oregon Court of Appeals and remand to the Employment Division for entry of an order denying benefits.
- Neither party would ask for attorney fees from the other.
- Smith and Black would pay the costs assessed by the Supreme

Court for dismissal, which might amount to two hundred dollars, but the state would seek no other costs from them.
- Smith and Black would repay the state for any "nonrefundable travel expenses" incurred as a result of the cancellation of oral argument.

The settlement fully addressed the concerns of the state and of NARF and its client, the NACNA, but offered precious little to Al Smith and Galen Black. Everyone in the conference room that night knew that Frohnmayer was agreeing to fold a winning hand (Steve Moore recalls remarking to Dorsay that he believed Smith and Black had at most a 5 percent chance of prevailing in the Supreme Court); in exchange for doing so, he was asking Smith and Black to make sure their court victories could not become troublesome precedents later. Frohnmayer saw it as a good deal for everyone involved with the future of peyote religion: "They got the brakes put on a decision which everyone, except Al Smith, believes will be seriously adverse to the interests of the Native American Church, reserving for another day the criminal law issue—which, from our standpoint, would never be pursued anyway."

But to Al Smith, the issue was not quite so clear. Dorsay had called him promptly after signing the memorandum. In any formal settlement, the client, not the lawyer, has the final say. Dorsay was frantically trying to find Galen Black as well, but no one knew where he was. In the days after the meeting, it came down to Al Smith's decision.

Al Smith was not a lawyer. All he knew was that he and Galen had fought Frohnmayer in court over and over and that they had won every time. Now Frohnmayer was offering to let Al Smith surrender unconditionally—not just to drop his claim but to repay the money he had gotten as unemployment compensation. How could that be right? Steve Moore assured him that no money would come out of his family's pocket. But there was a symbolic humiliation to so abject a surrender.

NARF and the Church wanted the settlement to happen. Suddenly Al Smith found himself subjected to a lot of advice from people—white and Native—whom he hardly knew. He had not sought this confrontation; the eagle feather had propelled him into the fight. Now elders he respected, and leaders of the church, were urging him to drop it. They believed he could not win, that he would harm the Church and Native people generally by fighting on.

Indian people, as a rule, don't much like to be told what to do by white people. And if that's true in general, it's triply true of Al Smith, who had survived for nearly seventy years by sheer stubbornness, a stern refusal to bow down. Now white people, too, were telling him to drop his fight. One local attorney sympathetic to NARF began calling and dropping by, telling Al in no uncertain terms it was his duty to step out of this case. He persisted, brushing aside Al's reservations, until Al told him to go away and never come back.

There were late-night phone calls, too, from Indian people all around the country. Somehow the word had gotten out that Al Smith was single-handedly pushing forward with a case that might destroy peyote religion. At night the phone would ring, and Al would hear the voices of elders, people he had never met, begging him not to "take our medicine away."

But there were one or two voices telling him to stay the course. One came from Stanley Smart, the Road man who had introduced him to peyote. Stanley wasn't a Church leader or a politician. And now he told Al Smith that the case ought to go forward just to see what would happen. For all his lifetime, Smart said, peyote religion had existed half in and half out of the First Amendment. Peyote leaders had done everything they could to pacify the white man. They called themselves a church, they talked about Jesus, they explained over and over that peyote kept them sober and productive, the way white people said they wanted Indians to be. But still no one was sure whether peyote worshipers were real Americans like Catholics or Methodists. They had an exemption from the drug laws, true; but the exemption came from the DEA, which could revoke it anytime the white man changed his mind. White people had changed their minds before. Maybe it was time to find out whether the white man's Constitution had room for the Church; maybe it was time at last to know where Grandfather Peyote stood.

And Al's other confidante was Jane. Jane let Al know that she supported whatever he did. But she was incensed at Steve Moore and NARF, because she felt they had promised to help Al and then turned on him, that they told him they were his friends before the settlement and then got ugly when he refused to obey their orders. In a diary entry at the time, she wrote:

> Craig [Dorsay] says to be on g[u]ard for possible character bash-
> ing. Steve Moore has already commented to Craig—Al was just
> a flake, not a *real* member, just hangs out w/ white women, *not*
> traditional. This hits below the belt—all trust is gone. How can
> Al take advice from these men who have shown themselves this
> way[?] The effort began as an appeal to clergy for "moral support
> for Mr. Smith" and to urge A[ttorney] G[eneral] not to appeal
> decision of Oregon Supreme Court "persecution of the members
> of the N.A.C. [a]s a way to solve the drug problem in Oregon
> or elsewhere." . . . Al's case was negotiated away to nothing.
> NARF's stand was a heavy pressure on Al to give up whatever
> he had to "save the church"—threatened him with full respon-
> sibility of "killing the church because he was too pigheaded to
> back out." . . . They are willing to sign away everything that was
> gained here in Oregon—the S[upreme] C[ourt] decisions grant-
> ing NAC protection, they want Al to admit his wrongdoing in

going to church, admit his peyote ingestion was criminal, pay back $$, (NARF will) and withdraw his constitutional right to practice in the case. Is this not the same persecution NARF has pleaded to end? Is this moral support for Smith? How can one deny an individual his freedoms and justice in order to save those freedoms for this larger community?

For Al, it came down to a dark night of the soul a few days after the draft settlement was signed. He sat awake in bed as Jane slept beside him, staring into the dark and thinking of his long years as a pilgrim and a stranger, never quite at ease with whites, never fully at home in the Native world. Now he was alone again, with voices from both sides telling him to disappear, not to make trouble, to drop the eagle feather to the ground. "In the wee hours in the morning here, it came to me," he said later. "Your kids are going to grow up and the case is going to come up one of these days and someone will say, 'Your dad is Al Smith? Oh, he's the guy that sold out.' My kids are going to say, 'That's my dad, all right.'

"I'm not going to lay that on my kids. I'm not going to have my kids feel ashamed. Even if we lose the case, they are going to say, 'Yeah, my dad stood up for what he thought was right.' So I got a couple of hours sleep. I phoned Craig and told him, 'Well, let's go to court.' "

11

HUMAN SACRIFICE

Preparing for oral argument before the U.S. Supreme Court is an agonizing process—the legal equivalent of programming a space shuttle launch. Lawyers, like engineers, want to control events—to ask questions to which they already know answers, to use precedents certain to be compelling, to make arguments that have been tested and retested in court. But before the Supreme Court, the lawyers don't have control. The justices ask the questions, and they take pride in their ability to stump even the best-prepared advocate. The Court may overrule its own precedents, and the justices may decide that well-worn arguments no longer have any force.

For most lawyers appearing in front of the Court, final preparations center on a series of "moots"—mock oral arguments in which team members and outsiders play the role of justices and do their best to throw the advocate off stride by asking new questions or casting doubt on arguments. Frohnmayer's rule of thumb was that he would not argue a Supreme Court case that had not been through at least five full-dress moots following the protocol of argument before the Court. Once he and his team reached Washington in the fall of 1989 for the oral argument in *Smith II*, their moots were run by the National Association of Attorneys General (NAAG). Frohnmayer had helped develop the NAAG mooting program, which offered a chance for any state attorney general's office to hone its arguments with the help of lawyers for the U.S. Justice Department, advocacy-group experts, and knowledgeable private lawyers who played the role of justices and pushed the advocates to meet expected questions and objections from the bench.

The NAAG moot was the first time that Frohnmayer had exposed his arguments to outsiders—people who did not work for him and did not share the state's perspective on the long, tortuous history of the case. He expected some tough questions. But the initial moot for *Smith II* went much worse than expected. The "justices" hated his argument.

The problem was that Frohnmayer didn't want to appear before the Court as a vengeful prosecutor seeking to jail peaceful peyote worshipers. The issue at the heart of the case now—put there by the Supreme Court itself—was whether the state could ban the peyote ceremony as part of its prohibition on peyote. But the state of Oregon didn't really want to formally ban peyote religion; Frohnmayer had no plans to arrest Road men or seize ceremonial peyote. What Oregon wanted was the right to refuse unemployment compensation to religious claimants who had broken state drug laws. And so Frohnmayer decided to begin his argument by discussing *Sherbert* v. *Verner* and the other unemployment-compensation cases that had established the "compelling interest" test.

Frohnmayer argued that *Sherbert* and the cases that followed it were different from this one in a key respect. This case was about a flat, absolute ban on certain conduct. Oregon's statute, as construed by its own courts, prohibited possession and use of peyote for any reason at all. There was no exception for religion; there was no exception for anyone. This was different from *Sherbert*, Frohnmayer argued, because in that case and those that followed, the law allowed some people to quit their jobs or refuse new work for some personal reasons, such as the need to move to a new community or to care for a sick relative. Claimants who were unemployed for these reasons would still get their unemployment compensation. But as written, the state statutes had refused to include religious scruples as one of the personal reasons worthy of exemption. Frohnmayer's argument was that the Free Exercise Clause went only this far—that if the state law exempted some secular behavior, it couldn't refuse to exempt religiously motivated reasons. Because Oregon's law had no exemptions, he planned to argue, *Sherbert* didn't apply.

It was possibly a valid argument, but the "justices" at the NAAG moot swept it aside in a couple of minutes. "I remember all of the NAAG judges sitting there with their faces screwed up as Dave began his argument. And they just jumped him quickly. They pushed the argument past that and they got into the other part of the case with questions almost immediately," Virginia Linder recalled later. "I think their immediate feedback was, 'What are you doing talking about that? The Court didn't bring you here for that.' "

After the moot, the Oregon team huddled quickly and decided to begin its argument with the issue of criminal prohibition of religious conduct. Frohnmayer was used to going into oral argument with a neat script, typed by his staff in an easy-to-read large Orator typeface. But now he and his assistants began hastily reordering the pages, adding scribbled notes and arrows, and crossing out huge blocks of text.

Meanwhile, Frohnmayer had other distractions to deal with. He was an announced candidate for governor of Oregon. Each day brought political inquiries by the press; once he even had to stop in mid-moot to respond to a deadline query from National Public Radio. Each night he struggled to focus his thoughts and refine the arguments he would make before the Court. The centerpiece of his argument was the contention that, in the midst of a drug crisis, requiring states to exempt religious use of a controlled substance might put the courts on a slippery slope that would eventually destroy the nation's efforts to end drug abuse.

"Slippery slope" arguments are very common in law, but they are often not terribly convincing. We are all familiar with the talk-radio host who argues that if the state allows legal abortion for any reason at all, "the next step" will be jackbooted shock troops herding the aged into death camps. But Frohnmayer believed that in this case—partly because of Oregon's unique constitution—the argument was valid.

There was, of course, a counterargument he could expect Dorsay to offer: the Native American Church was a force for sobriety and abstinence. Its religious tenets centered around the need to avoid alcohol and drugs and to use peyote only in the controlled environment of the tipi ceremony. A generation's experience with the federal peyote exemption suggested that these restrictions were sincere and effectively enforced. There was no real report of problems with peyote intoxication at ceremonies or of sacramental peyote finding its way onto the street.

The answer came to Frohnmayer after dinner one night shortly before argument. It was an answer that held an echo of the Rajneeshpuram episode, with its sudden and dizzying shifts in the cult's theology and practice. "Why can't you argue that the internal controls of the religion are sufficient for the state to cede over regulatory authority to the religion itself rather than retaining it with the government?" Frohnmayer recalls asking himself. "The answer is this—that religions change. Once authority to regulate practices is ceded out of government hands for all eternity, you have ceded away the possibility of regulating something that could become very dangerous. That is a killer argument. All of us heard it at the same time and said, 'That's a killer.' "

Craig Dorsay, meanwhile, traveled to Boulder and underwent a full moot of the case, with NARF attorneys and others versed in the issues as mock justices. Dorsay had sat as second chair in one argument before the U.S. Supreme Court. Though more experienced than Lovendahl, Dorsay was keenly aware that a complex, high-stakes case like this one might be better presented by an experienced Supreme Court advocate. Months before the argument, he called Laurence Tribe, a professor at Harvard and a high-profile appellate lawyer who frequently appeared before the high court. Tribe said he would serve as lead counsel if Dorsay would turn the case over to him entirely and withdraw. Dorsay proposed this arrangement to Smith. "Al wasn't comfortable," Dorsay recalled. "He wanted someone local to talk to him." In the end, Dorsay prepared the argument himself, with Steve Moore and Walter Echo-hawk as second chairs.

Al Smith and Jane Farrell-Smith and their two children had come to Washington for this argument, their way paid for them by supporters. Stanley Smart was with them. They stayed at the Capitol Hotel on Capitol Hill, not far from the Phoenix Park, and toured the city on the weekend before argument, reveling in the crisp autumn weather. Jane Farrell-Smith recalled being trapped at a street corner by the fourteen thousand runners of the Marine Corps marathon. She and Al filed by the marble statues of the white men who had founded the United States; they wondered whether the legal system these men had built included people like them.

Smith was a higher-profile case this time than it had been in 1987. Indian religious leaders had come to Washington to bear witness to the importance of peyote religion to their traditions. They held a prayer ceremony outside the Court the night before oral argument. And the next morning, many Native people were in the courtroom when the chief justice called Dave Frohnmayer to the lectern to give his argument.

"The question is this," Frohnmayer told the Court. "Does the Free Exercise Clause require every state to exempt the religious peyote use by the Native American Church, or perhaps even beyond that, other substance use by other religions, from the reach of generally applicable criminal laws regulating the use of controlled substances by all citizens?" The Oregon Supreme Court's opinion compromised the state's interest in controlling the use of hallucinogenic drugs, he said.

Justice John Paul Stevens asked Frohnmayer whether Oregon could constitutionally ban the use of wine in Christian Communion ceremonies. This was a question the state had been expecting and had spent a lot of time preparing for. Frohnmayer's answer was carefully noncommital. There might be less of a state interest in regulating the "small quantities" of wine used in church. Besides, he argued, there was a difference. Christians did not drink sacramental wine for its physiological effect, but peyotists eat their sacrament "at least in part for its very hallucinogenic properties."

Frohnmayer returned to his "slippery slope" argument:

[W]e have a claim by Respondent that line drawing of the kind that we find so objectionable in pursuit of our interests in reli-

gious neutrality is easy. And we point to the lower federal court
cases suggesting that other persons using peyote, other persons
using hashish, LSD or marijuana for sincere religious reasons,
that those cases can be easily distinguished. We simply invite
this Court's careful review of those cases, which are shamelessly
result-driven and involve religious gerrymandering from which
no consistent neutral principle emerges. And our point is that if
we cannot accommodate on equal grounds, then the requirement of accommodation must fail.

He then moved on to his "killer argument" that peyote religion,
even if now safe, might become unsafe in the future if granted
affirmative constitutional protection:

And there is a final and critical point here related to our health
and safety interest. That is that denominational practices, and
indeed individual believers, even in long-standing religions, can
and do change. They change the nature of their religious beliefs,
they change the nature of their doctrine, and that is the very
essence of freedom of religion and belief. . . . But then we must
ask, before we let [regulatory] control pass in the form of a constitutional exemption . . . what are the contours of that exemption and how will it be conferred. Because if the denominational
or church controls weaken or change, there [will be] still en-
shrined in the Bill of Rights a permanent exemption for the practices of that religion.

Craig Dorsay then rose to speak for Smith and Black. "I am
compelled as an initial matter to address the subject raised by
Justice Stevens relating to the use of alcohol," he began. "[I]f
Indian people were in charge of the United States right now . . .
you might find that alcohol was the Schedule I substance and

peyote was not listed at all. And we are getting here to the heart of an ethnocentric view . . . of what constitutes religion in the United States."

Peyote, Dorsay argued, was not dangerous when used in ceremonies. "There is . . . no evidence that peyote, as used by the Native American Church, has been misused in the sense that i[t] has been misused by society." The Church's long history had produced at most "one or two anecdotal instances" of adverse reactions, he said.

Dorsay then turned to the point he had planned to begin with:

> [T]his case is indistinguishable from previous unemployment cases before this Court. The Oregon Supreme Court has now decided twice, as a matter of state law, that the criminality of Respondent's conduct is immaterial to Oregon's unemployment compensation law. . . . [T]hat is the reason the Oregon Supreme Court did not address its constitutional question under state law[,] because the criminality was not relevant. . . . I believe what the [Oregon Supreme Court] did [in their opinion on remand] is [to] respond to the dissent's invitation to say this is what we said the first time. We meant it, we are saying again.

Dorsay tried to direct the Court's attention to the *Sherbert* test. But the drug issue would not go away. Justice Sandra Day O'Connor asked him whether an exemption for the Native American Church would apply to other sincere claims for religious peyote use. "I do believe it would be required under normal constitutional analysis," Dorsay said. What about religious marijuana use? O'Connor asked. "I don't want to go down that road too far," Dorsay began.

"I'll bet you don't" was O'Connor's dry answer. The courtroom dissolved in laughter. For Virginia Linder, sitting at the counsel table for the state, that moment was the key to the oral argument. She concluded that the state had O'Connor's vote and, with it, probably a majority of the Court.

For Dorsay, though, the defining moment was just ahead. He returned to his argument that a state could not outlaw a religious practice without showing that it caused actual harm. Justice Scalia interrupted him: "Well, I suppose you could say a law against human sacrifice would, you know, would affect only the Aztecs. But I don't know that you have to make . . . exceptions. If it is a generally applicable law." Years later Dorsay still remembers that moment with sharp resentment. However interesting the hypothetical may have seemed to Justice Scalia, to Dorsay it seemed to slur Native Americans and their religions. "It was just sort of disrespectful, I thought, the way Scalia approached it. . . . You could hear Indian people—there were a large number in the courtroom—just sort of exhale, a large sigh, like, 'Oh, God, we got this jerk again.' "

After a brief rebuttal by Frohnmayer, *Smith*'s time was up. The Court rose for lunch. Looking back, the argument was mostly striking for what was not said. Not one word from counsel, not one question from the bench suggested that this case turned on anything except the appropriate application of the *Sherbert* "compelling interest" test. The issues were whether drug prohibition was a compelling interest, whether *Sherbert* allowed that interest to be considered even if it was not mentioned in the state's unemployment statute, and whether the interest was "compelling" even though the state had little evidence that religious peyote use had ever harmed anyone. Since its petition for certiorari, filed in 1986, the state had not even suggested a new look at *Sherbert*. All the briefs in the case took the test for granted, and no justice had suggested otherwise.

After the argument, the lawyers huddled on the Court steps to answer reporters' questions and compare their projected vote counts. The Native American Church leaders gathered as well to state their case to the press. Steve Moore recalled Al Smith during these informal proceedings, surrounded by leaders of the church that had tried to stop his case from going forward. "I think Al felt very, very alone in that moment," he said.

But Smith's most vivid memory is not of his own loneliness but that of another—Stanley Smart, the Northern Paiute Road man who had been his spiritual guide and who, like him, had incurred the wrath of Church leaders and of NARF staffers. "I was up being surrounded by press and I happened to look over, kind of off in the distance over there was Mr. Smart. I wanted to call him up. I wish I had now. He was just standing out there by himself. Standing in the background. Now that he's gone, dead, you know, I wish I had called him up."

12

INCIDENTAL
BURDENS

Early on the morning of April 17, 1990, Dave Frohnmayer got a call from a reporter. Public figures on the West Coast are used to hearing the phone ring before sunrise; the three-hour time difference with the East Coast means that broadcast reporters are already facing deadlines while people in Oregon and California are still driving to work. The reporter told Frohnmayer that the state had won the *Smith* case, which did not surprise him greatly. But the reporter also seemed concerned that the Supreme Court had "taken away" religious freedom. Frohnmayer dismissed that idea; the case was limited to a special set of facts. Nonetheless, the question suggested that the opinion went much further than he had expected.

Not until he got a copy of the slip opinion by fax, though, did he have a chance to analyze what the Court had done. He and his staff read the opinion page by page, and as they did so, their confusion grew. Jerome Lidz recalls that "my first reaction was, 'This sweeps too broadly, this is really trouble and I don't like this.'" Rives Kistler recalls thinking that a page of the opinion must be missing. "I remember when I read Scalia's opinion, I thought, 'It stopped.' It came to an end, and I thought, 'Well, there's going to be another section here.'"

What they were realizing is that the Court had done something no one had asked or expected it to do. All of the state's arguments, all of Smith and Black's counterarguments, were couched in terms of the "compelling interest" test of *Sherbert* v. *Verner*. But the Court, in an opinion by Justice Scalia, had thrown *Sherbert* out the window.

The majority opinion in *Smith* was joined by Chief Justice Rehnquist and by Associate Justices Byron White, John Paul Stevens, and Anthony Kennedy. But in style and tone, it was clearly the work of Justice Scalia, who signed it. Like most of Scalia's major opinions, it was radical in its approach and less than respectful of Supreme Court precedent.

Scalia began by defining the Free Exercise Clause as protecting "first and foremost, the right to believe and profess whatever religious doctrine one desires." But, Scalia noted, religious believers often want more than that: they want to do something, to carry their beliefs into practice. Some religious behavior would be protected by the First Amendment, he said—but not much. "It would doubtless be unconstitutional, for example, to ban the casting of 'statues that are to be used for worship purposes,' or to prohibit bowing down before a golden calf"—in other words, to forbid actions that had *only* religious meaning. But Al Smith and Galen Black, he wrote, "contend that their religious motivation for using peyote places them beyond the reach of a criminal law that is not specifically directed at their religious practice." The correct meaning of "free exercise," Scalia said, was that it protects religious worshipers only against laws *specifically aimed* at religious practice. Oregon's law had a health and safety rationale rather than an antireligious origin; thus, "free exercise" did not bar its application to peyote religion.

As precedent for this proposition, Scalia cited *Minersville School District* v. *Gobitis*, a 1940 case in which the Court held that a local school district had the right to expel children who were Jehovah's Witnesses when they refused—as required by their faith—to say the Pledge of Allegiance. The Witnesses regarded the flag as a "graven image" and saluting it as blasphemy. "Conscientious scruples have not, in the course of the long struggle for religious toleration, relieved the individual from obedience to a general law not aimed at the promotion or restriction of religious beliefs," Justice Felix Frankfurter had written in *Gobitis*.

At this point in the opinion, constitutionally sophisticated readers would have begun to suspect that something was seriously wrong. That's because *Gobitis* is widely considered one of the Court's worst mistakes. In fact, just three years after *Gobitis*, in a case called *West Virginia State Board of Education* v. *Barnette*, the Court had made a stunning turnaround, overruling *Gobitis* and holding that the First Amendment *did* after all protect children who did not wish to recite the Pledge. But a reader of Scalia's opinion would not have known that; as far as the *Smith* opinion was concerned, *Gobitis* remained good law. It was almost as shocking as citing *Dred Scott* v. *Sandford*, the case that held that black people could never be American citizens, or *Plessy* v. *Ferguson*, which approved racial segregation by law. It was the kind of thing that would earn a first-year law student a failing mark on an exam.

Scalia's citation of *Gobitis* was not the result of sloppy research. He knew about *Barnette* as well as anyone. But in a trademark move, he had found a rationale to "distinguish," or explain away, the second case—and to explain away other cases like *Wisconsin* v. *Yoder* that would seem to offer support to Smith and Black. These cases, he explained, were not *free-exercise* cases at all; they were instead something called *hybrid cases*, a term that had not existed in constitutional law until then. A hybrid case, he explained, was one that involved "the Free Exercise Clause in conjunction with other constitutional protections, such as freedom of speech and of the press . . . or the right of parents . . . to direct the education of their children." Here, in one of the long strings of case names and page numbers that lawyers unlovingly call string citations, Scalia stuck his explanation of *Barnette*. That case, he explained by indication, was one of many "decided exclusively upon free speech grounds."

Technically, Scalia was correct. The Witnesses in *Gobitis* had argued first and foremost their own religious scruples against the Pledge, and the Court had rejected their argument. Three years later—after the Witness sect had suffered a wave of persecution—the Court repented; but in *Barnette* it had couched its decision in terms not of free exercise but of free speech. Not only Witnesses had the right to refuse the Pledge, Justice Robert Jackson wrote for the Court in *Barnette*; government had no right to make *anyone* recite political beliefs he or she did not hold. "If there is any fixed star in our constitutional constellation," Jackson wrote in an often-quoted paragraph, "it is that no official, high or petty, can prescribe what shall be orthodox in politics, nationalism, religion, or other matters of opinion or force citizens to confess by word or act their faith therein."

This interpretation of *Barnette* is one that only a Supreme Court justice could hope to get away with. Whatever the pleadings may have said, *Gobitis* had not been written as an opinion about freedom of religion only; anyone reading the opinion would have to conclude that the Court was empowering government to override *any* sort of objection to the Pledge. The point of the Pledge, Frankfurter had written, was to enforce national unity, which was "the basis of national security." To allow any children to refuse to participate would weaken the vital lesson, he said. *Gobitis* was a strong, sweeping opinion, and very few observers over the past fifty years have doubted that the Court had repented and decided to withdraw the case—except Antonin Scalia.

Unlike *Gobitis* and *Yoder*, Scalia continued, "the present case does not present such a hybrid situation, but a free exercise claim unconnected with any communicative activity or parental right." Instead, he said, Smith and Black "urge us to hold, quite simply, that when otherwise prohibitable conduct is accompanied by religious convictions, not only the convictions but the conduct itself must be free from governmental regulation." Again, Scalia was exercising his prerogative to rewrite the record. Smith and Black had never challenged the right of government to *regulate* peyote religion; the Native American Church exists happily and has for nearly a century within a complex web of state and federal laws designed to make sure that ritual peyote is not abused. What they objected to was a state law that *prohibited* their religious practice; even so, they did not "quite simply" argue that their religious beliefs were above the criminal law. Instead, they contended that the law must be weighed in the balance, using the "compelling interest" test.

Smith and Black argued that there was no compelling state interest that required banning peyote use to the faithful; the state of Oregon had argued that its anti-drug policy was such a "compelling interest." No one at any point had argued *simply* one way or the other. The entire case had taken place within the context of the *Sherbert* test.

That test Scalia now relegated to minor status. "In recent years we have abstained from applying the *Sherbert* test (outside the unemployment compensation field) at all," he explained, citing cases where government tax, military, and prison policy had prevailed over free-exercise challenge. The argument is so brisk that a reader might forget that *Smith* itself was an unemployment-compensation case. The question of criminal law was entirely the Court's invention; having forced Smith and Black to step out of the unemployment context, Scalia now, like a character in Lewis Carroll, explained to them that they were losing because they had not stayed within it.

When the case concerned an "across-the-board criminal prohibition on a particular form of conduct," Scalia explained, *Sherbert* didn't even apply anymore. "We conclude today that the sounder approach, and the approach in accord with the vast majority of our precedents, is to hold the test inapplicable to such challenges." If courts applied *Sherbert* to "neutral, generally applicable laws," Scalia explained, they would destroy the power of government to make any rules at all. "Any society adopting such a system would be courting anarchy," he wrote, "but that danger increases in direct proportion to the society's diversity of religious beliefs." America was a religiously diverse society, he explained; "precisely because we value and protect that religious divergence, we cannot afford the luxury of deeming presumptively invalid, as applied to the religious objector, every regulation of conduct that does not protect an interest of the highest order."

Religious minorities penalized—even outlawed—by "neutral" laws, Scalia explained, shouldn't look to the courts anymore for protection. Their only hope lay in the state legislatures and Congress, which could, if they chose, protect religious belief. But that was a matter of politics, not law. "It may fairly be said that leaving accommodation to the political process will place at a relative disadvantage those religious practices that are not widely engaged in," Scalia conceded, "but that unavoidable consequence of democratic government must be preferred to a system in which each conscience is a law unto itself or in which judges weigh the social importance of all laws against the centrality of all religious beliefs."

Americans, even those who don't get to worship services often, are used to hearing public officials speak respectfully about the people's piety and wisdom. The average American, in fact, might be likely to name "freedom of religion" as the most important of the liberties the Constitution protects. They are not used to being told that their freedom depends on the legislature's whim or to hearing that the courts have no interest in hearing from individuals oppressed by the political process. But Scalia's style does not sugarcoat.

Justice Sandra Day O'Connor, who wrote a separate opinion in *Smith*, understood better the customary rhetoric of freedom. She scolded Scalia for his rule that "neutral" laws were not subject to free-exercise scrutiny. "To reach this sweeping result," she wrote, "the Court must not only give a strained reading of the First Amendment but must also disregard our consistent application of free exercise doctrine to cases involving generally applicable regulations that burden religious conduct." O'Connor wrote that the First Amendment "does not distinguish between laws that are generally applicable and laws that target particular religious practices. Indeed, few States would be so naive as to enact a law directly prohibiting or burdening a religious practice as such. Our free exercise cases have all concerned generally applicable laws that had the effect of significantly burdening a religious practice. If the First Amendment is to have any vitality, it ought not be construed to cover only the extreme and hypothetical situation in which a State directly targets a religious practice."

O'Connor insisted that *Sherbert* was a valid and workable test for many situations, not only unemployment cases. "To me, the sounder approach—the approach more consistent with our role as judges to decide each case on its individual merits—is to apply this test in each case to determine whether the burden on the specific plaintiffs before us is constitutionally significant and whether the particular criminal interest asserted by the State before us is compelling. Even if, as an empirical matter, a government's criminal laws might usually serve a compelling interest in health, safety, or public order, the First Amendment at least requires a case-by-case determination of the question, sensitive to the facts of each particular claim."

Scalia's reference to legislatures as protectors of minorities was mistaken as well, O'Connor argued. She quoted Justice Jackson in *Barnette*:

> The very purpose of a Bill of Rights was to withdraw certain subjects from the vicissitudes of political controversy, to place them beyond the reach of majorities and officials and to establish them as legal principles to be applied by the courts. One's right to life, liberty, and property, to free speech, a free press, freedom of worship and assembly, and other fundamental rights may not be submitted to vote; they depend on the outcome of no elections.

The best way to preserve the Bill of Rights, O'Connor wrote, was to use the *Sherbert* test and decide free-exercise cases one by one. "The compelling interest test reflects the First Amendment's mandate of preserving religious liberty to the fullest extent possible in a pluralistic society. For the Court to deem this command a 'luxury' . . . is to denigrate '[t]he very purpose of a Bill of Rights.'"

O'Connor's opinion used the voice of justice that Americans are used to hearing. It cast the Court as the protectors of embattled minorities like the Native American Church. But her defense of American liberty actually did not include Al Smith and

Galen Black. O'Connor asked the Court to apply the "compelling interest" test that protects us all—all, that is, except the Native American Church. O'Connor—a former state judge with a hard-line view of drugs—was willing to administer the *Sherbert* test; peyote religion, she said, flunked it. It was dangerous, and the state was free to ban it.

"Oregon's criminal prohibition represents that State's judgment that the possession and use of controlled substances, even by only one person, is inherently harmful and dangerous. Because the health effects caused by the use of controlled substances exist regardless of the motivation of the user, the use of such substances, even for religious purposes, violates the very purpose of the laws that prohibit them." Since Oregon didn't want to make an exemption for peyote, she explained, it had a compelling interest in not doing so.

O'Connor's concurrence reads more gently than Scalia's harsh manifesto, but it provided no more comfort to the Church, and indeed probably less. Scalia at least was saying to religious groups that they were all in the same boat, at the mercy of the lawmakers. O'Connor's soothing tone seemed to reassure ordinary Americans that *their* liberties were safe; it was only "drug users" who were in danger from the law.

Justice Harry Blackmun dissented from the result, joined by the Court's other two liberals, Justices William Brennan and Thurgood Marshall. He ridiculed the rhetoric of Scalia's opinion: "I do not believe the Founders thought their dearly bought freedom from religious persecution a 'luxury,' but an essential element of liberty—and they could not have thought religious intolerance 'unavoidable,' for they drafted the Religion Clauses precisely in order to avoid that intolerance." But Blackmun skipped quickly over most of Scalia's opinion and instead argued with O'Connor about the application of the "compelling interest" test. It read as if it had been written before Scalia unveiled his opinion—as if Blackmun had assumed that the majority would do what most people thought it would, and decide *Smith* within the "compelling interest" framework. "Oregon's interest in enforcing its drug laws against religious use of peyote is not sufficiently compelling to outweigh respondents' right to the free exercise of their religion," Blackmun argued. "Since the State could not constitutionally enforce its criminal prohibition against respondents, the interests underlying the State's drug laws cannot justify its denial of unemployment benefits." This argument, though persuasive, was irrelevant. A five-member majority of the Court had now established a new rule, henceforth known as the *Smith* rule: if a law didn't target religion, then minorities whose practice was destroyed were out of luck.

Looking back on Scalia's maneuvers during *Smith*'s first hearing at the Court, it was hard not to conclude that this result was what the justice had been after all along. He had helped the Court mold *Smith* into a case that would let him get rid of *Sherbert*, a case he didn't like. The Court's crown prince had struck another blow. Religious freedom, after *Smith*, was a whole new game. And Nino Scalia set the rules.

13

GIDEON'S ARMY

William Nouyi Yang is a Hmong immigrant from Southeast Asia; he came to America after the defeat of the secret CIA-funded Hmong army that fought on America's side during the war in Indochina. Yang moved to Springfield, Massachusetts; other members of his extended family ended up in other parts of New England. There he found more terror and death than he had lived through in the killing fields.

The Hmong traditional religion teaches that if a person is mutilated after death, or buried without all the parts of his or her body, the spirit of the deceased cannot find its way to heaven. Instead, it remains on earth to torment the members of its former family. That is what had happened to his family since they came to the United States, Yang later said. One nephew had died in an automobile accident in 1984. State authorities performed an autopsy, which involved cutting open the body and removing organs. Since that first autopsy, two other members of the family had died suddenly, without explanation. Each death took place around Christmas. In each case, the state insisted on an autopsy. Yang later testified that "we knew it is a curse on us because we didn't prevent it from happening in the past."

On December 21, 1987, a fourth nephew, Neng Yang, fell into a coma without explanation. William Yang attempted to revive Neng, then rushed him to the hospital. Doctors at Rhode Island Hospital restored his breathing and heartbeat. They determined, however, that his brain function would not return; they advised the Yang family to terminate life support. The Yangs asked the doctors to promise that no autopsy would be performed. Although they thought they had been assured of this, the state medical examiner's office seized the body as soon as breathing stopped and performed an autopsy without notifying the Yangs or seeking their permission. Under state law, all unexplained deaths had to be investigated by autopsy, officials explained. There were no exceptions.

Neng Yang's father and mother went to federal court, seeking damages and a declaratory judgment that the state's action had violated their free-exercise rights. On January 12, 1990, District Judge Raymond J. Pettine ruled that the medical examiner's action had violated the Yangs' First Amendment rights. Though the state asserted "health and safety" as a reason for performing autopsies in all unexplained deaths, Pettine applied the "compelling interest" test and found that, without specific evidence of some kind of infectious disease, negligence, or foul play, the state's general interest in explaining Neng Yang's cause of death did not override the Free Exercise Clause. He granted a declaratory judgment that no more such autopsies should be performed if other family members died, and he set a hearing to determine the amount of monetary damages the Yang family should receive.

"The decision sent out a very strong and positive message to the local Hmong community, and also all the Hmong community in the United States of America, that they don't have to fear the government violating their basic religious rights," Yang said later. "We feel that as a minority in this great nation, we can trust our government to protect our religious rights under the U.S. Constitution."

But the judge's determination of damages was not complete on April 17, 1990, the day the Supreme Court handed down its decision in *Smith*. When Judge Pettine read the decision, he realized that the "compelling interest" test he had used in ruling for the Yangs was no longer the law. "It is with deep regret that I have determined that [*Smith*] mandates that I withdraw my previous opinion," he wrote in an order dated November 12, 1990. "My regret stems from the fact that I have the deepest sympathy for the Yangs. I was moved by their tearful outburst in the courtroom during the hearing on damages. I have seldom, in twenty-four years on the bench, seen such a sincere instance of emotion displayed. I could not help but also notice the reaction of the large number of Hmongs who had gathered to witness the hearing. Their silent tears shed in the still courtroom as they heard the Yangs' testimony provided stark support for the depth of the Yangs' grief." But Justice Scalia's sweeping language left the judge no choice; the Yangs would receive no damages—and no assurance that another family member would not be mutilated after death.

William Yang told his story to the U.S. Senate Judiciary Committee on September 18, 1992. He was the star witness in a campaign by the American religious community to overturn the *Smith* decision by passing a measure called the Religious Freedom Restoration Act.

The hearings came after more than a year of meeting and negotiating among those outraged by *Smith*. That, as it turned out, was a large group, stretching across America's religious spectrum.

Nino Scalia, the faithful Catholic and father of nine, made an unlikely antichrist. But his opinion in *Smith* earned him as many harsh words from the American religious community as had ever been hurled at liberal justices for their opinions in school-prayer cases. In the wake of *Smith*, Scalia learned the truth of Alexis de Tocqueville's analysis of the latent power of America's variegated religious community: "In the United States," de Tocqueville wrote in 1835, "if a politician attacks a sect, this may not prevent the partisans of that very sect from supporting him; but if he attacks all the sects together, everyone abandons him, and he remains alone."

Some court observers have suggested that the justices saw the *Smith* opinion as unremarkable, a routine summary of previous case law. If so, that perception simply underscores the isolation of the Court in its marble palace, where outsiders dare not approach except with hushed voice and downcast eyes. The religious community was unschooled in the deference due the nine oracles of America's secular religion; it reacted with a collective scream of outrage heard across the country.

The daily press was scathing. "Almost in time for the celebrations of the bicentennial of the Bill of Rights, Justice Scalia has interpreted this quintessential part of the First Amendment to be a majoritarian rule rather than a protection of individual conscience," sniffed pundit Nat Hentoff in *The Washington Post*. "Maybe it's just as well James Madison isn't around for the champagne." Columnist Edwin Yoder called the decision "disconcerting" and added that "[i]n theory, all religions are equal under the First Amendment; but in the eyes of the court some are clearly more equal than others. Alcohol, the sacramental element of choice for Christians and Jews, is allowable; peyote, the element of choice for Indians, is not."

In *The Christian Science Monitor*, Samuel Rabinove wrote that "history tells us that unpopular religious minorities, such as Mormons or Jehovah's Witnesses, have had problems with legislatures that were insensitive, if not hostile, to their concerns. Under the Supreme Court's ruling the free exercise clause no longer protects against such eventualities." Even *The Economist* of London, a staunchly conservative journal that usually fawned over Scalia's every word, wrote that *Smith* "has stunned church leaders, both Christian and Jewish. During Prohibition, the large Catholic minority won congressional support for communion wine. Now, apparently, a smaller minority simply takes its lumps."

In short order, a coalition of religious organizations and law professors joined Al Smith and Galen Black in asking the Court to rehear the case and to permit argument and briefing on the issue of "neutral, generally applicable" laws and the Free Exercise Clause. The coalition prepared a "friend of the court" brief designed to convince the justices that deciding the issue without alerting the parties had been a breach of Supreme Court practice. Supreme Court rules, however, don't allow parties to file briefs in connection with petitions for rehearing. The Court turned down the petition in a one-sentence order dated June 4, 1990.

The author of the brief, Douglas Laycock, later published it in the *Journal of Law and Religion*. He argued that the Court's decision was "inconsistent with the original intent, inconsistent with the constitutional text, inconsistent with doctrine under other constitutional clauses, and inconsistent with precedent."

Critics of the decision weren't content to savage it in the newspapers and law reviews. Within months of the decision, an extraordinary coalition of religious organizations and public-interest groups had come together. Their strategy was an audacious one: they would overturn *Smith* in Congress. Legislative revision is common in cases interpreting statutes: the theory is that Congress wrote the statute, and it has the authority to amend it when, in the members' judgment, the Court gets it wrong. *Smith*, however, was a constitutional decision; and short of a constitutional amendment, the Court is supposed to have the final word on interpretation of the Constitution.

However, in the fall of 1991, a coalition of groups began to meet to plan such a legislative override of *Smith*. The group was remarkable for whom its breadth: conservative Christian groups like Pat Robertson's American Center for Law and Justice, the antifeminist Concerned Women for America, and the Southern Baptist Convention sat down with representatives from the American Civil Liberties Union and People For the American Way. But the group was also remarkable for a few omissions. Like Gideon in the Bible, the coalition felt the need to send away some of its potential recruits.

Early in the process, Reuben Snake, a birthright peyotist, prominent Road man, and member of the Winnebago tribe, asked the coalition to adopt as one of its objectives the repeal of *Smith* as it applied to states' power to ban possession and use of sacramental peyote. The answer was that peyote was "controversial." What the religious groups wanted was to restore the "compelling interest" test; if they tried to go beyond that, the fragile coalition would dissolve.

To Snake, this was an ominous reply. The *Smith* court had included six votes to permit Oregon's ban on peyote to stand; five had signed on to Scalia's broad rule, while the sixth, Justice O'Connor, had no trouble in applying the "compelling interest" test and concluding that peyote religion flunked it. A statute that restored the test without mention of peyote might leave the Church still a six-to-three loser, while the "mainstream" religious groups scurried back within the protection of the First Amendment. "They asked the church to basically get their own coalition, get their own law," Walter Echo-hawk recalled later. "We felt snubbed."

With the losers in *Smith* safely in the background, the new religious army marched into battle with a sound of trumpets. Representative Steven Solarz, a liberal New York Democrat, introduced a bill called the Religious Freedom Restoration Act (RFRA). RFRA was the brainchild of Douglas Laycock, the Texas law professor who wrote the amicus brief that was never filed in support of the petition for rehearing.

The act baldly told the Court that it had screwed up. In the "findings" section of the statute, the law said that "in *Employment Division* v. *Smith* . . . the Supreme Court virtually eliminated the requirement that the government justify burdens on religious exercise imposed by laws neutral toward religion." Congress "found" that the Court was wrong: "the compelling interest test . . . is a workable test for striking sensible balances between religious liberty and competing prior governmental interests." Therefore, Congress was now overruling the Court, stepping in "to restore the compelling interest test . . . and to guarantee its application in all cases where free exercise of religion is substantially burdened." From now on, *Smith* wasn't the law: no government, state or federal, could "substantially burden a person's exercise of religion even if the burden results from a rule of general applicability" unless the law passes the "compelling interest" test. And where the old *Sherbert* rule had applied only in a few contexts, RFRA directed the courts to apply it across the board. From now on, the statute provided, the test would apply "to all Federal and State law, and the implementation of that law, whether statutory or otherwise, and whether adopted before or after the enactment of this Act."

The act was based on Congress's power to enforce civil rights under the Fourteenth Amendment. The amendment, one of the Civil War amendments that radically transformed American democracy, forbids states from denying anyone within their borders "the equal protection of the laws." A later section gives Congress "power to enforce, by appropriate legislation, the provisions of this article." This power, the bill's sponsors reasoned, would allow Congress to enact a rule of decision for free-exercise cases that would, by going beyond the minimum protection set by *Smith*, guarantee the integrity of the First Amendment right.

It was a risky strategy, because the Court, during the nineteenth century, had shied away from the prospect of enforcing racial equality and sharply limited the enforcement power. Proponents of the Civil Rights Act of 1964, in fact, had concluded that their best hope of passing a bill that would survive a court challenge lay in grounding the act on the congressional power to regulate "interstate commerce" rather than on the Fourteenth Amendment. The argument made in the Civil Rights Act's legislative history was that discrimination was bad for business—it made traveling, eating in restaurants, buying gasoline, and so on more difficult and dangerous for black Americans. While clearly true, this was a far less noble basis for a civil-rights law than a moral commitment to human equality.

The coalition, meanwhile, was not willing to ground religious freedom on its supposed effect on business. They decided to proceed, reasoning that civil rights were by now so deeply rooted in American law that the Court would not reject a measure that guaranteed a right that most Americans regarded as inviolable.

First, though, they had to produce a bill and get it through both houses of Congress. And despite their best efforts to avoid controversy, the bill nearly foundered on the abortion issue. In 1990 a small group called the Religious Coalition for Abortion Rights had published an article in its newsletter, *Options*. If, as seemed possible, the Supreme Court overturned *Roe* v. *Wade*, the author wrote, then supporters of abortion rights would turn to the Free Exercise Clause. The author cited Roger Williams, the Rhode Island Puritan who first championed separation of church and state, as authority for those who believed that choosing an abortion was a matter of free exercise. "An individual's right to have an abortion is as much a matter of religious liberty as Williams' choice to preach his religion. Abortion is a religious issue because the issue of when the fetus becomes a person is a matter of religious belief."

The argument was somewhat far-fetched, but it spooked parts of the religious community who were committed to a hard-line anti-abortion stand. The National Right to Life Committee, the umbrella anti-abortion group, announced its opposition to the bill; in short order, so did the U.S. Conference of Catholic Bishops. Representative Henry Hyde, the anti-abortion point man in the House, withdrew his sponsorship. At first, the anti-abortion forces said they would drop their opposition only if the bill included language making clear that it did not protect abortion rights. But such an amendment would alienate pro-choice groups, like the ACLU, who supported the bill. When Congress adjourned at the end of 1992, the act died in the House.

It took months of careful persuasion before aides to Senator Edward Kennedy were able to convince the bishops that the bill would be read by courts as neutral on abortion—neither creating a new basis for the right nor revoking any existing one. Even after the anti-abortion forces dropped their opposition, state attorneys general fought to get an amendment that would make it easier to brush aside inmates' religious complaints. But finally, in 1993, the logjam broke. The reintroduced Religious Freedom Restoration Act passed the House of Representatives unanimously on May 11. In the Senate, it received ninety-seven votes to only three against. In November 1993 President Clinton signed the bill.

"Let us respect one another's faiths, fight to the death to preserve the right of every American to practice whatever convictions he or she has, but bring our values back to the table of American discourse to heal our troubled land," the president said at the signing ceremony. At the time, J. Brent Walker, general counsel for the Baptist Joint Committee on Public Affairs, exulted that "the Religious Freedom Restoration Act is the most significant piece of civil rights legislation dealing with our religious liberty in our generation."

Gideon's army, it seemed, had swept the field. But the legislative history of the act contained an interesting reference to peyote religion. In the House report accompanying the bill, the authors wrote,

> In terms of the specific issue addressed in Smith, this bill would not mandate that all states permit the ceremonial use of peyote, but it would subject any such prohibition to the aforesaid balancing test. The courts would then determine whether the State had a compelling governmental interest in outlawing bona fide religious use by the Native American Church and, if so, whether the State had chosen the least restrictive alternative required to advance that interest.

In other words, the drafters were saying, the Smith rule was being overturned—except maybe not for peyotists. O'Connor had found against Smith under the "compelling interest" test. This language in the committee report seemed to hint rather broadly that other courts should do the same.

Oregon did not accept the invitation. At its first meeting after the Smith decision was announced, the Oregon legislature amended Oregon's Controlled Substances Act to exempt from prosecution any defendant who possessed peyote as part of a practice associated with a "good-faith religious belief." The bill was sponsored by State Representative Jim Edmunson (D-Eugene). Al Smith helped Edmunson lobby for passage of the bill. The Oregon attorney general's office took no position for or against the bill.

A year after the passage of the Religious Freedom Restoration Act, Reuben Snake's national crusade bore fruit, with the enactment of a statute protecting religious use of peyote by members of Indian tribes. Sponsored by Senator Daniel Inouye (D-Hawaii), the amendments provide that peyotists who are members of Indian tribes may not be "penalized or discriminated against" by state or federal governments on the basis of "use, possession, or transportation" of peyote "in connection with the practice of a traditional Indian religion." This protection explicitly bars "denial of otherwise applicable benefits under public assistance programs." For the first time in its history, the Native American Church stood on firm statutory ground. The law, however, also gave the federal government the right to decide who could be a member of the Church. Al Smith would be protected by the new law; Galen Black would not.

This would be a happy place to end the story, with the sound of trumpets and the rumble of the walls falling before the Lord's anointed. But real life is often less cheerful. In 1997 the Supreme Court briskly rejected Congress's attempt to tell it how to rule on religious-freedom issues. In a case called *City of Boerne* v. *Flores*, Justice Anthony Kennedy wrote for the majority that "RFRA was designed to control cases and controversies, such as the one before us; but as the provisions of the federal statute here invoked are beyond congressional authority, it is this Court's precedent, not RFRA, which must control." The Fourteenth Amendment enforcement power could not be used to create rights the Courts had not already recognized, he wrote.

If the story were left here, then, it would be almost the mirror image of the one above—Gideon's army routed by the keepers of the temple. But the huge outpouring of criticism that followed *Smith* had an impact on the Court. Finley Peter Dunne's Mr.

Dooley used to say that the Supreme Court follows the election returns. It's also true that even the justices, isolated and imperious as they are, hear from their spiritual advisers. The Court has begun, in its ponderous, impassive way, to back away from *Smith*—without admitting that it is doing any such thing.

The first sign of discomfort came in the case of *Church of the Lukumi Babalu Aye, Inc.* v. *Hialeah*, decided in 1993. The case was a foretaste of the diversity of American religion in the twenty-first century. A group of black Cuban Americans wanted to build a church in Hialeah, Florida. Most cities welcome most churches, but Hialeah was settled by white Cuban Americans, and the church of the Lukumi Babalu Aye was devoted to Santeria, a religion that worships traditional African gods and Catholic saints. Santeria is a kind of Cuban version of voodoo; in its services, spirits of the gods possess ecstatic worshipers, and priests, or *santeros*, sacrifice chickens and other animals. Hialeah didn't want these uncouth intruders carrying out pagan rites within the city limits. The city council quickly passed an ordinance banning the "unnecessary kill[ing], torment, torture, or mutila[tion of] an animal in a public or private ritual or ceremony not for the primary purpose of food consumption."

In his opinion in *Smith*, Justice Scalia had mentioned this case, which was then working its way up through the federal courts. Ruling against Oregon in *Smith* might lead to absurd results, he wrote, such as voiding "animal-cruelty laws" like the Hialeah ordinance. But either Scalia or his clerk hadn't read the case carefully; the Hialeah ordinance wasn't an animal-cruelty law at all, but a law against *ritual sacrifice*. It still allowed citizens to kill animals for meat or for hunting purposes, or even in religious rituals designed to produce kosher meat products. The Hialeah ordinance, in fact, was the closest thing imaginable to Scalia's hypothetical law against bowing down to golden calves.

So *Lukumi* was an easy case, even after *Smith*. But the Court, in an opinion by Justice Kennedy, didn't treat the case as easy. Instead, it went through a laborious parsing of the law, as if laying out for lawyers and judges the way to strike down laws affecting religion, even after *Smith*.

To begin with, Kennedy wrote that "the minimum require- ment of neutrality [for application of the *Smith* rule] is that a law not discriminate on its face." The words must not single out religion. Under this rule, *Lukumi* was an easy case: the ordinance used the words "ritual slaughter," which certainly seemed to sin- gle out religion.

Kennedy refused to accept that, however. He wrote that "[t]he words 'sacrifice' and 'ritual' have a religious origin, but current use admits also of secular meaning." It is hard to imagine a sec- ular "ritual sacrifice," but Kennedy insisted that the statute was ambiguous. So he proceeded to examine the statute's "effect . . . in its real operation" and the political history of its passage. The statute exempted every other form of slaughter—including slaughter of animals for kosher food; the Court concluded that the law's effect was to single out Santeria practice for "discrim- inatory treatment."

Still not satisfied, the opinion ground forward to consider the words of Hialeah's politicians who supported the ordinance. City officials had said that in Cuba "people were put in jail for prac- ticing this religion" and that "the Bible says we are allowed to sacrifice an animal for consumption." All these facts together, Kennedy wrote, meant that "the ordinances are not neutral."

This conclusion should have doomed the ordinance even un- der Scalia's test. But Kennedy pressed on to discuss whether the law was "generally applicable." The law exempted hunting and animal slaughter by small breeders, so Kennedy concluded that the law "pursues the city's governmental interests [in preventing cruelty and safeguarding public health] only against conduct mo- tivated by religious belief."

Having finally concluded that *Smith* did not apply, the Court then applied the *Sherbert* test, which, it said, *Smith* had not "watered down." The Hiahleah law failed both requirements: it did not further a "compelling interest," and its means were not "narrowly tailored" to further the interest it did advance. Thus the law was void.

Kennedy's opinion suggests that *Smith* might not apply in many cases: where laws specifically mention religious practice, for example, or where there are hints of antireligious motives by the legislature or where the law affects religious practice alone. In those cases, *Sherbert* is still the rule.

Lukumi seemed to suggest that the Court had learned something from the reaction to *Smith*. Scalia's tone had been brisk, sweeping. The Court wasn't in the business of weighing and resting laws that impinged on religion, he had said. Now, after *Lukumi*, balancing was back, and the test was so strict that good lawyers would be able to find dozens of ways of arguing that their clients' cases were not covered by the *Smith* rule. Some observers suggested that there might not ever be another *Smith*-style case; the opinion in *Lukumi* offered ways for courts to get out of applying the harsh *Smith* rule to any real factual situation that might arise.

There was another ominous sign for *Smith*. Justice David Souter, who had joined the Court shortly after *Smith* was decided, attacked Scalia's rule in a separate opinion. Souter was named to the Court by President Bush, but he had emerged as an intellectual antagonist of Justice Scalia, far less willing than Scalia to abandon minorities to the vagaries of politics. Now Souter wrote that the Court should "re-examine" the *Smith* rule at the first chance it got. Scalia's distinction between "hybrid" and "pure" free-exercise claims was "ultimately untenable," he wrote.

A year after *Lukumi*, the court again took up the issue of religious "neutrality." *Board of Education of Kiryas Joel Village*

School District v. *Grumet* involved the Satmar sect of Hasidic Jews. The Satmars relate to modernity much like the Old Order Amish of *Yoder*. They dress in distinctive and modest clothing; speak Yiddish as their primary language; shun television, radio, and secular publications; and follow strict sexual segregation outside the home. Under a New York state law allowing incorporation of neighborhood "townships," they had created a self-governing village inhabited solely by Satmars. Within the village of Kiryas Joel, Satmar children attended privately funded religious schools. But Satmar private schools weren't set up for kids who needed special education. At first, these children had attended public special-education classes outside the village. But Satmar parents objected: exposure to secular teachers and students was traumatizing and corrupting their children, they said. Previous Supreme Court cases barred the state from sending special-ed teachers onto the grounds of the religious school, so the New York legislature had formed a special school district that included the village by itself. The new school district provided nonreligious special-education classes in a separate, publicly owned school building.

Now, though, by a six-to-three vote, the Supreme Court voided the special school district. Justice Souter, the critic of *Smith*, wrote the majority opinion: "A state may not delegate its civic authority to a group chosen according to a religious criterion." The legislature had done a favor for the Satmars by passing a special statute. There was "no assurance that the next similarly situated group seeking a school district of its own will receive one."

Kiryas Joel made it harder for lawmakers to accommodate religious groups: such special deals must be narrowly drawn to avoid conflict with the Establishment Clause and must be available to all similarly situated religious minorities.

Kiryas Joel had serious implications for *Smith*'s theory that accommodating religion is best left to the legislatures. If courts defer to a legislature's decision not to offer exemptions, they ought logically to approve a legislature's decision to go ahead and provide them. But *Kiryas Joel* suggested that courts would not give lawmakers much leeway in cutting deals for minority faiths.

Justice Scalia dissented in *Kiryas Joel*, joined by Chief Justice Rehnquist and Justice Thomas. This case, he argued, was simply none of the Court's business: "[I]n the Land of the Free, democratically adopted laws are not so easily impeached by unelected judges." The "mere risk that the State will not offer accommodation to a similar group in the future," he argued, was a pretext. In fact, the majority were power-hungry activists, driven by "*this Court's* inability to control the New York Legislature's future denial of accommodation."

In the wake of *City of Boerne* v. *Flores*, the law of religious freedom remains unsettled. Some in Congress have called for a new law, this time keyed to "interstate commerce." Others, more ominously, have begun to call for a constitutional amendment that would guarantee the "right of the people" (meaning the majority) "to publicly recognize their religious heritage." But ironically, the Native American Church retains its statutory protection because it was not part of RFRA. The stone that the builders rejected has become the cornerstone.

Justice Scalia, too, must also sometimes ponder the ironies of *Smith*. In the years after the decision, the Court seems to have turned away from the direction in which he was leading it in 1990. One commentator noted that the other justices had begun to take notice of Scalia's "intellectual contempt" for them. At the end of the 1995–96 term, National Public Radio's Nina Totenberg, who has covered the Court for nearly two decades, broadcast what almost seemed to be an intellectual epitaph for Scalia: "Whether he is a happy or unhappy warrior is the subject of some debate, but Scalia has been content to write dissenting opinions often only for himself and Justice Clarence Thomas and to win no converts to his often ultra-conservative point of view."

By 1996 Scalia was allowing his bitterness to show. In a much-criticized speech to a prayer breakfast in Mississippi, he cast himself in the role of the lonely religious dissenter ridiculed by a trivial, secular culture. "We are fools for Christ's sake," he said. "We must pray for the courage to endure the scorn of the sophisticated world." And in the wake of Bill Clinton's landslide reelection that year, friends and associates of Scalia even began to hint that the justice would consider a conservative draft as the Republican presidential candidate in the year 2000.

The presidential talk was far-fetched and almost silly; it soon died out. But it underscored the fact that much of Scalia's unhappiness was due to presidential politics. In 1986, when he took office, he and other conservative jurists looked confidently forward to an unbroken string of Republican nominations to the Court, which would solidify right-wing dominance and make coalition-building unnecessary. But in another of history's surprises, two-party politics reemerged, and Bill Clinton, not George Bush, named the next two justices. Now the future of the Court hinged on the results of the 2000 election, and Scalia and his conservative colleagues reached out aggressively to determine that result. On the dramatic Saturday in December 2000 on which the Supreme Court ordered a halt to the counting of votes in Florida, Scalia could not resist a little victory lap. In an unusual statement accompanying the order, Scalia seemed to boast that he had five votes already lined up for his position. That position, by coincidence, would make his George Bush President of the United States.

The plot had twisted: Scalia was no longer Tonto, or even the Lone Ranger. For Bush and the GOP, Scalia and his four conservative colleagues were now the cavalry.

14

SIMPLE GIFTS

By the time *Smith* was decided, Dave Frohnmayer's attention was fully engaged elsewhere. He had decided to run for governor in 1990. Frohnmayer's opponent was Barbara Roberts, the bubbly fifty-three-year-old secretary of state. Roberts came from an even more prominent Oregon political dynasty than Frohnmayer; her husband, Senator Frank Roberts, was a powerhouse in the state legislature. Barbara, his second wife, had been majority leader of the state House of Representatives. She was a warm and charismatic campaigner, with the ability to gain a crowd's trust and sympathy with her bright smile and quick wit.

But in the spring of 1990, most Oregonians who followed politics thought Frohnmayer was uncatchable. He had been raising money for his campaign for more than a year and would end up with nearly $3.5 million, the most ever raised by a candidate for governor. One breakfast fund-raiser alone featuring President George Bush netted $800,000. Frohnmayer's name recognition matched or exceeded Roberts's, and every observer granted him a grasp of state government that neither Roberts nor any other candidate could match.

But things went badly for Frohnmayer that year. For one thing, Oregon voters, like voters in many parts of the country, had been alienated by the presidential election two years earlier, in which George Bush's campaign used hard-edged "attack ads" to defeat Democrat Michael Dukakis. "Read my lips—no new taxes," Bush had promised; but once in office, he had reneged on his promise. Frohnmayer was a friend of Bush's, but the connection wasn't a political plus. Vice President Quayle visited Oregon to endorse a state initiative that would have given parents state vouchers to pay tuition for their children at private schools. Frohnmayer, a strong supporter of public education, pointedly declined to appear with Quayle at a press conference.

Bush, meanwhile, had become mired in the controversy over federal efforts to protect the northern spotted owl in Northwestern forests. When the Environmental Protection Agency designated the owl as an endangered species in June, Oregon's logging industry, already crippled by recession, ground to a virtual standstill. In many parts of the state, families, cities, and whole counties depended on timber jobs and revenue from state timberlands to put food on the table. These communities were angry at Bush and wanted more immediate help than he seemed inclined to offer.

Frohnmayer's worst troubles, though, came from within his own party. Oregon's Republican Party had always been the home of moderates and freethinkers. But the eighties were the decade of Ronald Reagan and the Religious Right; inside the Oregon GOP a faction had appeared that wanted Oregon Republicans to behave more like Republicans in Southern California or South

Carolina. This group had gathered around a far-right organization called the Oregon Citizens Alliance (OCA), which was dedicated to fighting atheism, abortion, and the "homosexual agenda." The OCA had managed to put a strict anti-abortion initiative on the November ballot; they were discomfited by having to share the ballot with Frohnmayer, who had always been outspokenly pro-choice. OCA leaders offered Frohnmayer a deal—their support, or at least their silence, in exchange for dropping his support for abortion rights, a hard-line stand against gay rights, and veto power over his human-services appointments. Dave Frohn-mayer—who had faced down the Rajneeshees—had no hesitation in rejecting this clumsy attempt at extortion. Enraged, the OCA nominated a third-party candidate, Al Mobley, for governor.

After that, the campaign turned into a slow-motion nightmare for Frohnmayer. Before his announcement, he had asked every member of the family whether he should make the run. They had all supported his decision, and he and Lynn believed that the girls' health was stable, for the time being at least. But only a few weeks after his announcement in the fall of 1989, Katie developed pains in her side and back; doctors had to remove her spleen. In June of 1990, while Dave was spending a week's vacation at home with the family, Katie suffered a stroke. It was an unusual symptom for an FA patient. She recovered quickly. But in the back of his mind was the worry about his daughters and the guilt about the time he was taking away from them.

The truth was that, as the race went on, Frohnmayer felt less and less sure that he even wanted to be governor. He enjoyed state government and was confident he could do a good job, but the office he had always truly hankered after was in Washing-ton—U.S. Senator. He had decided to run for governor in 1989 because he and his allies believed the incumbent, Democrat Neil Goldschmidt, wasn't pulling his weight. From the beginning, Frohnmayer had planned for an insurgent campaign against

Goldschmidt. Early in 1990, though, Goldschmidt had suddenly withdrawn from the race. That had left Frohnmayer as the front-runner against Roberts; but his inner edge, his focus, was gone. In politics, when the candidate has lost that, no battery of consultants and aides can supply it.

Looking back, Frohnmayer remembers a campaign that sailed along on its own momentum without being able to adjust to changing events: "We had a lumbering battleship when we needed a PT boat." Week by week his lead over Roberts drained away. His out-of-state ad agency unveiled ads attacking Roberts for her pro-environment stand on the spotted owl; polls showed that instead of helping, the ads hurt Frohnmayer. Voters associated them with Lee Atwater-style smears; in September Frohnmayer fired his ad agency and tried to return to the high ground. Barbara Roberts, with her chipmunk smile and winning personality, was a natural for TV, for mass rallies and fairground grip-and-grins. Frohnmayer, a warm and witty man in private, came across on TV as distant and cerebral. And Mobley, who started out at 2 percent in the polls, expanded his support toward 10 percent as the election drew near.

When the votes were counted, Mobley had siphoned off 130,000 votes statewide; Frohnmayer lost to Barbara Roberts by 67,000 votes.

After his defeat, Frohnmayer's name was floated by Oregon's senators, Mark Hatfield and Bob Packwood, as a possible appointee to the U.S. Court of Appeals for the Ninth Circuit. Frohnmayer would have made a superb judge. He was smart, learned, and a gifted writer; he had the willingness to listen seriously to arguments on both sides of an issue before making up his mind. But, like his campaign, Dave Frohnmayer's nomination fell victim to the increased polarization of the Republican Party. Some in the Bush White House had never forgiven his snub of Vice President Quayle; others were repulsed because his brother

John, the head of the National Endowment for the Arts, had become a favorite target of the party's right wing. In the end, the Ninth Circuit vacancy went to Andrew Kleinfeld, a federal district judge in Alaska who better fit the emerging Bush mold. No match for Frohnmayer in intellect (his nomination received the largest number of "not qualified" votes from the American Bar Association rating committee of any of that year's nominees), Kleinfeld had represented Alaska Right to Life and had argued a lawsuit seeking to ban "homosexual recruitment literature" from local school libraries.

As Katie recovered from her stroke, doctors began to treat her with intravenous injections of gamma globulin. The improvement was so dramatic that Dave and Lynn began to let themselves hope that this might be the "magic bullet" they had hoped for. In the summer of 1991, Dave and Lynn took the entire family for a family vacation in central Utah. Dave remembers taking Katie to the top of a ski lift so she could see the magnificent view of the mountains in summer. But she began to gasp for air; he had to take her back down hurriedly. A few days later, as Dave and Lynn were sleeping in their motel room, Kirsten rushed to their door in panic. Katie had fallen again and could move only one side of her body.

Hearts pounding, the Frohnmayers raced in their family car across fifty miles of central Utah, following an ambulance in which emergency medical technicians were giving Katie oxygen. When they reached a small community hospital, she was lying almost motionless, unable to speak. The doctors there summoned the medical evacuation helicopter to take her to Primary Children's Medical Center in Salt Lake City. When the Frohnmayers saw their daughter in intensive care, she still could not move her right side or speak. "She was trapped inside, but she could blink and she could smile, and so you knew that you were being heard and understood," Dave recalled later. "We kept looking for signs of improvement, didn't find them."

After nearly a month in the Salt Lake City hospital, Katie flew back to Eugene in an air ambulance. On September 26, 1991, Katie Frohnmayer died at a hospital in Eugene. She was twelve. Her sister Kirsten had entered Stanford a few weeks earlier.

After Katie's death, Dave Frohnmayer left politics. At the end of 1991, he resigned as Oregon's attorney general to become dean of the University of Oregon School of Law. In June 1994 he was named interim president of the university.

In January 1995 Frohnmayer led a delegation of boosters and fans to Pasadena to cheer Oregon's Ducks in their first Rose Bowl appearance in thirty-seven years. A few days after the New Year's Day game, Kirsten Frohnmayer noticed a bruise she could not account for. Without telling her parents, she got a blood test; the counts suggested leukemia, which often accompanies Fanconi anemia and is usually fatal. In February 1995, at the University of Minnesota, she received a bone-marrow transplant from an unrelated donor. The transplant, considered a long shot, went well, and the new marrow took hold without complications. But surgeons at the hospital accidentally connected a catheter to her carotid artery instead of a vein. When the catheter was removed in April 1995, Kirsten suffered a small stroke. She recovered enough to attend her graduation from Stanford University, where she received an honors degree in human biology and was awarded membership in Phi Beta Kappa. But in August 1995 her leukemia unexpectedly recurred and she returned to Minneapolis for chemotherapy.

Treatment brought the leukemia into remission. Then Kirsten and Lynn Frohnmayer traveled to Milan, Italy, where she was treated with cells from the bone-marrow donor that had been genetically altered by an experimental process not yet approved in the United States. Her remission ended in April 1996, and she was readmitted to the hospital in Minneapolis with a recurrence of leukemia. On June 20, 1997, Kirsten Frohnmayer died of Fanconi complications at Sacred Heart Medical Center in Eugene.

In the telling, it seems like a story of inevitable decline. But at the time—and to the Frohnmayers, even now—there was nothing inevitable about Kirsten's death. Each moment of the last two years of her life seemed to oscillate between improbable hope and black despair. The unrelated-donor transplant should not have worked—but it did. But then the inexplicable mistake with the catheter threatened her life and led to a stroke. She regained her speech and movement faster than the doctors believed she could, but then they found spots on her brain they believed to be a fungal infection. When that scare proved to be unfounded, the leukemia returned. In Italy genetically altered T-cells promised a complete remission from the leukemia. But X rays suggested an aspergillis infection of the lungs; for six agonizing weeks they waited while doctors treated it with antibiotics before going ahead with the T-cells. The leukemia cleared up again.

In 1994, meanwhile, doctors at the National Institutes of Health had been preparing for human trials of a gene-replacement therapy they hoped would literally end FA by substituting a proper gene for the defective one Kirsten had inherited. Kirsten might have been the first human being to undergo the treatment—but at the last minute, an NIH committee raised questions about safety. The Frohnmayers fumed while the scientists debated. To them, as to parents of all dying children, the safety debate was literally insane. FA patients were dying, all of them, sooner rather than later. Any risk seemed worth it if it held out hope.

But by the time the gene therapy was ready for human trials,

Kirsten had developed leukemia and was ineligible. The human trials did not produce a cure; but still, even afterward, Dave and Lynn Frohnmayer can't help wondering whether the results might not have been better for Kirsten, whether they might not have bought her another year or two or five while research on a cure went on.

Almost to the end, Kirsten fought the disease with the bitter intensity of a young woman who planned to do great things with her life. She wanted to go to law school; she had a college boyfriend (the family called him "little Dave," because he had the same name as the father she adored), and they had plans. Not until two days before her death did she speak the unspeakable: it wasn't going to work. Even then, Lynn was holding on to hope. They had missed death by inches so many times that the laws of probability no longer held much meaning for her. (Not long before, a sober-faced physician had warned Dave and Lynn that Kirsten's odds of survival were about 1 percent; he was astonished when they both began laughing—1 percent seemed like so much more than they had dared hope for.)

No, Kirsten told her, it wasn't going to happen. "And I'm not sad about that," she told her mother. "It's been a happy life: great friends, great boyfriend, great family, great experiences. Look what I got to do." Even now, at the end of a lifetime of only two dozen years, she could not think of anyone else she would trade places with.

Kirsten's memorial service was held in the auditorium of South Eugene High School, where she had been student-body president. A family friend read aloud a letter to Kirsten written by her parents, and the Frohnmayer Family Singers performed the ageless Shaker hymn, "Simple Gifts":

> 'Tis a gift to be simple,
> 'Tis a gift to be free,

'Tis a gift to come down where you ought to be.
When you find yourself in a place that's right,
You will dwell in the valley of peace and delight.

The liturgy of the celebration was, behind the scenes, the subject of careful negotiation. There was little mention of God. Neither Lynn nor Dave has turned to any form of religion for comfort. Both were raised in churchgoing families: Dave's parents were Presbyterian, Lynn's Methodist. Several times during the girls' illness they had remarked on the kindness of hospital chaplains and other clergy who had helped them, but they felt no pull of conversion.

When Katie died in 1990, they asked the pastor of Dave's parents' church to open the memorial service. But they gave him strict instructions: he was not to claim or imply that Katie's death was in some way willed or approved by God—or even that it was somehow all right that fate had taken their beautiful daughter, tormented her, and killed her. "It's not a time of comfort," Dave said later. "It's an occasion of deep anger that this thing should be visited upon our child. If there is a God, why should this happen?"

Amy Frohnmayer has shown no gross symptoms of Fanconi anemia, but doctors have begun administering medicine to respond to a decrease in the number of healthy blood cells her marrow is producing. In 1995 Lynn Frohnmayer told a reporter that "I asked Amy the other day if she wanted to ask me any questions. She said, 'Why do I have to have it?' That's the one thing I can't answer."

In August 1996 Galen Black moved back to Coos Bay, Oregon. On August 19 his daughter, Tamara, gave birth to his first grandchild, Zachary. Black found work on construction jobs in the area. In June 1997 he suffered a major heart attack. Two months later Galen Black underwent balloon angioplasty at Sacred Heart Medical Center in Eugene. His condition is stable, though he is unable to work; he receives disability-insurance payments.

Galen remains puzzled at how the struggle he set off has been transformed over the years into something that he never foresaw and that has little to do with him. The story, he insists to an interviewer, is that of a dispute over how to treat Native American alcoholics. He was fired for doing his job. Even today the state of Oregon does not offer peyote religion as a therapy for alcohol and drug abuse among its Native people. Sweathouse Lodge has closed, and nothing has taken its place. Galen is agonized that the real story, as he sees it, is yet to be told.

These days he takes care of his health, tends to his grandchildren, and gets out into the hills around Coos Bay whenever he can to pan for gold. There is no fortune to be found there, but Galen and the other hobby miners of the Oregon coast pursue gold as a way of remembering the history of the area, the fever that brought white settlers there and that has produced the odd, rootless culture of the miner, the trapper, and the cowboy. With his gaunt cheeks and graying beard, in fact, Galen Black looks like a gold miner in an old photograph. Like Al Smith, he has become a part of the history of the West.

After leaving ADAPT, John Gardin married his childhood sweetheart and began a private psychological practice in Laguna Beach, California. Not long afterward, he realized that his self-diagnosis as a recovering alcoholic had been based on the quasi-religious atmosphere of ADAPT. He began drinking socially again and has experienced no problems with it.

Gardin's psychological practice broke up in a dispute between him and a partner; the resulting losses forced him into bankruptcy. In September of 1991, he was diagnosed with cancer of the kidney and underwent surgery. The surgery has apparently succeeded; Gardin today practices on a more modest scale, including consulting for the MTV series *The Real World*. Since leaving ADAPT, he said, "I've done a lot of my own research, and the reality is that there are a lot of people with alcohol and drug problems who recover in all sorts of different ways, not just abstinence." Having played a central role in starting the dispute that led to *Smith*, Gardin had lost sight of the case. When a caller reached him in 1995, he asked, "Whatever happened with that case?"

After his dismissal from ADAPT, Al Smith and his family moved to Eugene. Perhaps because of the controversy surrounding the case, Al never again found full-time work in the field in which he had spent his life, alcoholism and drug treatment. Though he was able to do some consulting work, he ended up taking a job with Goodwill Industries, attending a collection station where people dropped off donations of used clothing, appliances, and furniture. As their two children grew, Jane Farrell-Smith entered graduate school at the University of Oregon, where she got a master's degree in special education in 1992. After her graduation, she took up full-time work in the field; today she follows a career not all that different from the one that Lynn Frohnmayer had begun in the years before her children became sick.

Meanwhile, Al Smith retired shortly before the case was decided. He was seventy years old, and he had two children to care for—driving, shopping, cleaning, attending soccer games and teacher conferences. With the entry of judgment, he took up a place in American constitutional history. On the whole, it is a position he is comfortable with—as a warrior who lost his last battle but never give up the fight.

When he lay awake wondering whether to go on alone, he had been afraid that someday his children would be ashamed of him. They are not. In the spring of 1994, his daughter Kaila participated with the rest of her class at Roosevelt Middle School in

the annual "Cultural Heritage Fair." At the fair, each child pre-
pares a poster exhibition on some aspect of his or her family
history and ethnic heritage. Kaila's was an account of the *Smith*
case, illustrated by newspaper clippings and, most prominently,
by Al Smith himself, who sat proudly in front of a photograph
of himself.

With his striking Native features and his air of calm dignity,
Smith had the look of an icon from American history, incongru-
ously transplanted into a school gymnasium as he acknowledged
greetings and answered questions. He recalled later that although
the organized peyotist community remains somewhat aloof from
him after the case, he often encounters support from ordinary
Native people at Sun Dances and powwows.

> Native people who work on a national level dress different. They
> travel a lot, they stay in motels, drive rent-a-cars, and I am fa-
> miliar with that because I used to do that, too. People who don't
> do that stuff wear sweatshirts and ball caps and tennis shoes,
> Levis. Don't wear any jewelry. So there is a difference there, you
> know, of people that go to these meetings all the time and meet
> with other people at the national level and people that don't. So,
> I have experienced both of them. The people that are meeting
> in Washington and around the states all the time I had very little
> contact with. I had more contact with people who are street
> people like us who would say, "Hey, Al, you did a good thing.
> Thanks a lot." Things from that level . . . It is ten years down the
> line now and I'm saying ten years later, "Well, I didn't do any-
> thing." They say, "Yeah, you did."

Al Smith turned eighty in November 1999. He was the guest
of honor at a traditional Indian meal attended by nearly two
hundred people at the Longhouse, the Native cultural center at

the University of Oregon in Eugene. The menu included venison, elk, turkey, salmon, and bear; it concluded with a chocolate cake inscribed, HAPPY BIRTHDAY, RED COYOTE!

Al's first wife, Dorleen, was there, and so were five of his six children: Mark, Maureen, Matthew, David, Marisha, Kaila, and Lalek. (One daughter, Josette, lives in North Dakota.) It was, Jane Farrell-Smith marveled, the first time all of them had been in one place at the same time. The feast included a "talking circle" at which each celebrant spoke briefly of what Al Smith had meant to him or her—as father, friend, alcohol counselor, and role model, or warrior for peyote religion. Earlier that day, Al had saluted Jane, Kaila, and Lalek. "They're what I call my intact family," he said. "I think I'm settling in."

In April 2000 Al was the guest of honor at a different gathering. It was a meeting of the South Coast chapter of the Native American Church—organized officially only after the Oregon legislature had made peyote religion legal in Oregon. Jane Farrell-Smith was the meeting's "sponsor"—she had asked the Road man to hold the meeting and paid the expenses for the sacrament. There was no formal invitation list; in the manner of social life in much of the Native world, the word had simply been sent out that there was a meeting for Al Smith and that those who ought to attend were expected to be there.

The meeting began about nine P.M. The congregation gathered around the twenty-five-foot-tall tipi, bundled up against the spring chill, while inside Jane and the officials of the congregation discussed the point of the meeting and asked the Road man to pray for Al and his family. Then the flap was opened, and the guests gathered in a circle for the all-night vigil by the fire.

The glowing logs burned in the center of the tipi; behind them, its back to the Road man, was a slightly raised bank of earth, carefully sculpted in the shape of a crescent moon, its ends pointing east toward the opening in the tipi. At its center, in front of the Road man, sat Grandfather Peyote himself, a small living peyote plant to whom the Road man's prayers would be addressed. Around the fire sat nearly three dozen people, young and old, male and female, Native and white. Some were close friends of Al's; others knew of him only from afar. Some were lifelong peyotists; for others, it was their first step along the Peyote Road.

At the outset, the Road man passed a bag of rolling tobacco and corn-husk wrappers. Each celebrant made a prayer cigarette to carry prayers to heaven. When the Road man gave permission to light up, the tipi was full of whispered intercessions to Grandfather—for healing of the sick, for long life for the young and old, for courage for the weak, for deliverance for prisoners and addicts. The smoke rose and vanished into the darkness at the top of the tipi.

The Road man passed the medicine: dried peyote buttons, soaked in water and ground into mush; green buttons, kept moist since they were picked in the peyote fields a thousand miles away; and tea made of dried peyote buttons.

The peyote was bitter, but not harsh. It tasted of earth.

Then the singing began. Each singer in turn accepted the eagle staff; the Drummer took a place next to him or her; and the singer would recite four peyote songs to the beat of the water drum. Some songs were in Native languages; some were in Spanish. *"Abuelito, peyotito, ayudenos esta noche,"* went one—Little Grandfather, little peyote, help us tonight. One singer, an Anglo from California, gave a lovely rendition of "Mockingbird," to the four/eight beat of the water drum.

At midnight, when the staff had passed around the circle, the Road man sent the group out for a fifteen-minute break, the only official recess of the all-night ceremony. Whites and Natives alike complained of back pain or of distended bladders. They stretched their arms and legs as they stumbled, in the inky mountain night, toward two portable toilets mounted on a flatbed truck.

After the break, peyote circled the tent again. The Road man talked about the sacrament. He called peyote a warrior, sent from "the green nation" of the plant world to help save humankind from extinction. He noted that here, in the South Coast chapter, whites were welcome if they sought sincerely to learn peyote's wisdom. At other meetings only Natives were allowed. Some pey-otists had criticized this meeting and its leaders for allowing whites to come, he noted. But this was their way, the way they had learned from Stanley Smart before he passed into the shadows. He remembered Stanley's funeral, when the Paiute Road man's body had been carried into the tent and lain before the altar during all-night singing and drumming designed to guide his soul into the spirit world. He warned everyone that peyote religion did not need advertising or publicity; they should be very careful what they said about the meeting to people who did not understand. Then he asked all those present, young and old, to pray and work against the dark forces that bear so many Indian people down—alcohol, drugs, violence, diabetes, cancer. Peyote came from the green nation to help us fight these enemies, he said, but Grandfather could not do it by himself.

The staff passed from hand to hand as old friends talked about Al Smith. First was Jane, who remembered the dark days when NARF was pressing him to acquiesce in the settlement it brokered, and strange voices on the telephone would threaten or cajole or beg him "not to take our medicine away." She told his children yet again how their father had stood fast and how Stanley Smart had been the one Indian elder to counsel him to take the case to the white man's altar of justice and determine once and for all whether the Constitution was big enough to include peyote as well as bread and wine. Then she spoke of her wishes for long life for her husband.

Al Smith that night still seemed strong as a tree, with the vigor of a man many decades younger. But in the ninth decade of life, he knew he was close to the spirit world. He had once worried that no one would know him when he arrived there. One by one, the other speakers told him that he had written his name there now. The longtime peyotists thanked him for his fight for their religion; had he not fought and lost before the Court, they noted, they would not have a statute to protect peyote, both in Oregon and around the nation.

One speaker told of his vision of Al Smith as a culture hero. Such a hero is not a warrior who goes forth seeking enemies to kill. A real hero, said the speaker, is one who seeks only to make life—to nurture a family, to pass on knowledge to those who will come after. But when the battle comes uninvited to his doorstep, the hero does not turn away. Others may warn him that he cannot win or that he should not win or that he is too unimportant to fight the giant with only his five smooth stones. But the hero knows that no good comes from running away. He calls for water to wash his face, then stands to fight.

Throughout it all, Al Smith sat placidly. In a special concession to his status as an elder, he sat in a low metal lawn chair, with armrests and support for his back. On either side of him were his two youngest children, Kaila and Lalek, and across from him was his adult son Matthew. They were seeing the ritual for the first time.

Also seeing the sacred fire for the first time was a writer, an Anglo born in the East who had spent five years writing about *Employment Division* v. *Smith*. Now he was sitting where Galen Black had sat at the beginning of the story, gazing "into the bare facts of me." He ate sparingly of the sacrament; after all this

time, it would not have done to greet Grandfather by vomiting.
But he did eat, and in a quiet way, peyote spoke to him that
night. At first the message was banal. *You're getting older*, it said;
you need to pay attention to your lower back. But then the pain
passed—thanks in part to peyote and in part to ibuprofen—and he
began to look within himself, at what had drawn him to the story
of the *Smith* case. Writing teachers often advise their students to
write what they know. But few writers follow this advice. Instead,
their concerns come from the empty places in their souls, as they
pursue in the work what they cannot find on their own. Those who
struggle with morals write of ethics; those who wrestle with fear
depict bravery. For more than twenty years, the writer saw in the
fire, he had written about faith. Inside himself he found only a genial skepticism about ultimate reality. He envied those who heard
God's voice clearly, whether in the burning bush or only in the still,
small voice. He had written about radicals, who see the world
moving toward political redemption; about scientists, who believe
that curiosity and method will unfold the secrets of existence; and
about fundamentalist Christians who speak directly to the Lord of
Hosts. He had walked on many roads to Damascus; nothing
stirred inside him but admiration for those who felt what he could
not. He admired the people around him in the tent, with their belief that the green nation took an interest in human affairs. He was
not the man to ask where God was to be found; but he thought
that if he had ever been near the Creator, he was near Him in
that tipi.

He admired, too, Dave Frohnmayer, with his faith in law, reason, and deliberation; but he saw in the story of *Smith* a cruelty in
the law that matched the cruelty of fate to the Frohnmayers' three
daughters. If there was a plan in the illness of Katie, Kirsten, and
Amy, it was a malign one; as malign as the plan of a great and powerful judge who had seen the *Smith* case not as a dispute between

real people but as a chance to play with the law, to take away part of our heritage of religious freedom.

Then those unhappy thoughts quieted. The writer saw images in the fire. These were not hallucinations, but the kind of images he had seen before in desert mirages outside Antelope or in storm clouds over the Pacific off Coos Head. They were faces and scenes he had seen over the past half decade as he pursued the story that courts and judges were too busy and too important to understand.

Finally he saw a scene from that very morning, April 1. Before setting out for the meeting, the writer had stopped by McMorran House, the Tudor-style mansion that serves as the official residence of Dave Frohnmayer, president of the University of Oregon. Though Frohnmayer kept up a bruising schedule of meetings and speeches, he was observing his Saturday ritual by cooking breakfast for the family.

The writer had stopped by to check a few factual points. As bacon crisped, Frohnmayer insisted that his hair was not red, nor reddish, not even reddish-brown. Brown and gray, he insisted, whatever the reporter's eyes might tell him. Amy Frohnmayer, thirteen years old, and her brother, Jon, fifteen, gathered for breakfast as their father held forth to the writer. Also at the table were Lynn and a young cousin, Paul Frohnmayer, from Germany, whom the Frohnmayers had met on a recent trip to the family home in Bavaria and pressed into coming to Eugene for his junior year at South Eugene High.

Serving out the eggs and maple bars, Frohnmayer next insisted on another factual point. He had not met Lynn for the first time after Otto told him to call her in Washington, he said. In fact, they had met years before, when Dave had driven to California with his brother John, who was giving her a ride back to Stanford. He remembered her vividly, he said, the beautiful blonde in the backseat; he had wanted to sit in back and talk with her but had lacked the nerve.

At once the table broke into derisive hoots, orchestrated by Lynn. "You ignored me, David," she said, and the children agreed, although, as with all good family stories, it had happened before they were born. In that moment, Dave was to all of them what Dad so often is for many happy American families—a lovable, good-hearted dolt, amiably clueless, as central and as comic as the family dog.

The ease with which the family laughed at Dave was remarkable, not just because to the world outside he is such a formidable figure but also because he had so nearly left them only a short time before. On October 22, 1999, Frohnmayer had attended a meeting of a citizens' advisory panel at the campus of the National Institutes of Health in Bethesda, Maryland. He was discussing the prospects for human-genome research when he suddenly fell silent and tumbled to the floor. He had suffered a full cardiac arrest and would have died almost at once had he not been in a conference room full of doctors and nurses.

Two of them gave Dave cardiopulmonary resuscitation while an emergency medical team rushed over from nearby Suburban Hospital. The technicians used electric-shock paddles in an attempt to restart his heart. They administered seven separate shocks; his heart remained inert. After rushing him to the emergency room, doctors tried again. It took another thirteen shocks before his heart began to beat feebly on its own.

Lynn Frohnmayer was in Eugene when word came of Dave's crisis. The doctors warned her that he would probably never regain consciousness. Such a prolonged arrest would almost surely cause brain damage. He might die within hours or linger for months in a vegetative state.

But by the time Lynn reached Suburban Hospital the next day, Dave was conscious, if somewhat confused. Because he was being kept alive by a respirator, he was unable to speak. But soon he scrawled a note: "When can I talk again?" (His former staff members joked that the second line of the note read, "I have three major points to emphasize.")

Dave recalled nothing of his near-death experience. He had simply faded out during his remarks to the conference and then come to on a table, surrounded by figures in green masks. *This can't be happening*, was his first conscious thought. *We haven't found a cure for Amy yet.*

Within a week, Dave was breathing on his own and hoarsely lecturing anyone who would listen on recent federalism cases before the U.S. Supreme Court. Medical tests showed that Frohnmayer's arteries were clear. His "heart attack" had been caused by a sudden arrhythmia—a mysterious scrambling of the electrical signals that maintain heart rhythm. There was no clear cause, but Lynn and the doctors made clear to Dave that his days of coffee, Scotch, and cheap cigars were over. He had always been a weekend athlete; from now on he would walk two miles a day, cut out caffeine, and be careful what he ate. A week after his collapse, doctors implanted an electronic defibrillator in his chest—a computerized device that would administer electric shock to restart his heart if arrhythmia struck again.

Since then, Frohnmayer had shown no signs of another attack. He seemed unscathed by his brush with death, perhaps because, like Al Smith, he lived each day in the suburbs of the spirit world.

The writer looked around the table at the laughing faces—Lynn Frohnmayer, who had grown up with a father teetering on the edge of death, who had feared above all else when young that she would allow a child to die and had then lost her two daughters, two friends and companions, to slow, inexorable death; Amy Frohnmayer, who carried in her blood the same destructive cells that had carried off her two beloved sisters, who had nearly lost her father, one of the centers of her world, to death, but who spent her days learning slide-dance steps and mastering Vivaldi on the violin; Jon Frohnmayer, whose parents worried with him over his upcoming SATs; Paul, who had come from Germany into the life of a family like few others.

Before his latest brush with death, Frohnmayer had reflected that his family's long ordeal had given him—the striver, the Rhodes scholar, the master of preparation and deferred gratification—the simple gift of enjoying each good day as it passed. "The passage from Matthew says, Sufficient unto the day is the evil thereof," he said. "If you're working as hard as you can, and listening to as many people who are smarter and are working harder than you are, then at least you're trying to do something. Maybe there is something redemptive about that. You can get small pleasures out of the things that you do in life. You can say, 'Yeah, the cure will come for Amy. It's going to be different for her.' There may be a huge dose of denial in that. That's functional denial."

The laughing vision faded from the fire, and the writer was back in the tipi as a weary night wore toward dawn. He looked up and saw Al Smith on his lawn-chair throne, his two youngest children gazing up at him with pride, and next to them, Jane Farrell-Smith, his wife and companion of more than two decades.

As the drums continued and the sparks flew upward, the writer thought—whether he or peyote thought it he did not know—that Tolstoy was wrong when he wrote that happy families are all alike but that each unhappy family was unhappy in its own way. Unhappiness is boring and banal—what is there to say about pride and ego and anger? Happiness is found, if at all, in a different way by everyone who seeks it. And yet these two families, so different in so many ways, had one thing in common. Each was a band of pilgrims, people who though thrown close together could have remained strangers but had instead joined hands and started together across the valley of the shadow.

A NOTE ON SOURCES

Those seeking extensive documentation should consult my article on *Smith* in the *Arizona State Law Journal*, vol. 30, no. 4, pp. 953–1022 (Winter 1998).

The most important sources for this book were the numerous interviews I conducted with the protagonists: Al Smith, Jane Farrell-Smith, Dave Frohnmayer, Lynn Frohnmayer, and Galen Black. Among the lawyers and staff who worked on the case, I was able to interview David Morrison, Eldon Caley, Bill Gary, Jerome Lidz, Rives Kistler, Virginia Linder, Sande Schmidt, John Echo-hawk, Walter Echo-hawk, Steven Moore, Allen Johnson, and Craig Dorsay. At ADAPT, I interviewed John Gardin and Bruce Piper. The Smith family also kindly made available a comercially prepared family history: Russell Duke, *Some Family Information on Alfred Leo Smith* (October 23, 1991). They further tried to explain to me the basics of many Native ceremonies that I have not seen myself; needless to say, they are not responsible for any culture-bound errors that remain.

The best single written source on the Klamath people is Theodore Stern, *The Klamath Tribe: A People and Their Reservation* (Seattle: University of Washington Press, 1966). For historical background on Klamath-Modoc relations and the Modoc War, I have relied on Arthur Quinn, *Hell with the Fire Out: A History of the Modoc War* (Boston: Faber & Faber, 1997), a well-written narrative history. A sensitive evocation of the landscape in the Klamath country is David Rains Wallace, *The Klamath Knot* (San Francisco: The Sierra Club, 1983). General information on Oregon history can be found in Carlos A. Schwantes, *The Pacific Northwest: An Interpretive History*, 2d ed. (Lincoln: University of Nebraska Press, 1996). The historical geography of Oregon is a rich subject. I have relied heavily on W. F. Loy et al., *Atlas of Oregon* (Eugene: University of Oregon, 1976), and Samuel F. Dicken and Emily Dicken, *Two Centuries of Oregon Geography*, 2 vols. (Portland: Oregon Historical Society, 1979 and 1982). On the Stewart and Chemawa Indian schools, see Margaret Connell Szasz, *Education and the American Indian: The Road to Self-Determination Since 1928* (Albuquerque: University of New Mexico, 1977).

Otto Frohnmayer's career was reviewed in an excellent oral history interview on file at the Southern Oregon Historical Society in Medford, Oregon. Perhaps fittingly, the most accessible source on Fanconi anemia is by the Frohnmayers themselves: David and Lynn Frohnmayer, *Fanconi Anemia: A Handbook for Families and Their Physicians*, 3d ed. (Eugene: Fanconi Anemia Research Fund, 2000), available free of charge from FARF, 1800 Willamette St., Suite 200, Eugene, OR 97401 or on the World Wide Web at http://fanconi.org.

Very little has been written about Edison Chiloquin's lonely struggle. The best sources I have found were newspaper accounts:

Sue Hobart, "Chiloquins Strive to Restore Former Reservation," *The Oregonian,* December 15, 1974, p. C11, and "Indian, U.S. Seek Way to Set Up 'Living Village,' " *The Oregonian,* May 7, 1975, p. A15; Roberta Ulrich, "Ed Chiloquin Told Them Not to Sell," *The Oregonian,* December 13, 1993, p. A10; Dick Johnston, "For Remaining Tribal Lands, Klamaths Offered $130.54 Million," *The Oregonian,* February 8, 1980, p. A1; Paul Manley, "Klamath Indians Weigh Voting for Tribal Status," *The Oregonian,* July 18, 1984, p. C4.

The two most important texts on peyotism are Omer C. Stewart, *Peyote Religion: A History* (Norman: University of Oklahoma Press, 1987), and Edward F. Anderson, *Peyote: The Divine Cactus,* 2d ed. (Tucson: University of Arizona Press, 1996).

For background information on the Indian movement of the 1960s and afterward, see Vine Deloria Jr., *Behind the Trail of Broken Treaties: An Indian Declaration of Independence* (Austin: University of Texas Press, 1985); Paul Chaat Smith and Robert Allen Warrier, *Like a Hurricane: The Indian Movement from Alcatraz to Wounded Knee* (New York: New Press, 1996). A useful discussion of Native alcoholism is Michael Dorris, *The Broken Cord* (New York: HarperPerennial, 1990). Standard works on Native religion include Ake Hultkrantz, translated by Monica Setterwall, *The Religions of the American Indians* (Berkeley: University of California Press, 1979), Ake Hultkrantz, edited by Christopher Vecsey, *The Study of Native American Religion,* (New York: Crossroad, 1983): American Academy of Religion, *Studies in Religion no. 29.*

The literature on Rajneeshpuram is vast. I have found particularly helpful the ongoing coverage of *The Oregonian* and the following books: Lewis F. Carter, *Charisma and Control in Rajneeshpuram: The Role of Shared Values in the Creation of a Community* (Cambridge, England: Cambridge University Press, 1990); Frances FitzGerald, "Rajneeshpuram," in *Cities on a Hill: A Journey Through Contemporary American Cultures* (New York: Simon & Schuster, 1986); James S. Gordon, *The Golden Guru:*

The Strange Journey of Bhagwan Shree Rajneesh (Lexington, Mass.: Stephen Greene Press, 1987); Win McCormack, ed., *The Rajneesh Chronicles* (Portland: New Oregon Publishing, 1987); Hugh Milne, edited by Liz Hodgkinson, *Bhagwan: The God That Failed* (London: Caliban Books, 1986).

For general background on alcoholism and drug-abuse treatment, I have relied on Marc A. Schuckit, *Drug and Alcohol Abuse: A Clinical Guide to Diagnosis and Treatment* (New York: Plenum Press, 1995). The basic text of AA is Bill W., *Alcoholics Anonymous: The Story of How Many Thousands of Men and Women Have Recovered from Alcoholism*, 3d ed. (New York: Alcoholics Anonymous World Services, 1976). A more up-to-date insider's account of AA is Nan Robertson, *Getting Better: Inside Alcoholics Anonymous* (New York: William Morrow, 1988). A summary of the knowledge about controlled drinking at about the time of the controversy at ADAPT can be found in Nick Heather and Ian Robertson, *Controlled Drinking* (London: Methuen, 1981). The original RAND report is David J. Armor, J. Michael Polic, and Harriet B. Stambul, *Alcoholism and Treatment* (New York: Wiley, 1978). The key source for the Sobells' research at the time is Mark B. Sobell and Linda C. Sobell, *Behavioral Treatment of Alcohol Problems: Individualized Therapy and Controlled Drinking* (New York: Plenum Press, 1978). The article attacking the Sobells' research is Mary Lou Pendery, Irving Maltzman, and John West, "Controlled Drinking by Alcoholics?: New Findings and a Reevaluation of a Major Affirmative Study," *Science*, vol. 217, pp. 169–75 (1982). An account of the anti–controlled drinking case by one of the authors of the *Science* article is found in Irving Maltzman, "The Winter of Scholarly Science Magazines," *Professional Counselor* (October 1992), and in numerous other papers by the same author. Useful information can be found in Ron Roizen, "Comment on the 'RAND Report,'" *Journal of Studies on Alcohol*, vol. 38, pp. 170–78

(1977). A helpful summary by the same author is "The Great Controlled-Drinking Controversy," in Marc Galanter, ed., *Recent Developments in Alcoholism*, vol. 5 (New York: Plenum, 1987), pp. 245–79. A summary of the history of abstinence, written by a supporter of controlled-drinking research, is found in Stanton Peele, "Abstinence," in J. Jaffe, ed., *Encyclopedia of Drugs and Alcohol* (New York: Macmillan, 1991, 1993), pp. 92–97. Another discussion by the same author is "The New Prohibitionists: Our Attitudes Toward Alcoholism Are Doing More Harm than Good," *The Sciences* (New York Academy of Sciences), March/April 1984, pp. 14–19. A good summary of the growth of the Temperance Movement and its religious aspects can be found in Sydney Ahlstrom, *A Religious History of the American People* (New Haven: Yale University Press, 1974), pp. 425–27, and in Mark A. Noll, *A History of Christianity in the United States and Canada* (Grand Rapids: Eerdmans, 1992), pp. 295–98.

The basic source on the framing of the Oregon constitution is Charles Henry Carey, ed., *The Oregon Constitution and Proceedings and Debates of the Constitutional Convention* (Salem: Oregon State Printing Dept., 1926). A narrative history placing the Oregon convention in its Western context is David Alan Johnson, *Founding the Far West: California, Oregon, and Nevada, 1840–1890* (Berkeley: University of California Press, 1992). Information on Hans Linde can be found in Ronald K. L. Collins, "Hans Linde and His 1984 Judicial Election: The Primary," *Oregon Law Review*, vol. 70 (1991), p. 747. A very useful collection of essays is Robert F. Nagel, ed., *Intellect and Craft: The Contributions of Justice Hans Linde to American Constitutionalism* (Boulder, Colo.: Westview Press, 1995).

Good sketches of both the Seventh-Day Adventist faith and of Jehovah's Witnesses are to be found in Paul K. Conkin, *American Originals: Homemade Varieties of Christianity* (Chapel Hill: University of North Carolina Press, 1997).

NOTES

PAGE 9
". . . he will tell you": Stern, *The Klamath Tribe* p. 54.

PAGE 13
"Indians as a whole—with a few exceptions—are a pretty irresponsible group" : Robert Olmos, "K-Falls Worries, but Does Little About Its Boiling Indian Problem," *The Oregonian*, January 17, 1974, p. 19.

PAGE 14
". . . mold him in the ways of civilization": James Patrick Kehoe, "History of the Catholic Missionary Activity Among the Indians of the Oregon Country 1839–1936," (unpublished master's thesis, University of Oregon, 1936) p. 103.

PAGE 49

". . . shipping AA concepts onto reservations": The Broken Cord, p. 87 ff.; James E. Royce, *Alcohol Problems and Alcoholism: A Comprehensive Survey* (New York: Free Press, 1989), pp. 179–82.

PAGE 50

"He was a *chief!*": Stern, *Klamath Tribe*, p. 61.

PAGE 57

". . . as their Creator made them." Thomas Jefferson, Second Inaugural Address (March 4, 1805), reprinted in Thomas Jefferson, *Writings*, edited by Merrill Peterson (New York: Library of America, 1984), pp. 519–20.

PAGE 58

" ' . . . the worship of God' ": Kate McBeth, *The Nez Perce since Lewis and Clark* (New York: Revell, 1908), quoted in Michael C. Coleman, *Presbyterian Missionary Attitudes Toward American Indians 1837–1893* (Jackson: University Press of Mississippi, 1958), p. 83; " ' . . . a people without God' ": Ibid., p. 84.

PAGE 60

". . . into the presence of Christ": Omer Stewart, *Peyote Religion: A History*, p. 89.

PAGE 61

". . . eat breakfast together, and disperse": Most of this description is drawn from J. S. Slotkin, "The Peyote Way," in Dennis Edlock and Barbara T. Edlock, *Teachings from the American Earth: Indian Religion and Philosophy* (New York: Livewright, 1992).

PAGE 64

". . . a system for healing some Native alcoholics": Robert Bergman, "Navajo Peyote Use: Its Apparent Safety," *American Journal of Psychiatry*, vol. 12, (December 1971), p. 128; "The Peyote Religion and Healing," in R. H. Cox, ed., *Religion and Psychotherapy* (Springfield, Ill.: Charles C. Thomas, 1974). Affidavit of Robert Bergman, M.D., Clinical Associate Professor of Psychiatry, University of Washington, March 29, 1984 (on file with author).

PAGE 64

"'... does not constitute an addiction in any sense of the word'": Paul Pascarosa, Sanford Futterman, and Mark Halsweig, "Observations of Alcoholics in the Peyote Ritual: A Pilot Study," *Annals of the New York Academy of Sciences*, vol. 273 (1976), p. 518 ff.

PAGE 64

"'... I ain't going to mess with that'": Deposition of Alfred L. Smith, *Equal Employment Opportunity Commission v. Douglas County Council on Alcohol & Drug Abuse Prevention and Treatment*, No. 85-C139-E, U.S. District Court, District of Oregon, September 26, 1985, p. 45 (with Exhibit I, affidavit of Al Smith during application for benefits).

PAGE 88

"... ontologically and theologically abhorrent": Gordon, *The Golden Guru*, p. 210.

PAGE 92

"... one of whom was a trainee": Deposition of John G. Gardin II, *Equal Employment Opportunity Commission v. Douglas County Council on Alcohol & Drug Abuse Prevention and Treatment*, No. 85-C139-E, U.S. District Court, District of Oregon, September 4, 1985 (Roseburg, Ore.).

PAGE 94

"... consider peyote a drug": Smith deposition; Gardin deposition; Smith deposition.

PAGE 95

"'... first day of employment'": Interview with Bruce Piper.

PAGE 96

". . . ordinary Jesus language": Gardin deposition.

PAGE 98

". . . resident assistant at the inpatient treatment facility": All information about Galen Black's life comes from my interviews with him.

PAGE 99

"It's your personal choice": Smith deposition.

PAGE 101

". . . penance and spiritual cleansing": Joel Bernard, "From Fasting to Abstinence: The Origins of the American Temperance Movement," in Suzanna Barrows and Robin Room, eds., *Drinking Behavior and Belief in Modern History* (Berkeley: University of California Press, 1991), pp. 337–53.

PAGE 102

". . . to relieve the compulsion to drink": Robert O'Brien and Morris Chafetz, M.D., *The Encyclopedia of Alcoholism*, 2d ed. (New York: Facts on File, 1991), pp. 19–25; Sydney E. Ahlstrom, *A Religious History of the American People* (New Haven: Yale University Press, 1972), pp. 337–53.

PAGE 110

". . . expect of an employee": Administrative decision of the Assistant Director for Employment, Employment Division, Department of Human Resources, State of Oregon (March 22, 1984).

PAGE 122

". . . the golden age of federal civil-liberties litigation was over": William J. Brennan Jr., "The Bill of Rights and the States: The Revival of State Constitutions as Guardians of Individual Rights," *New York University Law Review* 61:4 (October 1986), p. 535.

PAGE 132

". . . other family member to enroll?": Bruce Piper, "Peyote Case: What Went Missing," unpublished manuscript, n.d. Reprinted by kind permission of the author.

PAGE 135

"Gardin went first": All quotations are from the transcript of testimony, *In re Galen Black* (transcript of referee hearing, December 5, 1983).

PAGE 139

"This use despite severe occupational consequences constitutes relapse": Affidavit of John L. De Smet (June 27, 1984).

PAGE 139

". . , all we have": Affidavit of Al Smith (March 26, 1984) (hereinafter Smith Affidavit); affidavit of Stanley Smart (March 19, 1984); affidavit of Omer Stewart (April 5, 1984); affidavit of Dr. Robert Bergman (March 29, 1984); affidavit of Emerson Jackson (date unknown) (appendix to Smith I cert. petition). For an approximation of the date, see letter from Gary Forrester to Emerson Jackson (May 16, 1984) (acknowledging submission of an affidavit supporting Al Smith).

PAGE 140

". . . a milestone in the case": Gruber's decision about Black is set forth in *In re Galen Black*, case no. 83-E-268 (referee decision, December 8, 1963). The corresponding decision about Smith is *In re Alfred L. Smith*, case no. 84-E-1181 (referee decision, July 23, 1984).

PAGE 142

"The board found against Black and Smith": See *Black v. Employment Division, Department of Human Resources*, 707 P.2d 1274, 1276 (1985). See State of Oregon Employment Appeals Board Decision, *Smith v. ADAPT* (August 28, 1984) (no. 84-AB-1217) (on file with author).

PAGE 144

". . . won in front of the referee": Release agreement between ADAPT and Alfred L. Smith (March 5, 1986); "Confidential Final Release," *Black* v. *ADAPT*, signed by Eric R. T. Roost (March 26, 1986).

PAGE 149

"Sitting before the assembled lawyers . . .": The account of Choper's remarks is from the handwritten notes of Dave Frohnmayer, dated "3/2/87."

PAGE 154

" 'They were just stunned' ": The account of the meeting is based on my interview with Sande Schmidt and the Board's official minutes, Sept. 24–25, 1987.

PAGE 159

". . . the first civil right of every American": Rowland Evans Jr. and Robert D. Novak, *Nixon in the White House: The Frustration of Power* (New York: Random House, 1971), p. 160.

PAGE 159

"the counter-revolution that wasn't": Vincent Blasi Jr., *The Burger Court: The Counter-Revolution That Wasn't* (New Haven: Yale University Press, 1983).

PAGE 159

" 'that group of clowns we had had around here' ": David G. Savage, *Turning Right: The Making of the Rehnquist Supreme Court* (New York: John Wiley & Sons, 1992), p. 41.

PAGE 161

" '. . . He could have been a member of the Curia' ": Joe Morgenstern, "Scalia the Terrible: Supreme Court Justice Antonin Scalia," *Playboy*, July 1993.

PAGE 163

". . . into line for a judicial appointment under Reagan": *1986 Current Biography Yearbook*, p. 505.

PAGE 164

". . . a jurist uneasy with judicial authority": Richard Nagareda, "The Appellate Jurisprudence of Justice Antonin Scalia," *University of Chicago Law Review*, vol. 5.1 (1987), p. 705.

PAGE 165

"I don't think it hurt Mario Cuomo": Stephen J. Adler, "Scalia's Court," *The American Lawyer* (March 1997), pp. 16–21.

PAGE 165

"Do you think that he knows the rest of us are here?": John Jeffries, *Justice Lewis F. Powell, Jr.* (New York: Charles Scribner's Sons, 1999), p. 534.

PAGE 225

"William Nouyi Yang is a Hmong . . .": Hearing before the Committee on the Judiciary, United States Senate, 102d Congress, 2d session, on s.2969, September 18, 1992, serial no. J-102–82, Committee Print, GPO, 1003; *Yang* v. *Sturner*, 728 F. Supp. 845 (D. R.I. 1990), opinion withdrawn, 750 F. Supp. 558 (1990).

PAGE 229

" '. . . simply takes its lumps' ": Nat Hentoff, "Justice Scalia vs. the Free Exercise of Religion," *Washington Post*, May 19, 1990, p. A25; "Indian Religion," *The Economist*, October 6, 1990, p. 25 (U.K. edition p. 51); Edwin Yoder, "A Ban on Peyote's Ritual Use," *St. Louis Post-Dispatch*, April 24, 1990, p. 3C; Samuel Rabinove, "The Supreme Court and Religious Freedom," *Christian Science Monitor*, June 25, 1990, p. 19.

Page 229

". . . *Journal of Law and Religion*": Douglas Laycock, "The Supreme Court's Assault on Free Exercise, and the Amicus Brief That Was Never Filed," *Journal of Law and Religion*, vol. 8 (1990), p. 99.

Page 233

" ' . . . the issue of when the fetus becomes a person is a matter of religious belief' ": *Options*, Fall 1990, reprinted in Prepared Statement of James Bopp, general counsel, National Right to Life, Washington, D.C., in Hearings before the Subcommittee on Civil and Constitutional Rights of the Committee on the Judiciary, House of Representatives, 102d Congress, 2d session, May 13 and 14, 1991, Committee Print, serial no. 99, GPO (1993).

Page 234

". . . whether the State had chosen the least restrictive alternative required to advance that interest": Rep. no. 88, 103d Congress, 1st session, 1993.

Page 241

" ' . . . his often ultra-conservative point of view' ": Nina Totenberg, "Court Watchers Concerned with Scalia's New Tone," National Public Radio broadcast, *Morning Edition*, July 8, 1996, transcript no. 1906–9.

ACKNOWLEDGMENTS

To begin with, I must thank the protagonists of this story—Galen Black, Dave Frohnmayer, and Al Smith—as well as their families and friends for their generosity with their time and their memories about the events of the story. All three made available documents from their family archives that made my job much easier and more pleasurable. I thank them for their trust. Galen Black is at work on his own memoir of his experience with ADAPT. I look forward to reading it and regret that I did not have it to use in my own research. Both Al Smith and Dave Frohnmayer have become my friends. Frohnmayer, first as my dean and then as president of the University of Oregon, has never tried to influence my views or conclusions about the case, which are substantially different from his own. Al Smith was generous with his time and patient with my ignorance. I thank and salute them both.

ADAPT's present and former directors, John Gardin and Bruce Piper, were also willing to go the extra mile to help me understand their perspective and that of the organization. I owe them my respect and my thanks.

All my interview subjects were extraordinarily conscientious in attempting to warn me away from factual errors and misinterpretations. Those that remain are solely my responsibility.

Members of the South Coast Chapter of the Native American Church received me as a guest at their peyote meeting, smudged me well with cedar incense, and made sure I understood what was going on. I will treasure my meeting with Grandfather Peyote as long as I live.

My tutor in the use of historical documents and oral interviews is my wife, Spencie Love, who understood the project even before others did. She remains my role model, my good luck, and my heart of gold. My children, Daniel and Maggie, politely pretended to listen when I talked about my research. Maggie is my consultant in trial procedure; Daniel showed me how to write the opening chapter. My parents, A. C. and Rozanne Epps, have always supported my writing and remain two of the best readers I know. My closest friend, David Ignatius, provided encouragement during the darkest part of this project and was available almost every day to advise or to cheer me up with his rendition of "The Two-Thousand-Year-Old Man." No one could call him ill equipped. James M. Fallows, Sam Deloria, Richard Dillard, and Katherine Fulton, also old friends, were prompt and detailed in providing insightful feedback on the finished manuscript. Wendy Weil, who has been my agent for nearly thirty years, was both efficient and kind in bringing the book to market. I owe her more than I can say. Julia Pastore, my editor at St. Martin's, is a marvel of efficiency, skill, insight, and tact.

I received helpful comments from colleagues at universities around the country who took the time to read the book at one stage or another: Michael McConnell, William Forbath, Gerald Torres, Richard Delgado, Jean Stefancic, William Van Alstyne, Walter Dellinger, Milner S. Ball, Charles Wilkinson, Mark V. Tushnet, David Garrow, Marci Hamilton, Jeff Powell, and Sanford Levinson.

Colleagues at the University of Oregon School of Law were also important supports. I particularly thank Rennard Strickland, James O'Fallon, and Keith Aoki. The university has been generous during the long writing of the book, supporting my research with a John Luvaas Fellowship, a James O. and Alfred T. Goodwin Senior Faculty Fellowship, a Kenneth O'Connell Senior Research Fellowship, a Love-Moore-Banks-Grebe Summer Research Fellowship, a full-year sabbatical from the University of Oregon School of Law, and a residential fellowship at the University of Oregon Humanities Center. The staff of the *Arizona State Law Journal* were efficient and creative in their editing of the law-review version of this story.

I have also been blessed with the best cohort of research assistants any professor could ask for: Tony Gould, Russell Barnett, Michael Monnolly, Mary Bruington, Anne Devlin Lyman, Angela Otto, Credence Fogo, and Chris Michali all contributed to every page. They have all become great lawyers, but the memory lingers of late-night sessions checking facts, discussing old horror movies, and improvising oldies a capella. My administrative assistants at UO, Ginger Bellino, Pat Bray, Renae Larouche, and Jackie Snider, helped shepherd the project through multiple drafts. The staff of the Boston College Law Library were extremely helpful in helping me find sources and documents.

Finally, I must thank my friend and colleague David Schuman, who is drumming his fingernails at my failure to mention his suggestion of *Smith* as a case that might make an interesting book. Chopped liver he's not. Having given me a priceless idea, he asked only in return that I call his daughter Rebecca on the morning of her sixteenth birthday and sing "Sixteen Candles" to her in falsetto (a vocal style for which I receive relatively few specific requests). More than five years later, Rebecca Schuman—no longer a teenager but not one whit less brilliant, formidable, or sarcastic than when she was the author of "But I Digress" in *The Register-Guard*—was the acquiring editor who first brought the book to St. Martin's. Though she has since moved on from publishing into the land of dot-coms and stock options, I thank her and her parents, David and Sharon. You were and are important in my life in more ways than you know.

INDEX

ABOUT THE AUTHOR

Garrett Epps is a former reporter for *The Washington Post* and the author of two novels. His work has appeared in *The New York Times Magazine*, *The New York Review of Books*, *The Nation*, *The New Republic*, and *The American Prospect*. He is currently associate professor of law at the University of Oregon. He divides his time between Eugene, Oregon, and Chapel Hill, North Carolina.